Human Relations

EASTWOOD ATWATER

PRENTICE-HALL, INC
Englewood Cliffs, NJ 07632

Library of Congress Cataloging in Publication Data

ATWATER, EASTWOOD, (date)
  Human Relations.

  Includes bibliographies and index.
  1. Interpersonal relations. 2. Young adults—
Life skills guides. I Title.
HM132.A88 1986   302.3′4   85-6549
ISBN 0-13-445727-7

Editorial/production supervision and
  interior design by Martha Masterson
Cover design: Photo Plus Art
Manufacturing buyer Barbara Kelly Kittle

Photo Credits

p. 25 Marc P. Anderson; p. 33 Mark Mangold, U.S. Census Bureau; p.55 Ken Karp; p.61 Ken Karp; p.71 Teri Leigh Stratford; p.76 Ken Karp; p.92 Teri Leigh Stratford; p.100 Laimute E. Druskis; p.106 Teri Leigh Stratford; p.110 Marc P. Anderson; p.117 Teri Leigh Stratford; p.130 Laimute E. Druskis; p.154 Laimute E. Druskis; p.172 Irene Springer; p.179 WHO photo by E. Mandelmann; p.201 Laimute E. Druskis; p.220 Laimute E. Druskis; p.236 A.T.& T. Co. Photo Center; p.248 Irene Springer; p.259 Ken Karp; p.284 Colorado Department of Public Relations; p.306 Ken Karp.

Illustration credits

pages 37, 51, 59, 69, 81, 94, 112, 113, 142, 176, 182, 209, 243, 251, 262, 296, and 305: Nancy Andre.
pages 12, 21, 24, 36, 40, 44, 89, 97, 129, 132, 137, 151, 152, 157, 159, 191, 193, 196, 200, 216, 219, 223, 227, 266, 269, 271, 278, 280, 282, 286, 289, 302, and 304: Don Martinetti.

ISBN 0-13-445727-7 01

Prentice-Hall International (UK) Limited, *London*
Prentice-Hall of Australia Pty. Limited, *Sydney*
Prentice-Hall Canada Inc., *Toronto*
Prentice-Hall Hispanoamericana, S.A., *Mexico*
Prentice-Hall of India Private Limited, *New Delhi*
Prentice-Hall of Japan, Inc., *Tokyo*
Simon & Schuster Asia Pte. Ltd., *Signapore*
Editora Prentice-Hall do Brasil, Ltda., *Rio de Janeiro*

Contents

Preface   xiii

Introduction: How to Study   1

THE SQ3R METHOD   2

   Survey   2
   Question   2
   Read   3
   Recite   3
   Review   4

SCHEDULING STUDY TIME   5

NOTETAKING   6

Preview the topic   6
Be selective   6
Organize your notes   6
What if you miss something?   7
Use your notes   7

TAKING TESTS   7

General guidelines   8
Objective tests   8
Essay tests   8

1 Self and Others   10

THE NEED FOR OTHERS   11

Cooperation and Sharing   11
Alleviating Stress   13
Comparisons and Conformity   15

THE SEARCH FOR SELF   16

Seeking self-fulfilment   17
The self-fulfilment contradiction   19
Loneliness   20

RELATING TO OTHERS   22

The search for community   22
Mutuality   24
Commitment   26

SUMMARY   28

SELF-TEST   28

EXERCISES   29

2 Meeting People   31

FIRST IMPRESSIONS   32

Physical Appearance   33
Reputation   34
Speech   35
Nonverbal behavior   36

MISTAKEN IMPRESSIONS   37

Person or situation?   38
False cues   38

Stereotypes   39
The halo effect   40

MAKING A GOOD IMPRESSION   41

Act natural   41
Put your best foot forward   42
Show an interest in others   43
Emphasize what you have in common   43
Give sincere praise   44

SUMMARY   45

SELF-TEST   45

EXERCISES   46

3   Becoming Friends   48

WHAT ATTRACTS PEOPLE?   49

Nearness   50
Similarity   50
Physical attractiveness   52
Liking   53

FRIENDSHIP   54

Who are your friends?   54
What friends do together   55
Rules of friendship   56
Lasting friendships   57

FRIENDSHIP AND INTIMACY   58

Self-disclosure   58
Compatibility   60
Dealing with differences   62
Intimacy and growth   62

SUMMARY   64

SELF-TEST   64

EXERCISES   65

4   Male and Female   67

SEX ROLES   68

Sex-role stereotypes   69
Changing sex roles   71
Sex roles and sexuality   72

SEXUAL BEHAVIOR 73

    Masturbation 74
    Sexual intercourse 75
    Problem behaviors 77

CHANGING ATTITUDES TOWARD SEX 80

    Freedom and fulfilment 80
    Caution and commitment 81
    Love and sex 82

SUMMARY 83

SELF-TEST 83

EXERCISES 84

5 Love and Marriage 86

LOVE 87

    Romantic Love 87
    Styles of loving 88
    Mature love 90

MATE SELECTION 92

    A filtering process 93
    Compatibility 94
    A rational or emotional choice? 95

THE MARRIAGE RELATIONSHIP 96

    Why people marry 96
    Types of marriage relationships 98
    Happiness is a satisfying relationship 100

SUMMARY 101

SELF-TEST 102

EXERCISES 103

6 Marital Adjustment 104

HUSBAND AND WIFE 105

    Husband and wife roles 105
    Who's in charge? 108
    Marital conflict 109
    Changes in marriage over time 111

SEX IN MARRIAGE 112

Sexual compatibility 113
Common problems 114
Starting a family 117

DIVORCE AND REMARRIAGE 118

Causes of divorce 118
The divorce experience 119
Single-parent families 121
Remarriage 122

SUMMARY 123

SELF-TEST 123

EXERCISES 125

7 **Effective Communication 126**

THE PROCESS OF COMMUNICATION 127

Types of communication 127
Nonverbal messages 129
Common barriers 131
Improving communication 132

EXPRESS YOURSELF EFFECTIVELY 134

Be assertive 135
Use "I" messages 136

BE A GOOD LISTENER 138

The failure to listen 139
Nonreflective listening 140
Reflective listening 141

SUMMARY 144

SELF-TEST 145

EXERCISES 146

8 **Handling Conflict 148**

CONFLICT 149

Conflict is unavoidable 149
Types of confict 151

STYLES OF CONFLICT MANAGEMENT   153

Defensive styles   153
Cooperative styles   155
Your personal style   156

COOPERATIVE PROBLEM SOLVING   157

Basic steps   158
Helpful hints   160

SUMMARY   164

SELF-TEST   164

EXERCISES   165

9   Managing Stress   167

UNDERSTANDING STRESS   168

What is stress?   168
Stressful events   169
Individual, situational factors   172

REACTIONS TO STRESS   173

Physiological effects   173
Defensive coping   175
Other coping devices   178

EFFECTIVE STRESS MANAGEMENT   180

Modifying your environment   180
Altering your lifestyle   182

SUMMARY   185

SELF-TEST   186

EXERCISES   187

10   Exploring the Workplace   189

THE PLACE OF WORK IN OUR LIVES   190

Why do people work?   190
How work effects us   192

ATTITUDES TOWARD WORK   194

Changing attitudes toward work   194
Motivating the worker   195
What do people look for in a job?   197

THE PROCESS OF CAREER CHOICE   197

    Stages of career choice   198
    Influences on career choice   200
    Work experience   202

SUMMARY   204

SELF-TEST   204

EXERCISES   205

11   Choosing a Career   207

CHOOSING A COMPATIBLE CAREER   208

    Self-assessment   208
    Exploring careers   210
    Identifying compatible careers   210
    Making a decision   213

PREPARING FOR A CAREER   215

    Apprenticeship programs   215
    On-the-job training programs in business and industry   216
    Colleges and universities   217
    Vocational and technical schools   218
    Military service and other government programs   220

CAREER OUTLOOK   221

    Trends and projected growth   222
    Your career outlook   226
    Changing your career goal   227

SUMMARY   228

SELF-TEST   229

EXERCISES   230

12   Finding a Job   232

IDENTIFY POTENTIAL EMPLOYERS   233

    Creative job hunting   234
    Group job hunting   235
    Suggested resources   237

CONTACT POTENTIAL EMPLOYERS   239

    Telephone calls   239
    The résumé   241

The letter   243
The application   245

PREPARE FOR THE EMPLOYMENT INTERVIEW   246

Be prepared   246
Questions you can expect   247
Some do's and don'ts   249

KEEP AT IT   250

Be persistent   250
Make follow-ups   251
Keep a positive attitude   252

SUMMARY   253

SELF-TEST   254

EXERCISES   255

13   Getting Along on the Job   256

WORK ADJUSTMENT AND SATISFACTION   257

The first job   257
Job satisfaction   258
The challenge of technology   260
Growing in the job   261

WOMEN IN THE WORKPLACE   263

Women at work   264
Working mothers   265
Reducing the earnings gap   267

IS THERE A FUTURE IN IT?   268

Promotion   268
Discrimination   270
Changing jobs   271

SUMMARY   273

SELF-TEST   273

EXERCISES   274

14   Leisure   276

LEISURE AND NONLEISURE   277

What is leisure?   277

Types of leisure 279

WORK AND LEISURE 279

Views of work and leisure 280
Work and leisure patterns 281

USING LEISURE POSITIVELY 283

Outdoor recreational activities 284
Entertainment and cultural activities 286
Vacations 288
Leisure and personal growth 290

SUMMARY 291

SELF-TEST 292

EXERCISES 293

15 Coping with Loss 294

SEPARATION AND LOSS 295

Types of loss 295
The experience of loss 298

DEATH AND DYING 299

Awareness of death 299
The experience of dying 300
Dying the way you live 302

BEREAVEMENT 303

The grief process 304
Unresolved grief 305
Good grief 308

SUMMARY 308

SELF-TEST 309

EXERCISES 310

Answers to Self-Tests 312

Glossary 313

Index 319

Preface

"No man is an *Island,* entire of itself," wrote John Donne. Rather, we are deeply affected by other people. At times people get us down. They annoy us, they disappoint us, and occasionally they betray us. Ultimately the big problems in life turn out to be "people problems." At the same time, it is in our moments of sharing and intimacy with friends and loved ones that we feel most at home in the world. Not surprisingly, one of the most valued goals in life for young adults is to have satisfying and close relationships with their friends, their marriage partners, and their families.

The purpose of this book is to help you gain a better understanding of your relations with others, with an eye to achieving more satisfying relationships. We'll begin with an overview of self and others, putting into perspective recent concerns with self-fulfilment. Then we'll discuss the common areas of adjustment in our relationships, such as meeting people, becoming friends, relating to the opposite sex, falling in love, getting married, and married life. We'll also examine several areas of human relations in which people commonly encounter difficulty, including communicating effectively, handling conflicts, and managing stress. We'll devote several chapters to the all-important topic of careers: exploring the workplace, choosing a career, finding a job, and getting along on the job. The relationship between work and leisure will be dealt with in a separate chapter. In the final chapter we'll discuss one of the most crucial matters of all, coping with loss, especially the death of friends and loved ones.

As you read the book, you are encouraged to relate the material to your own experience. To this end, I have used numerous examples from everyday life. Many of these are true accounts, with fictional names used to protect the people involved. The boxed items also highlight material that is relevant to everyday life. A self-test has been included at the close of each chapter to help you check how well you understand what you've read. I've also added several practical exercises at the end of every chapter. These may help you to apply the material to your own experience in a way that is enjoyable as well as educational.

I'd like to thank the reviewers who read the manuscript and made suggestions for improving it. Included here are: Gladys J. Baez-Dickreiter, St. Philip's College; Bart B. Bare, Caldwell Community College; P. J. Giampocaro, Rappahannock Community College; William Jacobs, Lake City Community College; Richard A. Kribs, Motlow State Community College; Karl G. Krisac, Delaware County Community College; Denise Owen, New Hampshire Vocational Technical College at Manchester; Toni Powers, Dover Business College; Michael Scheible, Gateway Technical Institute; Frank Zarkowski, South Seattle Community College.

I'm grateful for the understanding and cooperation of my wife Kay throughout the writing of this book. I also want to thank John Isley, my editor, whose support and guidance have made this book possible, and Martha Masterson, my production editor, for her judgment and skill in transforming my manuscript into the completed book.

Eastwood Atwater
Blue Bell, PA

Introduction
How To Study

THE SQ3R METHOD
    Survey
    Question
    Read
    Recite
    Review

SCHEDULING STUDY TIME

NOTETAKING
    Preview the topic
    Be selective
    Organize your notes
    What if you miss something?
    Use your notes

TAKING TESTS
    General guidelines
    Objective tests
    Essay tests

Invariably after a test, a student will come up to me and say, "I don't understand why I did so poorly on the test." "Did you study for the test?" I ask. "Yes, I read all the chapters," the student says. "But did you really understand the material?" I inquire. "Did you outline the important points on paper? Did you review before the test?" *Silence*. A puzzled expression comes over the student's face as if to say, "You mean reading the chapters isn't enough?"

The secret of studying is to become actively involved in what you're reading. You need to read for understanding, digging out much of the meaning for yourself. You must also actively use the material, and you can do this by marking or underlining the important points, outlining the key ideas on paper, discussing the material with others, and finally reviewing everything before a test. A teacher can organize and present the course in such a way that you are encouraged to study, but no teacher, however interesting or outstanding, can take the place of studying. This is something you must do for yourself.

THE SQ3R METHOD

Fortunately, there is a time-tested method of studying which can help you. It's called *the SQ3R method,* and it's designed to actively involve you in the material you're learning. SQ3R is an acronym—a word formed from the first letter of a series of words—for survey, question, read, recite, and review periodically. Extensive experience has shown that the SQ3R method can improve your comprehension and memory and consequently your test performance. Let's see how.

Survey

When you survey something, you do so for a purpose, usually to determine its boundaries or limits. This is especially important when you're working with time limits. Of course, when you're reading a novel, you start at the beginning and read straight through because you don't want to spoil the surprise ending. But with concepts and factual material, it's just the opposite. Here, it's important to survey the material as a whole so you can put the details in perspective as you read.

> First, look over the chapter table of contents
> Then skim through the chapter, looking at the various headings and
> subheadings
> Read the chapter summary
> Now determine how much you want to read at a sitting

Question

After you've surveyed the chapter, start asking yourself questions about it. The easiest way to do this is to turn each bold-faced heading and subheading into a question. For example, the first major heading and subheadings for chapter 2 are shown below:

> *First impressions*
>
> Physical appearance
> Reputation
> Speech
> Nonverbal behavior

Now think of a question about each heading and subheading. Here are some sample questions. *How important is the first impression we make on others? What do people judge by? Which aspects of our physical appearance do people notice most? How important is our reputation? Which characteristics of our speech most impress others? What do people notice most about our nonverbal behavior?* The use of questions will prove even more effective if you'll take the time to write down your questions and, as you read, your answers.

Read

It's best not to attempt to read too much material all at once. In this book a reasonable goal would be to read one major section at a time. In this way you can understand and digest the material in one section before proceeding to the next. Simply reading through material without understanding it amounts to little more than skimming. However, when you take the time to understand the material as you read it you'll retain it much better. If you don't know the meaning of a word, look it up in the glossary in the back of the book. If the word isn't in the glossary, look it up in the dictionary. Feel free to make notes to yourself in the margins of the text page, either about the meaning of a word or a key idea in a paragraph.

You may find it helpful to mark or underline key passages in the book. This keeps you an active participant in reading and makes it easier for you to review. Some students mark or underline as they read. Others read through a section and then go back and mark or underline. I prefer the latter strategy because I have a better idea of what the key passages are after I've finished reading a section. Here are some guidelines for marking or underlining.

Read through the section before marking or underlining
Don't mark or underline too much, just the key passages or ideas
Mark or underline in ink. Pencil often smears

Recite

You've just looked up someone's telephone number in the directory. You close the directory. Now you're dialing the number—oops, what was that number? You reopen the directory and find the number again. But this time as you reach for the phone, you keep repeating the number to yourself silently (or perhaps audibly). You're improving your retention through *recitation*—the act of repeating or speaking aloud.

Recitation is one of the best-kept secrets of studying. Years ago, Professor Gates demonstrated that students who spent 80 percent of their time reciting lists and only 20 percent reading them, recalled *twice* as much as those who spent all of their time reading. Think about it. Recitation is probably the single most effective way to increase retention of what you read. And remember, there are many ways to recite.

One way is to close the book and mentally rehearse what you've read. Then open the book and check. A second way is to ask yourself questions about what you've read. You may use questions you formulated earlier, or you may stop periodically and ask yourself, "What does this mean? What is the author saying?" A third way is to recite aloud. One approach to this is to ask questions and share your reactions to the material in class discussions. Another is to talk with your classmates about what you've read.

A fourth way to recite is to make your own written outline of a major section or chapter. I highly recommend this because it forces you to select the key ideas in a section. After you've finished reading, go back and jot down the main idea or ideas for each subheading. Some students make the mistake of simply copying down the headings and subheadings with little else. Others include too much detail, which becomes cumbersome. Be selective. You should be able to outline an entire chapter of this book in about two written pages. The act of writing down the ideas is itself a form of recitation, and it also provides a convenient guide for review before a test.

The amount of time you spend on recitation depends on the material you're reading. When you're trying to remember isolated pieces of information, like numbers or names, up to 80 or 90 percent of your time should be spent in recitation. But when you're learning ideas or concepts that are very meaningful and well organized, perhaps only 20 percent of your time should be spent in recitation. Additional experience will help each of you to discover the amount of recitation time that works best for you.

Review

We need to *review* (look again) for several reasons. First, reviewing helps to solidify the material as a whole in our minds. Second, reviewing is itself a form of recitation and thus improves our retention of what we've read. Finally, reviewing is essential for filing the material away in the memory. When we read something for the first time, it simply registers in our momentary attention span, sometimes called *short-term memory*. But in order to retain what we've read we must go over the material again so as to transfer it to *long-term memory* for future use, especially in tests.

Once you've completed reading the chapter, you're ready to review. First, read the summary at the end of the chapter to get a view of the material as a whole. Then look back over the chapter, formulating questions about the material under each bold-faced heading. Pay special attention to the key ideas you've marked under each heading and subheading. If you've made a written outline of the chapter, review this as well. It's a good idea to review all your notes periodically, say within twenty-four hours of first reading the material, then again seventy-two hours later, and after that about once a week until you're tested on the material.

Finally, when you feel ready, do the self-test at the end of the chapter. Check your answers against the list of correct answers provided in the book. It's very important that you go back and look up the answers to the questions you missed. You'll notice that the sequence of test items parallels the order in which material appears in the chapter, thus facilitating your use of the questions for study purposes. You may be interested to know that all of the items in the self-test are also included in the test bank provided for the instructor, but are worded differently. Such items make up about half of the total number of test questions in the instructor's manual. In this way, as you master the material in the self-test you'll be preparing for the classroom test, provided, of course, that your instructor uses questions in the instructor's manual, as most instructors do.

SCHEDULING STUDY TIME

Once you've attended the first class in each course, you're ready to plan your study schedule. Keep in mind your class schedule, the workload for each course, and other commitments like a part-time job. Be realistic. Don't schedule too much for a given time slot.

First, set aside a place for study which is free from distraction, and use that place only for studying. In this way, you'll build up a set of associations that will help you to study. If you find yourself daydreaming, get up and return when you're ready to study. When you've finished studying, leave that place. If you do this consistently, you'll soon associate this place with studying and feel more like studying there.

Second, plan to study at particular times. Some students prefer to study in a given block of time and quit at the end of that time regardless of how much they've read. Others plan to cover a certain amount of material and study until they've completed their goal. Either way, it's best to study in reasonable blocks of time, about one to three hours. After this, fatigue and boredom set in. Also, study first, then socialize and play. A student who was having difficulty in school told me she usually telephoned friends and played her guitar before getting around to studying about ten o'clock each evening. I suggested she reverse the procedure: study first and then reward herself by doing something she especially liked to do, such as playing her guitar. This strategy worked so well she eventually made the dean's list.

Third, space out your study time. Students frequently try to learn too much in too little time, a practice called *cramming*. Years ago, Hermann Ebbinghaus found that students who studied a list of new information once a day for several days remembered more of that information than when they studied the list several times in one day. Since then we've known that people learn more efficiently by distributing their study time over a period of days or weeks. It's best to read the appropriate assignments before attending class. Then periodically review your notes on the material as described earlier. The evening before a test can be reserved for a final review.

NOTETAKING

Notetaking serves several purposes. First, recording what you hear makes you an active participant in the listening process. Second, writing things down is a form of recitation which helps to store information in your long-term memory. This is why it's so important to take your own notes. Third, your notes will allow you to review lecture material that may not be in the textbook.

Some students prefer taking notes on $8\frac{1}{2}$-by-11-inch pages in a looseleaf binder which allows them to add and remove pages. Others use the more familiar spirally bound booklets, probably out of convenience. Either way, here are some suggestions for taking better notes.

Preview the topic

The most obvious way to do this is to look up the lecture topic in your syllabus or course outline ahead of time. At the least you should read the appropriate assignment before going to class. Most professors announce their lecture topic and put some sort of outline on the board. Copy the outline, and refer back to it if necessary while taking notes. All of this will alert you to the main ideas in the lecture and what to listen for while taking notes.

Be selective

Students complain that it's difficult to listen and take notes at the same time, and it is. But a lot depends on how you do it. If you try to record everything a lecturer says, you're doomed from the start. Instead, concentrate on listening to what the speaker is saying. Then be selective in what you record. Jot down the main points and ideas in phrases rather than complete sentences. Listen for key words that signal material which should be recorded. For example, if the lecturer says, "There are four reasons for this," be sure you record the four reasons in your notes.

Organize your notes

Otherwise, they will end up looking like a disjointed grocery list. Ordinarily, it's advisable to use two or three levels of headings and subheadings with the appropriate indentations. But a lot depends on the information you're recording. For example, if you were taking notes on this article about notetaking, two levels of headings would probably be sufficient, as follows:

Notetaking

Introduction
    3 purposes of notetaking

Preview the topic
　Ways to do this

Be selective
　Record key ideas

Organize your notes
　Sample outline

What if you miss something?
　Obtaining missing information

Use your notes
　Importance of regular use

What if you miss something?

If you miss an important point, don't panic. Simply leave space for it and move ahead. You can ask a classmate for the necessary information later. Seek out someone who takes good notes. You can also ask the instructor. Although students are reluctant to ask their instructor for such information, I find it reassuring when they do.

Use your notes

Most students take reasonably good notes, but fail to use them properly. Don't wait until the night before the test to review your notes. By then you've forgotten the meaning of much of what you've written. Instead, use your notes regularly. Review your notes for the previous lecture before attending your next class in that subject, or perhaps even in class while waiting for the next lecture to begin. Also, refer to your notes when reading the same topic in your textbook. Some students prefer to tape-record class lectures. But you should be aware that concrete names and factual information are best remembered in the visual memory track and should be put in writing. A better idea is to type up your notes after class. In this way, you'll be committing the material to memory as you type it, and you'll have a clear set of notes for review.

TAKING TESTS

The two keys to doing well on tests are preparing well and being reasonably relaxed and confident during the test. A little anxiety motivates you to study and keeps you alert during the test. But too much anxiety interferes with your thought and memory, causing you to miss things you really "know" in your less anxious moments.

General guidelines

Here are some guidelines to follow in preparing for a test, whether it's a multiple-choice or an essay test. About a week before the test, ask your instructor what the test will cover. How much of the test will come from the class notes? How much from the textbook? Also, ask what kinds of questions will be asked. Will the questions call for names and factual information, or mostly concepts? Are there topics of special importance? After you have an idea of what the test will cover, begin your study at least several days in advance. Then save time the night before the test for a final review. You might also schedule study sessions with other students. Discussing the course material with others helps to clarify your views and store the material in your memory.

Objective tests

Included here are multiple-choice or true-false questions as well as matching terms. In each case, you have to select the correct answer. Here are some suggestions for answering multiple-choice questions more effectively:

Read each question through carefully. Don't jump to conclusions.

Note key terms. Words such as *all, always,* and *never* imply extreme views which are often false. Words such as *some, sometimes,* and *may* imply more moderate views and are more likely to be true.

Rule out the most unlikely answers first. Then concentrate on deciding between the two most likely answers. This way, you've got a fifty-fifty chance of being correct.

When you've selected the correct answer, reread the question to make certain your answer matches the question.

If you have difficulty answering a question, put a light pencil check in the left margin and answer it after you've completed the other questions.

Should you stick with your first choice? It all depends. When you've studied reasonably hard and feel confident about your answer, stick with it. But when you haven't studied much or have *strong* doubts or uncertainty about an answer, it often pays to change it to one you feel more certain of.

Essay tests

Essay tests draw on your ability to recall material with a minimum of cues. Your ability to organize ideas and express them clearly also helps. If you'd like to improve your essay answers, try following these suggestions:

Read each question carefully.

Pay attention to key words, such as *compare, explain,* and *illustrate.*

Jot down a brief outline of important points. Then rearrange your points in the order you wish to write them.

Glance at your outline from time to time as you write. Otherwise you may digress from your main points.

Pace yourself according to the number of questions you must answer and the time allotted.

Answer the easier questions first. Then work on the more difficult ones.

Use separate paragraphs to distinguish major points. Express your main point in the opening sentence. Then provide supportive details and examples in the rest of the paragraph.

You can improve your test-taking ability by learning from your test results. If your instructor goes over the test results in class, be sure to attend this session. Find out what you missed and why. Was the instructor's emphasis different from yours? Did the instructor ask questions different from what you expected, demanding, say, factual material rather than concepts? When you changed your answers on a multiple-choice test, were most of the resulting answers right or wrong? If the latter, you might use more restraint in changing your initial answers next time. If you didn't do well on an essay test, ask your instructor how you can improve your answers. In any case, don't waste time sulking or blaming your instructor or yourself. Find out what you need to do in order to do better on the next test. Good luck!

Self
and Others

1

THE NEED FOR OTHERS
     Cooperation and sharing
     Alleviating stress
     Comparisons and conformity

THE SEARCH FOR SELF
     Seeking self-fulfilment
     The self-fulfilment contradiction
     Loneliness

RELATING TO OTHERS
     The search for community
     Mutuality
     Commitment

SUMMARY

SELF-TEST

EXERCISES

Dave and Karen, both in their mid-twenties, have been going together for about three months. They get along pretty well except for one major difference: Dave likes times when just the two of them do things, but Karen prefers a more active social life. She feels uneasy about his possessiveness, but so far she's tried to go along with his wishes. This evening, Dave has dropped by Karen's house for an informal visit.

"Did I catch you at a busy time?" asks Dave.

"Not really," Karen says. "I was writing a letter to a girlfriend."

"I've been thinking about what we might do Saturday evening," Dave says.

"I'm glad you mentioned that," says Karen. "A friend of mine is having some people over for a small party Saturday evening. I'd love to go. What do you say?"

"Well," Dave replies slowly, with a sour look on his face, "you know how I feel about parties."

"I know," Karen says reassuringly. "You work with people all day long, and you'd rather that just the two of us go out together."

"You've got it," says Dave.

Karen breathes a quiet sigh, then says, "You've got to admit I've tried to respect your wishes for privacy so far."

"Yes, you have."

"But I miss seeing my friends. Besides, some of them keep asking me, 'What's Dave like?' "

"Just tell 'em he's handsome, successful, and very sexy," says Dave with a laugh.

"Oh, come on," protests Karen. "Why not let them see for themselves?"

"Okay, okay," Dave says, throwing up his hands in mock-surrender. "If you feel that strongly about it all, I guess I'll go."

"Is that a *yes*?" asks Karen.

"Yes, I'll go to the party with you."

"You'll really enjoy it," Karen says enthusiastically. "I think you'll like my friends too."

"We'll see," Dave says.

THE NEED FOR OTHERS

Each of us needs people. We need to feel close to at least one person, like a parent, lover, or spouse. But as Karen's remarks remind us, we also need the companionship of other friends. A well-rounded life includes both types of relationships, as Dave and Karen are both discovering.

We'll begin the chapter by describing some of the other ways we need people, such as to achieve a common goal. We'll also point out how too much of a need for others leads to conformity, or to an excessive dependence on others. Then we'll examine the recent emphasis on self-fulfilment and the impact this has had on such relationships as marriage and friendship. Finally, we'll discuss the importance of balancing the claims of self with those of others in achieving mutually satisfying relationships.

Cooperation and sharing

"Man is by nature a social animal," wrote Aristotle over two thousand years ago. People join together not only to survive but to fulfil their human strivings. We band together in families to procreate and preserve human life. Infants must be fed, clothed, and protected until they can take care of themselves. We

Figure 1-1 We like to socialize especially when we're happy.

also cooperate in the exchange of services. Some people grow food, others build houses and schools, and still others heal the sick. We also cooperate with others to satisfy a wide range of needs and to attain mutual goals. We depend on the services of a variety of community organizations, like the local, state, and federal governments as well as our hospitals and fire, police, and postal departments. And just think of all the different groups we belong to: family, school classes, teams, churches, clubs, as well as a variety of interest groups.

We also seek out other people for the pleasure of sharing experiences. We may invite a friend out to celebrate a special occasion such as a birthday or a promotion, or we invite others to share a weekend trip. Sharing the good times heightens our enjoyment and makes the occasion even more special. Sometimes, when we're bored or restless, we may simply need the stimulation of others. People who go through an extended period of social isolation tend to become preoccupied with their own thoughts, memories, and dreams, and become less efficient in their thinking. In extreme cases, solitary prisoners and shipwrecked sailors report being overwhelmed by feelings of desolation.

Our desire to be with other people fluctuates somewhat, depending on our moods and the needs of the moment. To illustrate this a survey was made of some college students. One hundred students were asked to indicate whether they wished to be with others, to be alone, or had no preference, when they were in thirteen different situations. A majority of students wanted the company of others when they were in a good mood, on Saturday night, doing something new, or in a strange situation. In contrast, most students wanted to be alone when they were physically tired, embarrassed, or in a crying mood. The majority of students also wanted to be alone after being with others for a long time, like on a long weekend. Yet there was no consensus in some situations, such as being depressed, worrying about a serious problem, feeling mildly ill, and feeling very guilty about something. In these situations, some students wanted company; others preferred to be alone.[1] See Table 1–1.

Alleviating stress

We're also likely to seek out others when we're under a lot of stress, especially when we're afraid. Even patients who ordinarily prefer a private room in a hospital feel comforted having a roommate to talk with. Sharing new experiences helps them to feel more at ease. This has also been demonstrated in other settings. In one study, people who were threatened by an electric shock were much more inclined to affiliate with others to reduce their fears that those who were not expecting an electric shock. The presence of others provides reassurance and comfort. This is especially true when those facing the same situation remain calm. You begin to think: "If they aren't too upset, why should I be?"[2]

The calming effect of other people depends partly on how well you know them. In one experiment, people were exposed to a stressful situation under three conditions: alone, with a friend, and with a stranger. Then the amount of stress experienced by each person was measured for each condition. Those tested in the presence of a friend reported the least stress of all. There was little or no difference between the stress of those tested alone and those with a stranger.[3]

The presence of a friend helps in several ways. First, you may feel open enough to discuss your fears frankly, thus helping to alleviate them. You may also feel free enough to joke about your predicament, a classic way to reduce stress. Also, the physical presence of a friend may evoke all kinds of pleasant associations of strength and comfort. Yet the presence of friends does not always reduce stress, especially when your friends become more excited or frightened than you. If you have friends who overreact in

---

[1]Patricia Niles Middlebrook, *Social Psychology and Modern Life,* 2nd ed. (New York: Alfred A. Knopf, 1980), 258.

[2]D. Amoroso and R. Walters, "Effects of Anxiety and Socially Mediated Anxiety Reduction in Paired-associate Learning," *Journal of Personality and Social Psychology* 11 (1969): 388–396.

[3]S. Kissel, "Stress-reducing Properties of Social Stimuli," *Journal of Personality and Social Psychology* 2 (1965): 378–384.

Table 1-1. When Students Wish To Be Alone or with Others.

	PERCENTAGE OF STUDENTS WHO:		
	Wished to Be with Others	Wished to Be Alone	Had No Preference
Situations in which most want to be with others			
When very happy	88	2	10
When in a good mood	89	0	11
On Saturday night	85	1	14
When you are in a strange situation or doing something you've never done before	77	13	10
Situations in which most want to be alone			
When physically tired	6	85	9
When embarrassed	16	76	8
When you want to cry	8	88	4
When busy	12	70	18
After an extensive period of social contact—after being with others for a long time	12	75	13
Situations in which there was no consensus			
When depressed	42	48	10
When worried about a serious personal problem	52	44	4
When mildly ill (e.g., with a cold)	32	49	19
When feeling very guilty about something you have done	45	43	12

Situations in which 70 percent or more of the students wished to be with others or alone are listed separately from those situations in which there was no such level of consensus. As you look over the student reactions to each situation, try to figure out *why* the students answered as they did.

Source: Social *Psychology and Modern Life,* Second Edition, by Patricia Niles Middlebrook. Copyright © 1980, 1973 by Alfred A. Knopf, Inc. Reprinted by permission of Alfred A. Knopf, Inc.

certain situations, such as on an important test, perhaps it would be wise to avoid them at these times to escape the "contagion" effect of their anxieties.

There are also other instances when strangers may be more comforting than friends, especially when stress involves embarrassing or intensely personal experiences. In one demonstration, some men watched a color film vividly portraying puberty rites in a primitive society, in which incisions were made into the genitals of young men. Half of the men watched with a friend; the other half with strangers. The results showed that men felt less tension with strangers than with friends. Apparently, in such a situation, we're less embarrassed and less responsive to the reactions of others when we're with strangers.[4]

Comparisons and conformity

Another reason we seek out people is to share our feelings and opinions. Many life experiences would remain subjective and confusing, if not meaningless, if we didn't have the opportunity to compare our reactions with those of others. This is especially true in times of uncertainty and change. In fact, the more unsure you are about something, the more likely you are to turn to others. For example, suppose you leave a controversial meeting with mixed feelings. Perhaps you're uncertain how you really feel about the meeting. You may ask other people who attended, "How do you feel about that meeting?" Whatever they say, chances are that sharing your feelings will help to clarify your own reactions. The same thing happens in matters of personal taste, though to a lesser extent. How often have you heard someone ask a friend, "How do you like my new car?" or "How do you like my new dress?" While a consensus of responses, whether positive or negative, may confirm our private opinions, mixed responses may create doubt or lead to needed improvements.

Not surprisingly, we seek out people like ourselves for purposes of comparing opinions. The most likely reason is the desire to confirm our own ideas and feelings. Suppose you ask a classmate, "What did you think of that test?" and your classmate replies, "I thought it was hard." If you agree, you'll probably ask that person's opinions again or share your own on the next suitable occasion. On the other hand, if that person says, "I thought it was an easy test," and you disagree, you would be less inclined to ask that person's opinion next time. Otherwise, such disagreement might be unsettling for you. You might wonder, "Who's right here?" As a result, people gravitate toward those who hold similar views to their own.

In the process of comparing our opinions with those of others, there's a tendency to *conformity*. Essentially, conformity is the willingness to change our behavior because of real or imagined pressure from others. Sometimes we conform out of the fear of authority; at other times we act out the desire for other people's approval. Often we conform in our outward behavior without changing our minds. Suppose you are with a group of friends and all of you agree to see a movie. You'd like to see the latest horror film. But all of your friends have heard it's bad, and they agree on another movie. Chances are you'll go along with your friends, though you'd prefer to see the horror film.

In itself, conformity is neither good nor bad. A lot depends on the purpose it serves in our lives. Much of the time conformity has a beneficial effect as it adjusts our behavior in response to others. We usually stop at red

---

[4]A. Gordon, "Friends, Strangers, and Manipulated Stress" (Doctoral dissertation, Columbia University, 1970) Dissertation Abstracts, 1971, 23, 2366.

traffic lights, stand in line to register for classes or buy things, and display good manners in public. Unfortunately, we often conform when we don't have to. Students hesitate to speak up in class because they fear being wrong or looking foolish. Workers are reluctant to disagree with their bosses for fear of getting fired. Too often we say things that conflict with our honest opinion because of the desire for another's approval. As a result, we may go through life afraid to be ourselves.

THE SEARCH FOR SELF

Fortunately, there's more emphasis on the individual today than there used to be. The upheaval in traditional values which occurred throughout the 1970s has led to a greater appreciation of personal freedom, self-expression, and individual lifestyles. In many ways, these changes have encouraged each of us to be ourselves. These changing values have also led us to modify the "getting/giving contract" between ourselves and our environment—the unwritten rules that govern what we give in our marriage, work, and relationships with others, and what we expect in return. Although such changes were first evident among college-aged youth, many of these changes have filtered down into the general population.

For example, our marriage and family-life values have changed. Until recently, it was commonly expected that people would marry and have children. Those who didn't were regarded as selfish. Fred and Marie are typical of couples who married in the 1950s. They married in their early twenties and had four children as a matter of course. Marie grew up assuming she would devote most of her time to being a homemaker and mother. She took a part-time office job only after their youngest child was in school. Fred identified strongly with the breadwinner role and put off pursuing some of his own interests until retirement. Both parents have worked hard and sacrificed for their children's education. Now well into middle age, Fred and Marie realize they are no longer happy in their marriage. But they're staying together for the sake of their children, at least until their youngest son completes college.

Brad and Cheryl, married in the 1970s, have a different outlook. They didn't decide to have children until they had been married for five years, and then not until Cheryl was assured of a maternity leave. Furthermore, they agreed to have only one or two children. Typical of the "new breed" of parents, i.e., the younger and better educated, they have different ideas about parenting. Brad and Cheryl don't feel they should sacrifice for their kids. They frequently take weekend trips, leaving their kids with Marie's mother. Nor do they feel that kids should be a burden to their parents. They feel strongly that unhappily married couples should not remain together merely for the sake of their children.

Seeking self-fulfilment

None of our changing values has received more attention than the emphasis on self-fulfilment. Many of the terms of "pop" psychology have become familiar in everyday usage, such as the need "to be yourself" or to be a "real person," to "express your potential" or "do your own thing," or to "keep in touch with your true feelings."

Daniel Yankelovich has found that 80 percent of the general population is now engaged in the search for self-fulfilment in one way or another. About 17 percent of people manifest the *strong form* of self-fulfilment; the other 63 percent the *weak form*. Although the "strong formers" are in the mainstream of Americans who strive for self-improvement, their goals are different. Instead of working for material success and keeping up with the Joneses, these individuals are preoccupied with personal growth and fulfilment. About two-thirds of the "strong formers," compared to less than half of the weak-form majority, believe self-improvement is important and work at it, and prefer a creative life of self-expression and travel to a life of materialistic success.[5] See Figure 1-2.

Since the majority of people pursue the weak form of self-fulfilment, most of us fit in here. We may have many other concerns in our lives besides the search for self-fulfilment. We must deal with the realities of our jobs, our home lives, children with school problems, and the like. At the same time we too are questioning traditional patterns and values. Some of us wonder if we should be giving so much to our jobs, considering what we're getting out of them. Some of us compare what we're giving to our marriages and families to what we're getting from them. Many of us question the old rules of working hard, sacrificing for our kids, and defining success in materialistic terms.

Stan taught physical education at a community college. He worked hard at his job, introducing several new courses, and led the college baseball team to two championships. His wife Sue works with handicapped children. Instead of buying a nicer home Stan and Sue bought an old farmhouse and several acres of land in Vermont. For several summers they took their vacations there. They enjoyed Vermont so much they sometimes talked of moving up there. Then Stan's school, in extensive cost-cutting moves, eliminated many of his new courses and programs. Sue's job was also cut to part time. Instead of complaining about their frustrations as so many other couples were doing, they decided to move to Vermont. Stan took a combined teaching and coaching job at a nearby high school. Sue used her experience to get a job at the local hospital. During the summer they operate a camp for handicapped children. Stan and Sue enjoy their life in Vermont. At times, they miss some of their friends and the stimulation of living in a larger community. But most of the time they feel they made the right decision. Stan and Sue belong to the 63 percent of Americans whose lives and values are conventional in many respects.

[5]D. Yankelovich, *New Rules* (New York: Bantam Books, 1981), 75.

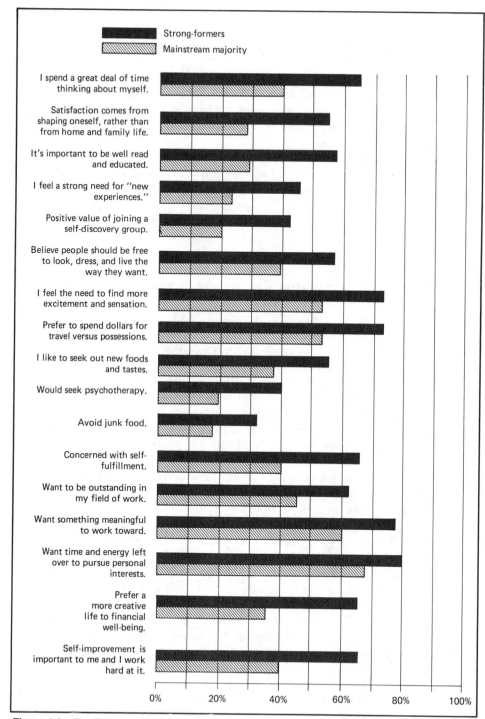

Figure 1-2. The Pursuit of Self-Fulfilment as a Lifestyle. Preferences of the "strong formers" vs. the mainstream majority.
Source: Daniel Yankelovich, "New Rules in American Life: Searching for Fulfilment in a World Turned Upside Down," *Psychology Today* (April 1981) 52.

But like many of us, they're redefining success, giving personal fulfilment a greater priority over the world of competition and material well-being.

The self-fulfilment contradiction

Things don't always work out so well. Even the best-laid plans may be undermined by economic reversals. Promising careers may become disappointing for reasons unforeseen at the outset. New relationships may fail to live up to our expectations. All of this suggests some of the contradictions within the search for self-fulfilment itself.

For one thing, it is difficult to pursue self-fulfilment without first satisfying the basic needs of food, clothing, and housing. Perhaps this is why such a lifestyle traditionally has been reserved for the rich. But in recent years, middle-class people have joined the search for the "good life" in increasing numbers. During the 1980s, however, economic forces have been moving us in the opposite direction. We've had to struggle with inflation, a tight job market, and high mortgage rates, for example, all of which threaten our survival rather than encourage our growth. People caught up in the clash between their personal aspirations and the economic realities become cynical and disillusioned. Young people who've grown up in an era of rising expectations are having to trim those expectations to match a world of diminishing resources and heightened competition.

Ken and Joan have been deeply influenced by the self-fulfilment movement. Unhappy in his engineer's job for years, Ken set up a management-consulting firm. As the kids reached school age, Joan began taking college courses part time. Eventually she enrolled full time. Unfortunately, Ken and Joan made their long-awaited moves at a time when there was a sharp downturn in the economy. Ken was caught between rising expenses for his kid's education and a lowered income. He also had to put his ailing mother into a nursing home. Reluctantly, Ken took another engineering job, keeping up his consulting practice on the side. Joan remained in school full time, but took a part-time job to help with expenses. Now Ken and Joan are under more stress than ever. They feel disenchanted about their opportunities for personal fulfilment.

Economic pressures have also intensified some chronic shortcomings of the search for self-fulfilment. One major flaw has to do with the impact of heightened expectations on our lives. Generally, when we expect more out of life we strive all the harder to achieve it. But when we expect too much, it tends to make us discontented and even more aware of our unhappiness. A common example is that of young people who have more choices than they would have had in the past, but are having trouble making those choices. Another flaw concerns focusing on inner needs at the expense of relationships. In recent years, some people have pursued their inner needs so intensely that instead of achieving the intimate relationships they desire, they have grown further apart from others. As a result, there are couples who are getting divorced for reasons that would not have led to divorce in the past.

Pursuing self-fulfilment on the basis of inner needs alone tends to lead to loneliness and depression.

Loneliness

We're all familiar with the symptoms of loneliness—the cold, empty feeling of being unloved, accompanied by the longing for companionship. Yet loneliness is more than the absence of people. Occasionally we choose to be alone without necessarily feeling lonely. We need solitude to sort out our thoughts and thus to relate better to those around us. At other times, we may be surrounded by people but still feel lonely. The truth of the matter is that loneliness comes from the absence of satisfying relationships.

We may experience different types of loneliness, corresponding to the types of relationships missing in our lives. One is an emotional isolation that comes from the lack of a close attachment to at least one other person. The other is a feeling of isolation that results from having too few social ties to others. Fulfilling our need for one type of relationship doesn't satisfy our need for the other type. Bart is happily married, but is so busy with his career he feels cut off from people beyond his family. On the other hand, Marianne, an unmarried career woman, has an active social life with a wide circle of friends. Yet occasionally she misses the closeness that comes from day-to-day sharing with a roommate or spouse.

Loneliness may be partly a state of mind too. When we seek intimacy and fail to find it, loneliness becomes more intense. This was brought out in a survey of loneliness showing that eighteen- to twenty-five-year-olds suffer the most from loneliness. Having loosened the ties with their parents, people of this age are actively seeking relationships outside the family. In addition, the idealism of youth, plus the recent stress placed on self-fulfilment, makes them especially sensitive to the gap that exists between their romantic expectations of intimacy and their current reality. Each successive age group, however, reports diminishing levels of loneliness. People over seventy suffer the least from loneliness. Although they spend much of their time alone, they've also learned how to take it in stride. Older people interpret things more realistically and can put the need for close relationships in better perspective.[6]

Unfortunately, loneliness has become a common experience for Americans. The growing popularity of telephone services for troubled people attests to this. Again and again, callers complain of loneliness in addition to their other problems. The loss of morale that accompanies loneliness is also a major reason why people seek psychiatric help.

Most college students suffer from loneliness at one time or another.

[6]C. Rubinstein, P. Shaver, and L.A. Peplau, "Loneliness," in *Personal Growth and Behavior 82/83*, ed. N. Jackson (Guilford, Conn.: The Dushkin Publishing Group, Inc., 1982), 152.

Figure 1-3

One survey of students in several American and Canadian universities yielded the following results: one-third of the students of both sexes reported occasions of quite upsetting, but not really severe loneliness. Another third of the students had experiences of very upsetting loneliness, but without psychiatric symptoms. Among the other students there was a wide range of reactions, from those who reported relatively mild loneliness to those whose loneliness was part of a psychological disorder, often accompanied by suicidal threats.[7]

The experience of loneliness doesn't feel the same to everyone. George feels lonely only on occasion; Ann feels lonely most of the time. People like Ann who are bothered the most by loneliness tend to feel abandoned, depressed, and desperate. Others suffer a milder kind of loneliness, the way you might feel when you find yourself alone on a weekend.

How Do You Cope with Loneliness?

Some people react to loneliness in passive ways. They may watch TV, cry, or sleep, all of which makes them feel even lonelier. Others take more active steps to alleviate their loneliness. They may work, read, or write a letter.

How do you handle loneliness? Do you sit and mope as if there's nothing you can do about it? Or do you take some initiative in overcoming your loneliness, like calling up a friend?

[7]V. Sermat, personal communication with the author, 1972. In Middlebrook, op. cit. 537.

RELATING TO OTHERS

So far we've seen that our need for people can make us oversocialized, so that we're overly dependent on the opinions and approval of others. Yet the concern with self-fulfilment of recent recent years carries the opposite risk of making us undersocialized. When each of us goes his or her own way, putting personal needs before satisfying relationships, we end up feeling lonely and cut off from others. Neither extreme will do. We need to balance the claims of self with those of other people. We must learn how to enjoy the give-and-take of human relationships while remaining true to our own needs. Our aim is mutually fulfilling relationships. In the rest of this chapter, we'll take a look at three important characteristics of such relationships—closeness, mutuality, and commitment.

The search for community

One of the most important qualities of a satisfying relationship is intimacy, the warmth and closeness that can exist between people. Yet a sense of intimacy is sadly missing in our everyday relationships. The single biggest reason is that we live in a complex, mobile society that is dominated by large institutions and threatened by impersonal routine. We come into contact with a wider circle of people than our grandparents did, but we soon learn that most of our relationships will be transitory and superficial. We buy an article from a sales clerk whose name we don't know. We talk with a telephone solicitor we've never met. Even at work, there's a tendency to form relationships on the basis of shared interests rather than deep emotional ties. The closeness of a personal relationship is often missing in our lives, leaving an emotional void. As a result, people are reaching out for more satisfying relationships.

Daniel Yankelovich labels this trend *the search for community.* Each year he and his colleagues do a survey to find the *search for community index,* which measures the need for forming close relationships with others. In 1973, one-third of the people expressed a need to compensate for the impersonal and individualistic aspects of society by seeking closer relationships with others. By the 1980s, almost one-half (47 percent) of Americans were engaged in the search for closer relationships. In some cases, people seek closer ties on the basis of common backgrounds, ethnic ties, or similar ages. In other instances they seek closer relationships on the basis of shared interests or personal values.[8]

Marriage and friendship continue to be the most common forms of close relationships. Today people marry primarily for love and companionship. They want a close relationship in which they can share their joys and problems. Not surprisingly, the quality of the marriage relationship itself determines

[8]Yankelovich, op. cit., 248.

TABLE 1-2. Shyness May Hold Us Back.

Situations	Percentage of Shy Students
Where I am focus of attention—large group—(as when giving a speech)	73
Large groups	68
Of lower status	56
Social situations in general	55
New situations in general	55
Requiring assertiveness	54
Where I am being evaluated	58
Where I am focus of attention—small group	52
Small social groups	49
One-to-one different-sex interactions	49
Of vulnerability (need help)	48
Small task-oriented groups	28
One-to-one same-sex interactions	14
Other People	
Strangers	70
Opposite-sex group	63
Authorities by virtue of their knowledge	55
Authorities by virtue of their role	40
Same-sex groups	34
Relatives	20
Elderly people	12
Friends	11
Children	10
Parents	9

In a survey of 800 high school and college students, Philip Zimbardo and his colleagues found that a majority of students (82 percent) describe themselves as having been shy at some time during their lives. Over 40 percent of them label themselves as presently shy—somewhat reserved, modest, and lacking in social skills. Shy people are especially apt to feel shy when they are the center of attention, in large groups, and among strangers. They are least likely to feel shy in small groups and among friends, i.e., in close relationships.

Source: P. Zimbardo, P. Pilkonis, and R. Norwood, *The Silent Prison of Shyness.* (Glenview, Ill.: Scott, Foresman and Company, 1974), p. 14A

whether people are happy in their marriage or not, as we'll discuss in the chapter on love and marriage.

But no matter how happily married we may be, we also need a network of friends, people with whom we share affectionate ties. Friendships supplement but do not take the place of intense love relationships like marriage. From adolescence on as we loosen the emotional ties with our parents, friends become our main support group. Friends become our functional family, the people whose opinions and support we care the most about. Friends help to shape our social identity and give us a deep sense of belonging. When we're discouraged, we'll often turn to a friend before a family member. Sometimes just having someone we feel close to who will listen and keep confidence is enough to see us through a crisis. Yet true friends are not easy to come by in our fast-paced society. According to one survey, 70 percent of Americans recognize that while they have many acquaintances, they have few close friends. About two out of five people say they have even fewer friends now than in the recent past. The search for community can be seen partly as the search for satisfying friendships.[9]

Mutuality

Mutuality has to do with people having the same level of involvement with each other. You'd think this would be the case for all romantic relationships, but this is far from being so. In about half of college-aged couples and married couples, one person is more in love or more on the giving end of the relationship than the other. Yet relationships in which one partner is more emotionally involved are about twice as likely to break up as those with mutual involvement. The same tends to be true in regard to other aspects of close relationships such as the distribution of power and sexual satisfaction. Here too, mutual relationships are more satisfying and lasting.

Figure 1-4 Let's keep it mutual.

[9]Yankelovich, op. cit., 248.

Mutuality between people tends to develop gradually; it overlaps with many of the other qualities of intimate relationships, like sharing, compatibility, and trust. People who have come to know each other well or have worked closely together may discover common interests and share a lot about themselves. The more they share, the more they like each other. And the greater their mutual liking and satisfaction, the closer they feel to each other. Mutuality also involves trust, or the willingness to let go rather than to control the relationship. More often than not, the feeling that "she trusts me" has its own way of activating us to justify that trust in return. Finally, mutuality involves respect for each other as individuals, such that people can disagree without threatening their relationship, at least up to a point. All these qualities have a contagious effect that further strengthens mutuality. That is, the more someone trusts and respects me, the more I want to relate to that person in the same way.

Mutual friends and lovers engage in a great deal of give-and-take in their relationships. Sometimes the giving-getting ratio will be eighty-to-twenty; at other times it is closer to twenty-to-eighty. But good friends don't keep books. They're willing to understand and wait for the ebb and flow to right itself in due time. I have a neighbor who is also a good friend. Sometimes he asks me to help him move a heavy piece of furniture. At other times, I'll ask him to pick up our mail and newspapers while we're out of town. Both of us would be hard pressed to say whether either of us has given or received more than the other in our friendship. What counts the most is that we feel comfortable asking such favors of each other because we're *mutual* friends. Do you have such a friend?

It takes teamwork to win

At its best, mutuality is expressed in the "we" identity so characteristic of successful sports teams and happy families. The people involved begin to think of themselves as "we" rather than a collections of "I's." Each retains his or her individuality, but is usually willing to subordinate self-interest for the good of the relationship or group. Here again, this is not always the case in close relationships. In informal conversation, a husband will say something like, "When I bought our house," only to be corrected by his wife, who asks, "When *you* bought our house?" "Oh," the husband explains hastily, "I mean when *we* bought our house." "That's more like it, dear," says his wife. In some instances, such first-person references may be chalked up to absent-mindedness, especially among the newly married. But happily married couples who have achieved a strong "we" identity are more apt to express themselves accordingly.

Commitment

Equally important to a satisfying relationship is commitment—the pledge or promise to make it work. There are many ways of committing ourselves to a relationship, ranging from an informal expression of interest to a legal contract like marriage. Sometimes a verbal remark such as "I'd like to see you again" is sufficient to strengthen a budding friendship. Also, when you love someone, you're making an important emotional commitment to that person, which partly explains why we don't fall in love easily. When such love is shared by both persons, their commitment to each other is even stronger. Pairing off as couples, going steady, and living together are further ways of committing ourselves to another person. Marriage and parenthood tend to be even more lasting types of commitment, partly because of the long-term emotional investment in the relationship as well as the legal contract involved. Married people usually don't realize the full extent of their commitment until years later when they're agonizing over their unhappy relationship or coping with a troubled teenager.

Sometimes we hesitate to make a lasting commitment out of fear that it will threaten our personal freedom. Such reluctance is understandable among young people facing major life commitments like a college education, career choice, or marriage. At this point in their lives many lack the knowledge, experience, and judgment to make a wise decision. They need to realize that such choices, though serious, are not irreversible. Unfortunately, the emphasis on personal freedom and fulfilment in recent years has diminished the number of lasting commitments made by people of all ages. People aspire to be free, to keep their options open and maximize opportunities for their own fulfilment. Consequently, more people are living together without bothering to marry. People also feel less loyalty to the institutions in their lives, whether it's the company they work for or their government. Yet a life of tentative commitments leaves us insecure, if not emotionally unsatisfied. After going with Hal, a law-school student, for three years without a hint of a marriage proposal, Nancy began pressing the matter in his senior year. But the more she asked about marriage, the more Hal resisted. "I'm not ready to make a commitment yet," he explained. However, when Nancy began dating other men, Hal became furious and accused her of betraying their relationship. Nancy replied, "If you aren't ready to make a commitment after all this time, I feel free to date other guys." For the next several weeks they engaged in heated arguments, mutual self-searching, and numerous late-night phone calls. Finally, they resolved things by becoming engaged. Both realized they need a firm mutual commitment in order for their relationship to grow and thrive.

There are advantages and disadvantages in making a firm commitment like marriage. An obvious disadvantage is the risk of getting trapped in an unhappy marriage, plus the emotional and financial penalties that go with divorce. A major advantage of marriage is the greater incentive for couples to work at their relationship during the low moments of their life together. Most married couples experience times when they doubt the wisdom of their marital choice. Having the firm commitment of a legal contract may motivate them to work all the harder at their marriage. Occasionally I see a couple whose marital problems seem overwhelming. Even marriage counseling doesn't seem to help. Then, perhaps partly out of desperation, one partner arrives at the conviction, "I've got to make this marriage work." When both partners reach this conclusion, it's amazing how their marriage improves.

Ultimately, commitments to enduring relationships are as essential to our personal fulfilment as to the satisfaction of the relationships themselves. The term *commitment* itself points us away from ourselves, whether in self-denial or self-fulfilment, toward our connectedness to others. We're reminded that we are social beings. We not only have needs for things like individual achievement and recognition, we also have needs for belonging, sharing, and helping others. Fulfilling ourselves as social beings requires that we learn to get along with others. In so doing, we must constantly balance the claims of self with those of others. We may easily overdo either side of this balance. Hans Selye, the famous authority on stress, noticed that patients suffering from stress-linked illnesses also have a warped code of behavior, one that emphasizes either too much selfishness or too much sacrifice. Instead, he advocates that we adopt the attitude of "altruistic egoism"—looking out for ourselves by making ourselves necessary and helpful to others.[10]

In this chapter, we've introduced the general theme of self and others. The remaining chapters in the book will explore ways of helping us to achieve mutually satisfying relationships in specific areas of life, like friendship, marriage, sex, communication, work, and leisure. But the need for balancing the claims of self with those of others remains the same throughout.

---

[10]Hans Selye, "On the Real Benefits of Eustress," *Psychology Today* (March 1978): 69.

SUMMARY

1. As "people who need people," we're constantly seeking out others for a variety of purposes. We join with others to achieve common goals. We seek out people to alleviate stress and to share our special moments. Also, in times of uncertainty and change we feel a need to compare our opinions with those of others. All of this results in a great deal of conformity in everyday life.

2. Changing values in recent years have brought about a greater emphasis on self-fulfilment, resulting in less social conformity. Yet we pointed out certain contradictions that make the search for self-fulfilment disappointing, such as periodic downturns in the economy as well as the inner pressure of exaggerated expectations. As a result, the search for self-fulfilment may end in disillusionment and loneliness, with couples getting divorced for reasons that would not have led to divorce in the past.

3. In the last part of the chapter we discussed how we must learn to balance the claims of self with those of other people in order to achieve mutually satisfying relationships. Such relationships tend to be characterized by a warmth and closeness, mutuality, and a commitment to make the relationship work. Commitment also points us toward our connectedness with others, reminding us that self-fulfilment and satisfying relationships go hand in hand.

SELF-TEST

1. People usually like to be alone when they are:
   a. happy
   b. embarrassed
   c. under stress
   d. confused

2. You would probably experience less stress before a test if you were:
   a. with a friend
   b. alone
   c. with a stranger
   d. talking to your teacher

3. When comparing our opinions with those of others, we tend to look for people who are:
   a. experts
   b. unlike ourselves
   c. like ourselves
   d. strangers

4. We seek the company of others for the purpose of:
   a. reducing stress
   b. achieving common goals
   c. sharing special occasions
   d. all of the above

5. The upheaval in traditional values throughout the 1970s led to a greater emphasis on:
   a. marriage
   b. self-fulfilment
   c. helping others
   d. all of the above

6. The search for self-fulfilment may be frustrated by things like:
     a. exaggerated expectations   c. an emphasis on inner needs
     b. a tight job market   d. all of the above

7. People in the _____ year-old age bracket tend to suffer the most from loneliness.
     a. 18 to 25   c. 36 to 55
     b. 26 to 35   d. 56 and over

8. _____ has to do with people reaching out for more satisfying relationships with others.
     a. self-fulfilment   c. alleviating stress
     b. the search for community   d. all of the above

9. _____ refers to two or more people having the same relationship toward each other.
     a. cooperation   c. mutuality
     b. self-fulfilment   d. conformity

10. We may commit ourselves to another person through:
      a. love   c. living together
      b. marriage   d. all of the above

EXERCISES

1. *Your preferences for being alone or with others.* Look over the thirteen situations in Table 1-1. First, select three of these situations in which you would want to be with others. Then, select the three situations in which you would want to be alone. Explain why in each case. How similar are your preferences compared to those of other students?

2. *When do you most want to compare your feelings and opinions with those of others?* Reread the material under the subheading "Comparisons and Conformity." Then think of several situations in which you're most apt to compare your feelings and opinions with other people's. Would you agree that we're especially likely to compare reactions in times of uncertainty and change?

3. *How important is self-fulfilment to you?* Look over the items in Figure 1-2 regarding the importance of self-fulfilment as a lifestyle. Then go down the list indicating how much you agree with each item as follows: *SA*—strongly agree; *A*—agree; or *D*—disagree. Considering your responses as a whole, which group do you most resemble—the "strong formers" or the mainstream majority?

4. *Obstacles to self-fulfilment.* Write a paragraph or two describing some of the factors which prevent you from actualizing your potential. How many of these obstacles, such as a tendency to procrastinate, lie within

you? How many of them come from your surroundings, like your job or financial situation? Are you actively working to overcome some of these obstacles?

5. *How do you cope with loneliness?* Recall several instances in which you felt very lonely. Then explain, in a paragraph or so, how you dealt with your feelings of loneliness. Did you react passively, by watching TV, eating, or sleeping a lot? Or did you take more active steps to decrease your loneliness, such as reading, working, writing a letter, or calling up a friend?

6. *Taking stock of your close relationships.* Think about the people you see on a regular basis, especially those you see every day. How many of these people do you have a close, personal relationship with? Also, to what extent is the emotional involvement and commitment mutual in your close relationships? All this considered, are you satisfied with your close relationships to family members and friends? Or are you searching for more satisfying intimate relationships?

Meeting People

2

FIRST IMPRESSIONS
  Physical appearance
  Reputation
  Speech
  Nonverbal behavior

MISTAKEN IMPRESSIONS
  Person or situation?
  False cues
  Stereotypes
  The halo effect

MAKING A GOOD IMPRESSION
  Act natural
  Put your best foot forward
  Show an interest in others
  Emphasize what you have in common
  Give sincere praise

SUMMARY

SELF-TEST

EXERCISES

Greg and Lisa climb out of the swimming pool and head toward two empty lounge chairs. As they pass a young woman in a string bikini, Greg whistles softly to himself. "Watch it," says Lisa in mock indignation.

"Aw, she's probably pretty stuck on herself, anyway," mumbles Greg, as he settles into his chair.

"How do *you* know?" asks Lisa. "You misjudged *me* when we first met. Remember?"

"Ah yes, I recall," laughs Greg. "I thought you were really stuck up too."

"See," Lisa points out, "and you were wrong. Admit it."

"Okay," admits Greg, raising his arms in playful surrender.

"I still can't figure out why you thought I was conceited," says Lisa.

"I dunno," says Greg. "I guess it was the way you avoided looking at me. Even after we began talking to each other, you kept looking away from time to time."

"I was shy," Lisa says. "I don't usually look people in the eye, especially new people. It wasn't just you."

"Well, now I know," adds Greg. "But for a while there I thought you were avoiding me for some reason. I almost didn't ask you out."

"I'm sure glad you did," says Lisa, as she smiled at him. "To be honest, I misjudged you too."

"How's that?"

"Well, when you said you were studying electronics, I thought, 'how boring.' I mean, I've always felt that people who worked with anything mechanical were kind of dull."

"Aha," Greg says, pointing his finger at her, "and you were wrong too, weren't you?"

"Okay, okay, I realize that now," admits Lisa. "I guess it was just another one of those dumb stereotypes."

"I'm glad you saw the light," chimes in Greg.

"Me too," adds Lisa, as she laughs softly and settles back in her chair.

FIRST IMPRESSIONS

Ever notice how quick we are to judge others? You pass a stranger in the hallway. Or you hand your deposit to a new teller at the bank. Or you may speak with someone you don't know on the phone. You know little or nothing about any of these people, but if you're like most of us, you'll quickly form a definite impression about them. Maybe it's the way this person looked or walked. Perhaps it's one's mannerisms or tone of voice. But in all cases the fundamental principle of *person perception* is this: we form extensive impressions of people on the basis of very little information about them.

Why are we in such a hurry to judge others? One reason is curiosity. Even when someone is apparently avoiding us, as Greg felt Lisa was doing, we're intrigued. We want to know why. Another reason has to do with anxiety and our need to understand the people around us, particularly in case we have to respond to them. The greater our fears about others, the more we misjudge them. Also, we assume a lot about people and often don't bother to confirm our hunches. As a result, we're continually discovering new things about people we thought we knew.

Fortunately, we modify our impressions of others as we know them better, as Greg and Lisa did. In some cases, we're reluctant to do so. Perhaps we hate to admit we were wrong. Or it may be a bit unsettling to realize we don't fully know what another person is like. In either case, we may minimize our misjudgments of people by being aware of our tendency to judge them too

Attractive people are judged more favorably, even on characteristics that have nothing to do with looks.

quickly. It also helps to realize how our impressions are influenced by such things as a person's appearance, reputation, manner of speaking, or nonverbal behavior.

Physical appearance

We're warned, "Don't judge a book by its cover." Yet it's hard not to, isn't it? A person's overall appearance makes a powerful impression on us. Someone's face, size, shape, and manner of dress all affect our senses and feelings. We're especially affected by how physically attractive someone is.

Physically attractive people evoke a wealth of associations in our minds, most of them positive. On being asked to give their impressions of photos of men and women of varying degrees of attractiveness, people attribute all sorts of positive qualities to the attractive ones. And the more physically attractive the person, the more favorable the impression. Many of the attributed qualities logically have little, if anything, to do with a person's appearance. Yet, the better-looking people are judged to be more interesting, kind, sensitive, poised, and sociable than others. Attractive people are also seen as more likely to achieve success in their careers and find happiness in their personal lives. Physical attractiveness is also associated with such diverse accomplishments as getting better jobs, faster promotions, winning national elections, suffering less serious psychiatric disorders, and receiving lighter sentences upon violations of the law.

Conversely, unattractive people may be viewed unfairly in terms of personal qualities that have nothing to do with physical beauty. As a result, we may unconscionably discriminate against unattractive people. Uglies Unlimited, an association of men and women who are concerned about this problem, are now taking such cases to court. Part of the difficulty they face is the lack of a standard definition of ugliness. Like beauty, ugliness is largely in the eye of the beholder. For some, baldness or fatness may qualify. To others, irregular features such as a large nose or discolored skin makes for ugliness.

We are not always so favorably impressed with "beautiful" people. Handsome men and beautiful women may strike us as egotistical and vain. They are also more likely to be rejected by their same-sex peers, partly because of jealousy. Although physically attractive people may be seen as more interesting and exciting than less attractive people, they are also viewed as less sincere or concerned about others. Rightly or wrongly, it seems that beauty is associated more with glamor than with deeper positive qualities.

Reputation

Suppose someone says, "I want you to meet Bill, a friend of mine. I think you'll like him," the chances are you will. Even before you meet Bill, you'll find yourself forming some kind of impression of him based on his reputation. If you hear good things about Bill first, you'll naturally form a favorable impression of him. Even if you later discover he also has some undesirable qualities, you'll probably give him the benefit of the doubt. On the other hand, if you hear bad things first, you're more likely to form an unfavorable impression of Bill, however undeserved this may be.

This point was strikingly demonstrated when college men were asked to get acquainted, during a ten-minute telephone conversation, with a woman student they had never met. Before the call was made, the men saw a photograph of the woman. Actually, the photograph was of someone else. Half the men were shown photos of attractive women. The other half saw photos of women judged to be unattractive by an independent panel of judges. When the men were asked what they expected of their telephone acquaintances, those who thought they would be talking to an attractive woman said she would probably be sociable, poised, and have a good sense of humor. Those who thought they would be talking to an unattractive woman expected her to be unsociable, awkward, and overly serious. Not surprisingly, based on the telephone conversations with the women whom they thought they had seen photos of, the men thought the attractive women sounded warm, charming, and humorous. Similarly, they thought the unattractive women sounded cold, clumsy, and humorless.[1] Such is the power of reputation.

Speech

Whether speaking face-to-face or on the telephone, we pay a lot of attention to what people say and how they say it. Those who are confident and well-spoken impress us more favorably than those who appear uncertain and inarticulate. How much people talk also affects the impression we have of them. Generally, those who talk a lot are seen as leaders in a group, especially if they know what they're talking about. Otherwise, they may be seen as domineering or rude. In social conversation, both men and women tend to like talkative people, at least up to a point. Women who talk for up to three-quarters of the time in a conversation may be seen as more friendly, intelligent, and outgoing than less talkative women. Yet men who talk this much may not fare so well. Apparently men are assumed to have more power in social conversation, rightly or wrongly. But when they exploit it by dominating conversation with women, they may come across as impolite and inconsiderate. Furthermore, talkative men who disclose a lot about themselves may contradict the stereotype of the "strong, silent male."[2]

The impression people make depends on many other characteristics of their speech, such as volume, rate of speech, tone of voice, and accent. People with loud voices are apt to be seen as extroverts; those with quiet voices are seen as introverts, or at least shy. Those who speak rapidly may be seen as more intelligent or persuasive than others. But an excessively fast rate of speech may also indicate anxiety, either about what is being discussed or about the person with whom one is speaking. People who speak in a warm, relaxed tone of voice make a pleasing impression on us, whereas those who speak in a cold constricted tone of voice come across more unfavorably.

People's accents also affect our impression of them. Perhaps you've noticed how TV ads often feature someone with a polished foreign accent. It's as if the sponsor wants to associate the product with prestige, thus creating an image of glamor and desirability in our minds. Regional accents also make their mark on us. People who speak in a New England accent are apt to be judged favorably, partly because of the heritage associated with that part of the country. On the other hand, those who speak with a Southern accent are apt to be judged less favorably, often unfairly so, especially by the poorly educated. However, the popularity of country-and-western music in recent years has helped to emphasize the positive qualities associated with less sophisticated accents.

[1]M. Snyder, E. D. Tanke, and E. Berscheid, "Social Perception and Interpersonal Behavior: On the Self-fulfilling Nature of Social Stereotypes," *Journal of Personality and Social Psychology*, 35 (1977): 656–666.

[2]C.L. Kleinke, *First Impressions* (Englewood Cliffs, N.J.: Prentice-Hall, Inc., 1975), pp. 81–84.

Figure 2-1 Actions speak louder than words.

Nonverbal behavior

A person's posture, facial expressions, and gestures definitely affect how we see them. Someone who sits or stands erect while talking to us is more likely to make a positive impression than one who slouches in his chair or who puts her feet on the desk. Similarly, someone who points, glares, and interrupts a lot will make a negative impression compared to one who is relaxed and listens to what we say. Generally, we are more favorably impressed with those who look us in the eye, though not with a stare. People who look at us are more apt to be seen as trustworthy and likable. Those who avoid our gaze strike us as having something to hide, whether from guilt, deceit, or just plain shyness. Yet the aggressive sales person who looks us steadily in the eye may be overdoing it, leading us to resent such an intrusion into our privacy.

A word of caution is in order in regard to nonverbal behavior. Popular understanding has it that nonverbal expressions have some kind of universal meaning. There is the notion, for instance, that folded arms always mean defensiveness. But this simply isn't so. Nonverbal expressions are best understood in the particular situation in which they occur. For example, I once saw a hypnotist ask for volunteers to assist him in a demonstration on stage. But among the volunteers who raised their hands, the only ones selected were those who were sitting in a relaxed posture, with arms dropped by their sides. Many of them were slouched in their seats. No one with arms or legs crossed was chosen. I suspect the hypnotist interpreted such body language simply as an indication of the volunteer's attitude toward hypnosis. I doubt that he would have made the mistake of judging their personalities that way, i.e., of regarding all those with folded arms or legs as defensive people. We'll point out the importance of other aspects of nonverbal behavior in a later chapter on communication.

Smiling

People who smile at us usually make a more favorable impression than those who don't. This is probably why people in TV ads seem to smile indiscriminately. Smiling suggests willingness to please. Smiling is especially welcome in situations where we are anxious or uncertain. The smiling hostess in a crowded restaurant reassures those waiting in line that they haven't been forgotten.

Smiling is affected by so many different factors it shouldn't be taken at face value. For instance, people smile more on sunny days than rainy ones. Women tend to smile more than men. There are also regional differences. Southerners smile more readily than people in the crowded northeastern part of the United States. The "low-smile" region of the country stretches from upstate New York through New England. Maybe the cold weather has something to do with it.

Because smiling is affected by so many things, perhaps we should be careful in judging individuals by their smiles until we know what their smiling means.

MISTAKEN IMPRESSIONS

You're attending a party at a friend's house. He wants to introduce you to this terrific girl he knows. He nods in her direction; sure enough, she's very attractive. You're introduced, and you begin talking together. You discover you have a lot in common. But as you listen, you also get the feeling this person is somewhat opinionated, if not snobbish. You're getting mixed signals. Is she as terrific as you were led to believe? Or is this a mistaken impression? You'll never be sure until you get to know her better.

The above incident illustrates the most common source of mistaken impressions, namely, insufficient information. We misjudge people mostly because we don't know them well enough. Given our tendency to "size up" people rather quickly, this shouldn't be surprising. In some cases, we may not have known the person long enough. Or we may not have seen this person in

Figure 2-2 Smiling breaks the ice.

enough different situations. Perhaps we have not become emotionally involved with the person, having known him or her only at a distance. In the following section, several of the ways in which our lack of information leads us to misjudge people will be explained. These include the tendency to judge people in terms more of motives and traits than of circumstances. There's also our reaction to false cues, to a person's speech, and to various stereotypes. We'll also discuss the halo effect, or the tendency to label people good or bad on the basis of just a few good or bad qualities.

Person or situation?

We frequently misjudge people by underestimating the influence of situational factors on their behavior, and overestimating the role of personal traits and motives. We tend to think that people always behave in a certain way because they choose to, when if the truth were known they're often restricted by their circumstances. I saw an example of this in my own class. I announced that I was inviting Dr. Johnson, the college registrar, to give a special lecture in class. Immediately the class broke out in moans and protests. When I asked what all the fuss was about, students began recounting the usual horror stories about registration, such as having to stand in long lines and not getting the schedules they wanted. I explained that a lot of this had to do with the process of registration itself rather than Dr. Johnson's personality. But my words fell on deaf ears.

Sure enough, on the day my guest spoke several students skipped class. But those who attended gradually warmed up to him, and enjoyed the discussion following the talk. In the next class period I discovered that the students had formed a much more favorable impression of Dr. Johnson in the classroom setting than they had at registration. My positive remarks about the guest speaker or his reputation probably influenced their impressions of him. Yet in both instances—during registration and in class—student impressions of Dr. Johnson were heavily influenced by situational factors.

Perhaps you've had a similar experience. Someone you didn't care for too much in one situation came across much more favorably at another time and place. It's not that the other person is being deceitful; rather, everyone's behavior is a combination of inner traits and external influences. To avoid misjudging people, we should be aware of the powerful and changing influence of situational factors. Also, if you want to know what a person is really like, interact with that person in different situations.

False cues

Wrong impressions frequently result from false cues. The latter consist of signals and indirect suggestions which unconciously trigger off certain associations in our minds. The marks of success and wealth often become false cues, especially to the unsuspecting. Since people who are highly successful and financially well-off characteristically indulge in expensive items like lavish houses and cars, we may mistakenly assume that anyone who has such things is rich. Not so. In one instance, a man hoping to sell false franchises for a fictional fast-food chain established a temporary office in a prestigious building and rented a Rolls Royce car to impress his clients. He made a small fortune before a group of disillusioned customers took him to court. In another case, a couple living on social security payments transformed themselves into jet-setters by displaying signs of wealth. They spread the word that they were about to inherit millions of dollars from a rich uncle, and then proceeded to run up huge charge accounts against the anticipated fortune. In due time, as their creditors became suspicious at so many unpaid bills, the deception was uncovered.

I recall a resourceful student who solved his check-cashing problem by turning false cues to his advantage. It seems that bank tellers were reluctant to cash his checks because of the widespread belief that anyone who resembles a student, i.e., is dressed in jeans and the like, must be poor. Not to be outdone, he returned to one of the banks that had previously refused him; but this time he was dressed in a coat and tie and carried a handsome attaché case. He cashed his check with ease. Unfortunately, people with ulterior motives can do the same. During the rush of Christmas shopping, one man disguised himself as Santa Claus and then successfully robbed a bank.

The moral is, don't judge people by too few cues. Try not to be overly impressed by signs of wealth and status. When there's a lot at stake, take time to know more about the people you're dealing with.

Stereotypes

These are widespread generalizations that have little, if any, basis in fact. Yet they are so common we assume that they are true. When people preface their remarks by phrases like *all women drivers* or *all doctors*, we may rightly suspect that they are thinking in terms of stereotypes. An example of stereotypic thinking is the commonly accepted notion that people who wear glasses are smarter than those who don't. The unspoken assumption is that such people have used their eyes so much for reading and studying that they need glasses. The fact is that the need for glasses has more to do with hereditary weakness of the eyes than one's study habits.

Other stereotypes have to do with things like hair growth and hair color. Men with beards, mustaches, and an abundance of body hair are seen to be more masculine and virile than those with less hair. Redheads of both sexes are regarded as more hot-tempered than people with other hair colors. Women brunettes are viewed as more intelligent and responsible than blondes, while blondes are thought to be more fun and sexier. Perhaps this has something to do with the stereotype of the dumb blonde.

Figure 2-3

Referring to some of his teammates, a football player once said, "Whenever I hear a guy speaking with a Southern drawl, I think 'stupid.'" It probably didn't occur to him that other people may feel the same way about football players. And so it goes. The truth is, stereotypes—all stereotypes—distort our perception of other people. We see the person we want to see, or need to see, rather than the person right there in front of us. Have you ever felt you were a victim of stereotyping? If so, in what way? Are you sometimes guilty of misunderstanding others because of your own favorite stereotypes? Be honest.

Changing Stereotypes

Have you ever noticed how ethnic stereotypes keep changing?

Throughout the '30s and World War II, the Japanese were pictured as shrewd, sly people. *Made in Japan* became synonymous with inferior products. But in recent years, the increasing market in the United States for Japanese products such as cars and stereos has evoked admiration and imitation. The Japanese are now seen as intelligent and industrious. Western management experts visit Japan in hopes of learning their industrial secrets.

Blacks were viewed as lazy and superstitious throughout the '30s and '40s in our country. Since the rise of the civil rights movement in the '50s, however, blacks have been seen as more militant and politically active. Moreover, the increasing visibility of blacks in sports and musical groups has been accompanied by the emergence of the stereotype of blacks as especially talented in athletics and music.

Do you think these people have changed that much? Or do our stereotypes tend to reflect changing attitudes and social conditions?

The halo effect

This is the tendency to label people with global judgments like good or bad simply on the basis of a few good or bad characteristics. It's as if the person wears a halo (ring of light) over his or her head, like an angel, and can do no wrong. This is especially true in regard to key qualities like warmth and sociability. Once we see someone as warm and sociable, we're likely to attribute all kinds of other positive qualities to this person, like intelligence and industriousness. Conversely, when someone is seen as cold and withdrawn, we're apt to infer that this person possesses other negative qualities as well. In the latter case, we speak of a *negative halo effect,* or the *devil effect.*

Like stereotyping, the halo effect tempts us to view people in global, simplistic terms. In reality, of course, each one of us is a more complex mixture of positive and negative qualities than we appear. A colleague tells of one of her "poorer" students who drove her to distraction by taking every one of her computer courses twice. Sometimes he retook a course simply to pass; at other times he wanted to earn a better grade. "He was always asking questions," she said. "He nearly drove me crazy." Several years later she came across this student at a convention and discovered he had become highly successful in computers. In fact, he was making more money than his former teacher. Interestingly, he attributed much of his success to having learned everything in school "so well." My colleague was dumbfounded, though pleasantly so. Needless to say she's more cautious about labeling students these days. Watch that halo effect.

All things considered, it's amazing that more of our impressions of people aren't mistaken. This is especially true when you realize how quickly we judge others. Speaking personally, the longer I work with people, the more I try to delay judgment of someone until I get to know him or her better. I may be impressed at first by this one's beauty or that one's manner of dress. Sometimes a person reminds me very much of someone else I know. But in the back of my mind I always remember that each of us is a distinct individual with different strengths and weaknesses. As I get to know someone better, inevitably I discover this person is more complex and interesting than he or she appeared at first glance. Is this true in your experience?

MAKING A GOOD IMPRESSION

By now you may be asking yourself how you come across to people or what you can do to make a better impression. No set of instructions in themselves will guarantee success, for so much depends on the individual and the situation. However, you can use many of the principles we've discussed so far to make a better impression. What follows are suggested strategies that have proven helpful to others. But each of you must adapt them to your own personality and life situation.

Act natural

In their haste to make a good impression, individuals sometimes forget the most important point of all—be yourself. You usually make the most favorable impression when you act naturally. Otherwise, you may come across as stilted or phony.

Trying too hard is a common mistake. For example, in one demonstration some college women dressed, as they normally did, in blue jeans. Others put on dresses and high heels as they would for a special occasion. Half of the women in each group added a touch of perfume; the other half did not. Then a group of young men were asked which women they felt most attracted to. Surprisingly, the men preferred the women dressed in jeans and giving off a fragrant scent. The most likely explanation is that these women were seen as simply enhancing their natural manner of dress. Those who dressed up in heels and wore perfume were viewed as aloof and conceited, or trying too hard to make a good impression.[3]

Put your best foot forward

Acting naturally doesn't preclude looking your best. Whether you're attending a party or being interviewed for a job, it's natural to want to put your best foot forward. This includes being reasonably clean, well groomed, and well dressed. You have probably heard enough comments from your friends to know which clothes look best on you and what hairstyle is most becoming.

It is also important to dress appropriately for the occasion. I recall a young man who discovered this the hard way. Normally he dressed very casually, as did most of the other students. Then one day he spotted a newspaper

---

Opening Lines

You're seated alone in a bar. You see an attractive woman sitting with a female friend nearby. You'd like very much to meet her. But how? If you wait for an introduction or a suitable occasion it may never happen. Instead, if you are like many people in our mobile society, you are increasingly likely to take the initiative.

Some men, fearing rejection, use flippant lines such as, "Your place or mine?" or, "How would you like to take me home with you?" Yet most women are put off by such an approach. When questioned on the subject, individuals of both sexes overwhelmingly prefer a more tactful approach, preferably innocuous lines such as, "I don't think I've had the pleasure of meeting you," "Hi, I'm so-and-so," or, "Would you like to dance?"

Young women are also more willing than in the past to take the initiative with men they want to know better. In some cases, women may introduce themselves first, often while socializing in a mixed group. In other instances, a smile directed toward the men they are interested in is enough to encourage further contact.

What are the pros and cons of this approach? The hazards? Can you think of better ways of meeting new people?

---

[3]R.A. Baron, "Effects of a Pleasant Scent on Social Behavior" (Paper presented at meeting the American Psychological Association, Montreal, September 1980).

ad for a job he wanted. He responded by shaving off his mustache and beard and dressing up in a suit and tie. I hardly recognized him. Later, when he returned from the job interview, he looked depressed. He hadn't been given the job. I suggested he find out why so he could benefit from his experience in future job interviews. He was told that the company was looking for more of a "campus type," someone who would be easily accepted by students. The young man was devastated. Had he simply been himself and put his best foot forward he might have been given the job. He also learned an important lesson—dress appropriately for the occasion.

Show an interest in others

One of the best ways of making a good impression is to show an interest in others. Perhaps we should add—a *sincere* interest. Be attentive. Face the other person. Maintain eye contact with the person you're talking to. Eye contact generally enhances communication and the impression you make. You might also bear in mind that the usual pattern of eye contact during conversation is that of alternatively looking at the speaker and then looking away before rees-tablishing eye contact. Otherwise, a gaze turns into a stare which becomes an intrusion to the other person's privacy. Normally, the person doing the listen-ing is more intent on maintaining eye contact with the speaker. Perhaps this helps focus attention on what the other person is saying.

Be a good listener. Remember that people are much more interested in their own ideas and experiences than in other people's lives. The art of being a good conversationalist is learning how to listen, drawing out the other person's ideas and reactions. Unless your partner is a compulsive talker or a bore, he or she will respond to your interest by wanting to get to know you better.

Emphasize what you have in common

Because we are attracted to those with similar backgrounds and interests, build on what you have in common with others. This doesn't mean that you can't be yourself. Far from it. It simply means that in order to develop a rapport with others you begin talking about what you have in common before moving on to things on which you may differ. This is probably why so much "small talk" is about the weather or trivial events. At least it's a safe starting point while people get acquainted.

It is also important to maintain credibility. Everyone realizes that each of us is an individual. You're not expected to be just like everyone else. The world would be a boring place if you were, wouldn't it? But whenever possible it pays to agree on as many important issues as you can before expressing disagreement. You might say something like, "I agree on the need to strengthen our national security, but I disagree with the way our government is

Figure 2-4

going about this." Such a statement allows for more discussion than an outright disagreement. Interestingly, people are more likely to form a favorable impression of you if your views are believable. Although people who disagree with others all the time are the least liked, those who readily agree all the time are not necessarily the best liked. People who disagree sometimes, especially when they are open to change, are viewed more favorably by their partners than those who always agree or disagree.[4]

Give sincere praise

With few exceptions, people like to hear favorable comments about themselves, so sincere praise goes a long way in making a good impression on others. Compliments often come naturally by emphasizing the positive. For example, you may observe that your friend remains remarkably unruffled while driving in city traffic. So why not say something like, "I admire the way you stay so calm while driving in the city." Or you may notice that someone looks especially attractive for an occasion. Why not tell that person, "You look great tonight."

There are two important conditions to keep in mind. The first is that praise must be sincere to be appreciated. Insincere praise is flattery, which usually makes a negative impression. One possible exception is with low-esteem people who may be so starved for approval they will believe anything. But most of us resent flattery. The second condition is that you have nothing obvious to gain by giving a compliment. Otherwise, giving praise may be seen as an ex-

[4]J. Lombardo, R. Weiss, and W. Buchanon, "Reinforcing and Attracting Functions of Yielding," *Journal of Personality and Social Psychology* 21 (1972): 359–368.

pression of an ulterior motive. Such calculated compliments often occur in sales transactions, which may seduce the unsuspecting but more often offends those with good sense. So when you're talking with a client or with your boss, go easy on the compliments lest your motives be misunderstood.

By following these suggestions, you can make a better impression on others. But remember what was said at the outset. No strategies in themselves will guarantee success. So much depends on you, your life situation, and how well you apply these suggestions. Finally, keep in mind the most important point of all—be yourself.

SUMMARY

1. Each of us tends to judge people rather quickly, usually on the basis of very little information. Possible reasons for this include curiosity, anxiety, and our need to understand others before responding to them. Our impressions are influenced by many things, especially a person's physical appearance, reputation, speech, and behavior.

2. The most common cause of mistaken impressions is the lack of sufficient information about people. We tend to underestimate the importance of situational factors and overestimate the influence of inner motives and traits. We may also misjudge people because of false cues, stereotypes, and the halo effect.

3. You can use the principles of impression formation discussed in this chapter to make a better impression on others. Suggested strategies include acting naturally, putting your best foot forward, showing an interest in others, emphasizing what you have in common, and giving sincere praise.

SELF-TEST

1. When we first meet people, we tend to judge them mostly on the basis of:
   a. their family background   c. very little information
   b. how much money they make   d. their educational level

2. _____ people are more likely to be judged interesting, happy, sociable, and successful in their careers.
   a. highly intelligent   c. very tall
   b. physically attractive   d. wealthy

3. We tend to have a favorable impression of conversation partners who:
   a. look us in the eye   c. are physically attractive
   b. smile at us   d. all of the above

4. The most common source of mistaken impressions of others is:
   a. insufficient information
   b. regional speech accents
   c. conflicting information
   d. erroneous reputations

5. People frequently misjudge others because they underestimate the importance of:
   a. inner motives
   b. social status
   c. situational influences
   d. personal traits

6. _____ are widespread generalizations that have little basis in fact.
   a. reputations
   b. stereotypes
   c. compliments
   d. false cues

7. _____ tempts us to regard people as wholly good or bad simply on the basis of a few good or bad characteristics.
   a. reputation
   b. physical appearance
   c. the halo effect
   d. stereotyping

8. In going for a job interview, it's especially important to:
   a. wear expensive clothes
   b. speak up frequently
   c. dress appropriately
   d. give a lot of compliments

9. One of the best ways to make a good impression on others is to:
   a. express sincere interest
   b. ask favors of them
   c. compliment them a lot
   d. all of the above

10. People are more likely to form a favorable impression of us when our views:
    a. never agree with theirs
    b. are believable
    c. always agree with theirs
    d. are always correct

EXERCISES

1. *First impressions.* Select someone in your class you haven't met. Then jot down as many impressions of this person as you can. Now make it a point to meet this person and become better acquainted. To what extent were your first impressions accurate? Inaccurate? Would you agree that we tend to judge people rather hastily?

2. *Favorable and unfavorable impressions.* Think of several people who made a favorable impression on you. Also think of an equal number of people who made an unfavorable impression on you. In each instance, what most impressed you about these people? How influential were things like reputation, physical appearance, speech, and behavior?

3. *Do you see some people wearing "halos"?* Are there people you've generally labeled *good* or *successful*? Do these people have any faults? Conversely, are there people you regard as *bad* or *failures*? Do these people have any redeeming qualities? Would you agree that in everyone there is a

more complex mixture of desirable and undesirable personal qualities than is apparent to the superficial observer?

4. *Think of people you've misjudged.* How do you account for this? Can you relate your mistaken impressions to some of the things discussed in this chapter? Which ones? Would you agree we tend to judge people on the basis of too little information?

5. *List some common stereotypes in everyday life.* Examples would include stereotypes like *all women drivers* and *all teachers.* You might organize your list into categories like sex stereotypes, ethnic stereotypes, career stereotypes, and so forth. Is there any truth to these stereotypes? What purpose do they serve?

6. *What kind of impression do you make on others?* How do you know? Recall some unexpected compliments you've received. Think back to some of the critical comments others have made to you. You might ask your friends and colleagues to give their first impressions of you, preferably in relation to specific situations. List some changes needed to make a better impression on others.

Becoming Friends

3

WHAT ATTRACTS PEOPLE?
    Nearness
    Similarity
    Physical attractiveness
    Liking

FRIENDSHIP
    Who are your friends?
    What friends do together
    Rules of friendship
    Lasting friendships

FRIENDSHIP AND INTIMACY
    Self-disclosure
    Compatibility
    Dealing with differences
    Intimacy and growth

SUMMARY

SELF-TEST

EXERCISES

Marie meets her friend Jackie on their first day in Introductory Psychology. The instructor has divided the class into pairs so that they can get acquainted and introduce each other to the class. Since Marie is sitting next to Jackie, they introduce themselves and begin exchanging information about themselves.

"What are you studying?" Marie asks.

"I'm hoping to get into the nursing program," replies Jackie.

"What a coincidence, that's what I'm planning to study too."

"You and several hundred others," laughs Jackie. "I hear it's very difficult to get into the nursing program here."

"That's what I understand too," adds Marie.

Jackie asks, "Is this your first semester here?"

"Yes," replies Marie. "How about you?"

"This is my second semester. I waited until this semester to take the required Introductory Psych course."

"How hard are the courses?"

"It all depends on the instructor and the course," Jackie replies. "And how much you study," she adds with a laugh.

Marie says, "This is my first time back in school after eight years. I'm not sure how well I'm going to do."

"You'll get more confident after you've taken a few courses," Jackie reassures her. "A big problem for a lot of us with families is finding time to study."

"I'm worried about that too," Marie says. "I still have a little girl at home."

"I'm a little more fortunate," Jackie says. "My two boys are adolescents, so I can get a lot of my studying done before the boys come home after school."

"I'm planning to bring my little girl to the daycare center here at the college," adds Marie. "That should give me some study time in the library between classes."

At this moment they are interrupted by the instructor, who indicates that it is time for the students on the front row to begin introducing each other to the class.

WHAT ATTRACTS PEOPLE?

How did you meet your friends? Can you recall? Many friendships begin through chance encounters. You may have met your friends in the same class at school, as Marie and Jackie did. Or perhaps you live in the same neighborhood or work in the same company. Similarity also plays an important role in friendship. We're attracted to people we have a lot in common with; in some cases we're attracted to people who complement us in certain ways. Yet not everyone in the same course with the same career goals will become friends. A lot depends on the "chemistry," or subjective factors, in our relationships with others. Almost from the start, we seem to get along better with some individuals than others, don't we?

Psychologists have gathered a lot of information about interpersonal attraction and friendship. They've identified several key factors which influence our attraction to each other, including the following. We tend to like people who:

1. live or work near us
2. have a lot in common with us
3. are attractive and pleasant people
4. feel a liking for us

Nearness

The closer two people are geographically, the more likely they are to become friends. Think of who your friends are. Now visualize how you met them. Chances are that at some point your friends lived nearby, attended the same school, or worked in the same place. In some instances, you may have met your friends through other friends of yours.

Nearness facilitates friendship in several ways. First, coming into contact with people provides more opportunities for interacting with them. And there's a strong association between interaction and liking. That is, the more you interact with someone, the more you like that person. And vice versa: the more you like a person, the more you associate with him or her. Second, we tend to emphasize the positive qualities and play down the negative qualities of people we associate with. Feeling you're stuck with an unpleasant roommate or co-worker may otherwise arouse feelings of conflict and resentment. Also, social norms imply pleasant, cooperative relationships with others. We make a special effort to get along with the people who live or work closely with us. Otherwise, life might be miserable.

Nearness is especially important during the early stages of attraction. For example, in Julie's first year of college, her two best friends lived next door and across the hall. As she met more people on campus, she spent more time with other students. By her senior year, her two best friends were her boyfriend, who lived off-campus, and a girl who shared the same college major, who lived across the campus.

There are also limits to the connection between nearness and liking. When there are deep differences or incompatibilities between people, close interaction may work the opposite way, leading to overt conflict and alienation. Hence the saying "familiarity breeds contempt." In some cases, continued interaction among people who actively dislike each other leads to violence. It is well known by the police that in murder and assault cases the leading suspects are likely to be spouses, lovers, or co-workers.

Similarity

The old saying "Birds of a feather flock together" suggests another reason you're attracted to some people more than others, namely, similarity. This is especially true of such characteristics as one's attitudes and interests. When meeting people for the first time, notice how you gravitate toward those with attitudes and interests similar to your own. The more important the shared attitude is to you, whether in regard to work, sex, or religion, the more the bond of attraction will be strengthened. Similar attitudes also confirm your own opinions and beliefs, and this too makes for mutual attraction.

Having similar social characteristics heightens attraction in several ways. You feel more comfortable with those from the same background because you have more in common. Knowing that another person has been shaped by many of the same influences as yourself helps you to predict that person's behavior, putting you more at ease in his or her presence.

You're also attracted to people with personalities like your own. But the association between liking and similarity is weaker and less consistent in regard to personality than it is with other social characteristics. In one study, investigators found that the more similar in personality college freshmen were, the more they liked each other. But when they interviewed those students in their senior year, the link between similarity of personality and attraction had virtually disappeared. Maybe increased emotional and social maturity resulted in less need to have friends just like themselves. Or perhaps greater maturity makes people more tolerant of those who are different from themselves, at least in some aspects of personality.[1]

There's also some truth to the old adage, "opposites attract." This has been expressed in the theory of complementary needs. According to this view, when each person acts out of his or her needs in a way that simultaneously complements or satisfies the needs of another person, these two people may be

Figure 3-1

[1]C. E. Izard, "Personality Similarity and Friendship: A Follow-up Study," *Journal of Abnormal and Social Psychology* 66 (1963): 598–600.

especially attracted to each other. For example, a talkative dominant person may be attracted to someone who is more willing to listen and follow the lead. Together they make a good team. In actual practice, attraction based on complementary needs seems to apply more to specific traits than to one's personality as a whole. In one survey, when student nurses were asked their roommate preferences, most wanted someone with similar personal traits. Yet the follow-up questionnaire showed that roommates who remained together the longest were complementary in terms of dominance.[2]

Physical attractiveness

You're attending a party. You've spoken with at least two people of the opposite sex. One is strikingly attractive, but not especially friendly to you. The other person is not nearly as physically attractive, but seems interesting and enjoyable to talk with. Which person are you most attracted to? That's a difficult question to answer, isn't it? A lot depends of course on your values and the kind of relationship you're looking for. But there are other factors involved, and social scientists have shed some light on them.

In one study, students were evaluated on the basis of their personal traits, social skills, and physical attractiveness. Then they were randomly matched by a computer for a dance date. During the intermission, the students were asked how well they liked their partners. Six months later, they were asked the same question. As it turned out, physical attractiveness was the most important factor related to liking. What about each person's own looks? That's an important influence too, as was established in a related study. It seems that the more attractive you feel you are, the more you feel entitled to a partner of similar attractiveness. This is known as the *matching hypothesis.* According to this view, each of us might prefer the most attractive partner possible, but out of a fear of rejection, we'll settle for someone pretty much like ourselves.[3]

Attractiveness also varies somewhat between the sexes, as implied in a commercial computerized dating service which invited applications from "attractive" women and "successful" men. The unspoken assumption was that men are generally attracted to women on the basis of their looks and sex appeal, while women are attracted to men because of their personal qualities and achievements. Perhaps this has something to do with the traditional expectation that men be breadwinners. At the same time, men and women now view each other more similarly than in the past, as described in the boxed item below.

[2]E. Bermann and D. Miller, "The Matching of Mates," in *Cognition, Personality and Clinical Psychology*, eds. R. Jessor and S. Feshback (San Francisco: Jossey-Bass, 1967),

[3]E. Berscheid and E.H. Walster, *Interpersonal Attraction*, 2nd ed. (Reading, Mass.: Addison-Wesley Publishing Company, 1978), pp. 182–191.

What Makes Him So Attractive to Her?

When a woman is attracted to a man who is not obviously handsome, other men wonder why. Maybe he's rich or famous. But suppose he's not?

Actually, women are also attracted to men because of physical attractiveness. But women are attracted in a way that men are unaware of. When asked to imagine what physical attributes women most admire in men, men's responses usually emphasize muscular build (his chest, shoulders, or arms), the size of his penis (as suggested by tight pants), and to a lesser extent, such attributes as tallness and slimness. However, when women are asked what they really admire about a man's physical appearance, it's a different story. Women are likely to mention a man's eyes, his rear end (usually described as small and sexy), his slimness, tallness, and his flat stomach. A muscular chest and shoulders come at the bottom of the list. There are exceptions of course, such as the women who like a "hunk" of a man.

All this may come as a surprise to many men, partly because they aren't accustomed to judging their own sex in such terms. Men are apt to judge their male peers in terms of muscular development and athletic abilities. Actually, neither sex does too well in judging the physical attractiveness of their own sex, because the standards of attractiveness vary considerably between the sexes.

Liking

We're also attracted to people who like us. Deep within, each of us needs love and approval. People who are affectionate and friendly and do things for us touch a responsive chord within us. Those who are cool and critical toward us tend to be disliked. This is probably why people with warm, pleasant personalities are generally popular. It's also why we're attracted to people who say complimentary things about us, as long as we feel they are sincere.

"That's not always true," says Carol. "When Brad and I first met, he was so critical of me I couldn't stand him. But by the end of the semester we had become good friends." Carol's experience illustrates Elliott Aronson's *gain-loss theory* of attraction. According to this view, it's the gain or loss in someone's liking for us that determines our attraction to them. We're especially attracted to someone who increases his or her liking for us throughout the relationship. An example would be someone, perhaps like Brad, who at first doesn't care too much for us but then gradually increases his or her affection over a period of time. Conversely, we especially dislike those who have decreased their liking for us. An example would be a person we've cared a great deal for, perhaps in a romantic relationship or marriage, who has cooled his or her affection for us. In the latter case, the decreased acceptance arouses our anxiety and self-doubt. By contrast, in the former case the increase in affection strengthens our sense of acceptance and our self-confidence. In this way the gain-loss theory helps explain why we come to like people we initially didn't care too much for, and how long-term relationships may grow out of earlier disappointments and in-compatibilities. It's as if the more you have to work at a relationship, the more you come to value it.

Does this mean we won't appreciate or may take for granted those who've liked or loved us all along? Not necessarily. In one study, subjects were exposed to two conditions of liking: in the first, individuals went from a negative to a positive evaluation for the subject; in the second, individuals were consistently positive toward the subject. The comparison of these two conditions showed that those who consistently gave positive evaluations were preferred. Thus we're most attracted to individuals who *consistently* like or love us.[4]

FRIENDSHIP

Mutual attraction between two people often ripens into friendship—the affec-tionate attachment between friends. Ordinarily, we think of a friend as someone we've known a long time. Yet friendship has more to do with the quality of our relationships. Think of all the people you've known a long time but for one reason or another don't consider friends. You may also think of someone you've known only a short time but like very much. Perhaps the two of you have shared a lot of experiences in a short time, on a trip, say, or in a workshop.

Friendship is a unique kind of relationship in that it isn't regulated by law as are the ties between live-in lovers, spouses, and parents and chil-dren. Instead, friendship grows out of free choice. We choose our friends. Or more accurately, friends choose each other, as one-way friendships do not last long. Although friendship frequently develops within other roles, like co-worker or neighbor, it has its own subjective rationale—which is to foster feelings of warmth, trust, and affection between individuals. It's no accident that in an era of disillusionment with large impersonal institutions, younger people especially seek solace and satisfaction in their friendships and family lives.

Who are your friends?

Can you distinguish friends from acquaintances? Chances are you could list various types of friends. "Work" friends are people you enjoy sharing coffee breaks and gossip with. "Activity" friends are those you do different things with, such as bowling, camping, or playing tennis. Your "favor" friends are people who are willing to loan you something or help you in an emergency.

---

[4]E. Berscheid, T. Brothen, and W. Graziano, "Gain/loss Theory and the 'Law of Infidel-ity': Mr. Doting vs. the Admiring Stranger," *Journal of Personality and Social Psychology,* 33 (1976): 709–718.

Having an intimate talk.

Most people also distinguish between their casual friends and their close friends. A close friend is someone you can share freely with without fear of being betrayed.

People of all ages agree that the most important qualities in a friend are loyalty and the ability to keep confidence. Other desirable qualities in descending order of importance are: warmth, affection, supportiveness, honesty, and a sense of humor. When speaking of friends, people often say things such as, "I trust him"; "He makes time for me"; "She's so understanding"; and, "She accepts me even though she doesn't totally approve of the things I do."

What friends do together

According to a nationwide survey of friendship, the two most frequent activities among friends are "having an intimate talk" and "doing a favor for a friend." Among women, having an intimate talk ranked first: doing a favor for a friend came second. Among men, the rankings were reversed. Both activities presuppose a considerable degree of trust and acceptance. There was a great deal of agreement in regard to the other activities of friends.

According to the survey, men and women enjoy doing a variety of things together. Eating out in a restaurant, having a meal in someone's home, or sharing a drink are all social activities that combine companionship with the pleasures of the palate. Friends also report seeing a movie together, attending an organization they both belong to, playing a sport or watching a sporting event. They are also likely to go shopping together, do something with their children, or conduct a business transaction. Men and women in their twenties and beyond often enjoy similar activities as sex differences in this regard tend to diminish with age.[5]

Sometimes the greatest favor you can do for a friend is to listen. When faced with a crisis, many people turn to a friend before seeking out their families. Friends may serve as a sounding board and provide support without the complications of kinship. At the same time, people who lean on their friends when they really need a therapist may be asking too much. The author recalls two women who began sharing their respective marital problems to the point where they both became suicidal. Fortunately, the intervention of professional help saved them from personal and domestic tragedy, but only after considerable stress on their friendship.

Who Can You Turn To?

There's an old saying—"a friend in need is a friend indeed." Think of all the people you call your friends. Now list the names of those

whom you could ask for feedback on your job performance
with whom you could share personal feelings and problems
to whom you could turn for help in a personal crisis
from whom you can get support after a marital separation or death in the family

If you can name only two or three people, your personal support system may be too narrow. Perhaps your name isn't on enough other people's lists. After all, friendship is a two-way affair. How many people would seek you out in a time of need? Hopefully, this exercise will make you more aware of the importance of friends as a personal support system.

Rules of friendship

There are certain unwritten "rules" of friendship. One of them is that friends can confide in each other. Good friends feel comfortable sharing their feelings as well as the facts of their personal lives. They share the bad news as well as the good. Suppose you were separating from your spouse or were just fired at work. It's highly likely you would seek out a friend to have a heart-to-heart talk with.

---

[5]M.B. Parlee and the editors of *Psychology Today*, "The Friendship Bond," *Psychology Today* (October 1979): pp. 50, 53..

Ordinarily, friends won't tell on each other. When a friend has done something questionable in your eyes, you may discuss this with him or her, and perhaps give your personal reaction. But you won't go around telling others about it. When it comes to more serious matters like breaking the law or self-destructive behavior, other considerations arise. Most people wouldn't help a friend commit suicide.

How about having friends of the opposite sex? Some people are still skeptical about this. But today more people of all ages are choosing opposite-sex friends. One reason may be that in a highly mobile society we're selecting a greater diversity of friends than in the past. Also, now that men and women are working side-by-side just about everywhere, they feel freer selecting friends of both sexes. At the same time, most people agree that opposite-sex friendships are different from same-sex friendships. A major reason is the ease with which a friendship may turn into a sexual relationship. Almost half the respondents in the *Psychology Today* survey said they had experienced a friendship turning into a sexual relationship. One-third of them had engaged in sexual intercourse with a friend in the past month. Although this may strengthen some friendships, it poses a threat to others, especially when one person is married.[6] What do you think about married people having opposite-sex friends? Would you agree that a lot depends on how happily married the couple is? How about the importance of each partner being loyal and honest with his or her spouse?

Lasting friendships

Friendships, like old wine, tend to become better with age. Among old friends we can be ourselves without fear of being rejected. We're as familiar with their mannerisms and shortcomings as they are with ours. But given the increased mobility in our society, you may wonder just how many people have old friends anymore. Fortunately, most people do. The great majority of people in the *Psychology Today* survey on friendship said they had friends of six years or longer. About one-fifth of the respondents indicated they had friends of twenty years or more. This finding may be less surprising when you realize that the largest number of friendships are formed during childhood and adolescence. Perhaps friendships are more intense at that age, or perhaps we have invested so much in the relationship over time that its value has increased considerably. The second most common sources of friendships are college and other friends.[7]

The success of a friendship depends mostly on the special quality of the relationship, and to a lesser extent on the factors like the frequency of contact or the manner of keeping in touch. Most of us have friends we see infrequently, don't we? We may keep in touch by phone, card, or letter. Sometimes a vacation or class reunion provides the occasion for renewing old ties. Why do

[6]Ibid. pp. 50, 53
[7]Ibid. : 54.

friendships cool off? When asked about this, the *Psychology Today* survey respondents indicated that the top three reasons for friendships breaking up were: one of us moved away; I felt my friend betrayed me; and, we discovered we had very different views on issues of importance to me. Other reasons included one person getting married or divorced, one person becoming much more successful at work, or richer, than the other one, and one person borrowing money from the other. But apart from moving away, the single most common reason friendships break up is betrayal. Perhaps that's why people of all ages value loyalty and the ability to keep confidence as the most important ingredients of friendship.[8]

FRIENDSHIP AND INTIMACY

Friendship is a form of love. This shouldn't be surprising when you consider the term *friend* is derived from the word meaning to love. Many of us might agree with the young woman who said, "I wouldn't hesitate to tell my best girlfriend 'I love you.' " Conversely, lovers and happily married people of both sexes readily admit their lover or spouse is their best friend. Both friendship and love actually have to do with interpersonal intimacy—a warmth and closeness between people in which the partners feel free to be themselves, to share their innermost thoughts and feelings.

Each of us needs this kind of closeness with at least one other individual in order to develop fully as a person. Otherwise, we might go through life, as many people do, feeling cut off or superficially related to those around us. But when we feel very close with at least one other person, we're more apt to reach out and become friends with others.

Too often people shrink from intimate relationship because of the mistaken notion that intimacy is synonymous with sexual intimacy, which it isn't. Certainly the physical contact between lovers or partners in sexual intercourse can intensify their emotional closeness, although this isn't always the case. People may engage in sexual intercourse with little emotional involvement, as in casual one-night stands or the mechanical sex between unhappily married people. But all the same, it's desirable to form intimate relationships with others in a nonsexual way, as with same-sex friends or most of our opposite-sex friends, and it is this *interpersonal* intimacy we wish to focus on in this section. We'll discuss friendship and intimacy in terms of mutual self-disclosure, compatibility, dealing with differences, and personal growth.

Self-disclosure

A close friend says, "I'm having a personal problem," and proceeds to tell you about it. How do you respond? You could simply listen and keep the information to yourself without mentioning your own experiences, thereby establishing

[8]Ibid. : 49.

Figure 3-2

a power advantage over your friend. After all, she has made herself vulnerable by sharing personal matters not ordinarily revealed to others. But if you're like most people, your natural response will be to share similar experiences of your own. In doing so, you'll demonstrate that your friend's trust and confidence are well placed. The more you disclose about yourself, the more your friend will do the same. Also, the more you share, the closer you and your friend will feel to each other.

Ordinarily, the level of self-disclosure deepens as the relationship between two people becomes more secure. Sharing too much of yourself too quickly, say with a casual friend or stranger, is likely to have the opposite effect. Such hasty self-disclosure tends to dampen intimacy, with both partners expecting a rapid dissolving of their relationship. For example, Suzanne spent a long weekend at a mountain cabin with her new boyfriend Ken. Throughout the weekend they shared a lot about themselves as well as engaging in physical intimacies. Driving home, Ken suggested they see each other again Monday evening. Suzanne declined, saying, "I need some time for myself." Feeling disappointed, Ken said, "I don't understand." Suzanne replied, "I think we may be rushing things." Backing off a bit is not at all unusual in such situations in order for one or both partners to feel more secure. They may begin fighting over nothing, often after lovemaking. It's as if the fight serves the unconscious purpose of creating the needed distance between partners. More often than not, the person who most needs the distance in order to feel comfortable in the relationship picks the fight.

What do friends disclose? A lot depends on how close the friends are, their life situations, and their mood of the moment, to mention just a few factors that influence self-disclosure.

Some things are obviously easier to share than others. Safe topics include information about school, work, interests, personal tastes, and leisure activities. Personal feelings are riskier to share, though much of the conversation between friends consists of telling how they feel about things that interest them. Sometimes after you've experienced an important or trouble-some incident you can't wait to share your feelings about it with a friend.

Subjects like politics and religion are more emotionally charged, though much depends on how comfortable friends feel with each other. Some-times even friends are reluctant to discuss their financial affairs or matters pertaining to their bodies and sex lives. Yet, close friends may readily share such information, though sometimes not in great detail.[9]

Close friends are also likely to share secrets. Two of the most common themes of secrets among people, especially the college-aged, are sex and fail-ure. Ironically, secrets seem to be mostly for telling, with the sharing of secrets heightening the intimacy between friends.

How Much Do You Disclose to Your Spouse?

A young man in his mid-thirties told his wife about a brief affair he'd had while out-of-town on business several months earlier. He said he felt no emotional attachment to this woman and promised not to see her in the future. The young man also told his wife he felt better for having shared this secret with her, and hoped it would bring them closer together. But he was wrong. His wife became angry and resentful. Ever since, she has found herself wondering if he really loves her and what he is doing when he is out-of-town.

Should you share everything with your spouse? Or does it depend on how it would affect the relationship?

Compatibility

Good friends are usually compatible in some way, though by no means alike. Compatibility, or the ability to get along well together, is affected by so many different factors it's difficult to say what makes any given set of friends compat-ible. They may be compatible because they come from similar backgrounds, as with people who have grown up in the same area and attended the same schools. In other instances, friends may share similar interests or experiences, as with people who work for the same company or have gone through a lot together. Friends may also feel compatible because of their personalities and lifestyles, whether they are similar or complementary.

Fortunately, people are discovering they can be compatible with friends from a wider diversity of backgrounds than they could in the past. Part of this has to do with the greater social mobility and more relaxed social norms of our society. There's also a greater appreciation of individuality, or "being yourself," these days. One woman complained that too many of her friends shared not just one or two but all of the same interests. Acceptance into their group meant joining the same clubs, vacationing in the same places, and belonging to the

---

[9]Sidney Jourard and Ted Landsman, *Healthy Personality,* 4th ed. (New York: Macmillan Publishing Co., 1980), 269–270.

same religion. By contrast, she said, "I like being friends with different kinds of people. It makes life more interesting." Would you agree?

In some instances compatibility between friends is rather obvious, as with Marie and Jackie, mentioned at the beginning of the chapter. Both are older students, have family responsibilities, and are planning nursing careers. In other cases, it's hard to figure out what makes friends so compatible with each other. I think of three older students, two women and a man, who have lunch together each week throughout the school year. The one thing they obviously have in common is that all three of them are math majors. Otherwise, they are very different from each other. One of the women is single; the other woman and the man are married and have families. The married woman is also working with computers, though the other two are only mildly interested in computers. One woman has a highly organized personality; the other one has a casual and relaxed lifestyle. The man is highly emotional. Frankly, it's hard to know what makes them such loyal friends. Perhaps if we knew them better we would understand why they are so compatible.

Good friends feel comfortable with each other.

Dealing with differences

No matter how compatible two friends may feel, the more they get to know each other the more they realize that each of them is an individual. In fact, healthy intimacy itself consists of interpersonal closeness without the surrender of either person's individuality. Each person must come to terms with the "otherness" of his or her friend. You discover this person is somewhat different from what you earlier thought. You'll discover things about your friend you don't fully understand. You may also become aware of things about him or her you can't accept. And remember, your friend is discovering such things about you too.

Compatibility between friends depends largely on how well such differences, and in some instances conflicts, are handled. If you ignore them, especially when important issues are involved, they won't go away. They simply remain hidden. They may simmer in the unconscious, surfacing in disguised symptoms. You may suspect hidden conflicts when one or both of you is unduly critical or is always nagging the other. Repeated irritation with each other or boredom in the relationship are other symptoms of hidden conflict. Maintaining emotional distance or perhaps unexplained avoidances of each other are also signs of unresolved conflict. It is much healthier for the friendship when friends can recognize and deal with their differences openly. We'll discuss how this can be done in a later chapter on handling conflict.

Friends must also adjust to each other's style of intimacy, whether as friends or lovers. Two people may like or love each other to an equal degree. Yet each tends to *express* his or her affection somewhat differently. Some individuals prefer to let friendships and love affairs develop gradually; others jump into new relationships with intense involvement. Some persons readily express their feelings in words, while others follow the old "actions-speak-louder-than-words" approach. Also, some persons are more aware of the balance of payoffs in their relationships; others are more generous and giving. You can just imagine the misunderstanding that occurs when two people fail to adjust to each other's style of intimacy. For example, after a few dates Mark says he loves Marianne and wants to make love with her. Although Marianne is fond of Mark, she feels strongly that sex should come later in their relationship. Without talking this out or making some accommodation to each other, their relationship may dissolve. Or they may drift into a one-sided affair in which one of them does most of the giving, with resentment surfacing later in the relationship.

Intimacy and growth

Ideally, intimacy should foster growth in each friend as well as in their relationship, whether they are same-sex friends, lovers, or married people. But this isn't always the case, is it? Sometimes friends become jealous and manipulative. Or they may become so concerned with balancing the books, so to speak, that their friendship becomes snarled in a set of obligations. Friends may also become overly dependent on each other. Friendship turns into an "addictive" relationship. Like those addicted to alcohol or drugs, each person needs increasingly larger doses of affection and reassurance to feel secure in the relationship. This is especially likely to happen among opposite-sex friends, lovers, and married people. Preoccupied with their relationship, they may cut themselves off from other friends who might interfere with their security.

This is the case with Eric and Pam. Both are in their mid-twenties, share several common interests, and have become serious about their relationship. But Pam is uneasy about Eric's possessiveness. "Even when I go out with my girlfriends," she says, "he starts asking all these questions: 'What are you going to do? What did you two talk about?'" Throwing out her hands and rolling her eyes, she adds, "If a man shows an interest in me at a party, Eric drops what he's doing and comes running over to join us." Pam's friends have warned her about Eric's possessiveness. And Pam readily admits she's worried about the future of their relationship.

By contrast, healthy intimacy fosters growth in each person as well as in the relationship. Sensing that they are genuinely accepted, each feels free to keep up other friendships. They feel outside interests and friendships provide a variety and spice to life. Also, each welcomes change in the other as a way of adding to the vitality and richness of their relationship. However, in most instances our close relationships are neither extremely addictive nor fully mature, healthy intimacy. Most friendships and love relationships fall somewhere in between.

Consider Scott and Cheryl's relationship. Even though they are going steady, they enjoy keeping up other friends. Cheryl likes an occasional get-together with her girlfriends at work. She's also active in a community choral group, which includes men and women. Scott looks forward to his weekly game of golf with male friends. He also goes fishing occasionally. "I haven't got the slightest desire to go fishing," Cheryl says. "Thank God for those fishing buddies. Now, if I find him going fishing with an attractive blonde," she adds with a laugh, "that's another story." Sometimes Cheryl wonders about Scott's relationship with his ex-girlfriend, who works at the same place he does. But they've talked about this, and Cheryl feels there is nothing going on between them. Yet occasionally she has doubts. All in all, Scott and Cheryl are secure enough in their relationship to keep up outside interests and friendships. Both feel such involvement enriches rather than threatens their relationship.

How about your friendships? Do some of your friendships or love relationships resemble addictive relationships? Or are they mature, healthy relationships? Think over your intimate relationships, including same-sex friends, lovers, or your spouse. Then ask yourself these questions:

How does this relationship affect each of us?

Is each of us free to change and grow?

Does each of us keep up other interests and friendships?

If lovers, are we also friends?

Does each of us give as well as receive love?

Can we experience closeness without giving up our individuality?

Answers to such questions may help each of us to realize how healthy or addictive our friendships are.

SUMMARY

1. Generally, we're attracted to people who live or work near us, who have a lot in common with us, who are physically attractive, and who like us. In some instances, we're especially attracted to people who have "grown on us," with whom we've experienced a mutual increase in liking.

2. Friendship depends more on the quality of the relationship between two people than in the frequency of their contact. Not surprisingly, the two qualities most desired in a friend are loyalty and the ability to keep confidence. When friendships cool, it's often because one person feels betrayed or the individuals have grown apart in their views.

3. We've also discussed how close friends, whether same-sex friends, lovers, or married people, enjoy an intimate relationship. As such, they share a lot about themselves, and feel compatible with each other. Yet they must also make allowances for their differences. We've also noted that some friendships become restrictive, resembling addictive relationships. Healthy friendships by contrast foster growth in each person as well as in their relationship.

SELF-TEST

1. The _____ of others is especially important in the early stages of interpersonal attraction.
   a. educational level
   b. nearness
   c. physical attraction
   d. beliefs and values

2. Similar social characteristics heighten the attraction between people through their:
    a. having more in common
    b. confirming each other's beliefs
    c. predicting each other's behavior
    d. all of the above

3. According to the matching hypothesis regarding attraction between the sexes:
    a. females seek males who match their father image
    b. both sexes seek partners about as attractive as themselves
    c. males seek females who resemble their younger sisters
    d. both sexes prefer computer-matched dates

4. The two most important qualities of friendship are the ability to keep confidence and:
    a. warmth
    b. physical attractiveness
    c. sex appeal
    d. loyalty

5. The most frequent activity among women friends is:
    a. eating out
    b. doing a favor for a friend
    c. shopping together
    d. having an intimate talk

6. Friendships often break up because one or both persons:
    a. feels betrayed
    b. moves away
    c. grows apart in their views
    d. all of the above

7. Friends generally find it easy to discuss their:
    a. politics
    b. personal feelings
    c. work
    d. financial affairs

8. People are now more likely to choose their friends from:
    a. their own sex
    b. a wider circle of people
    c. the same ethnic group
    d. all of the above

9. In a healthy friendship, conflicts or differences are:
    a. encouraged
    b. avoided
    c. discussed openly
    d. mostly hidden

10. _____ promotes personal growth on the part of both partners in a friendship.
    a. healthy intimacy
    b. strong need for dependency
    c. the desire for security
    d. romantic love

EXERCISES

1. *Write a personal ad about yourself.* Suppose you wanted to meet a romantic partner through a classified personal ad. How would you describe yourself? How would you describe the type of person you are looking

for? Write a short paragraph about yourself for the classified personal ads of a magazine or paper devoted to this purpose.

2. *What attracted you to your friends?* List all the people you consider friends. Then review the various factors influencing interpersonal attraction discussed in this chapter. Now go down your list and check off the factors which apply to each friendship.

Nearness	Physical attractiveness
Similarity	Liking for me
Social/personal	Other factors?

Do you find that some factors played a more important role than others in forming friendships?

3. *Who can you turn to?* Which friends can you turn to when you need help or support? If you didn't do this exercise earlier in the chapter, go back and answer the appropriate question in the boxed item on page 56.

4. *Do you have a close friend of the opposite sex?* Are you sexually involved with your friend? How is this relationship similar to or different from your same-sex friendships? What do you think about the wisdom of married people having close friends of the opposite sex?

5. *Self-disclosure.* How readily do you share personal matters with close friends? To find out, jot down your answers to the following questions?

With whom do I feel most comfortable sharing myself? Least comfortable?

Which topics do I share least or most readily?

Do I share more with same-sex than opposite-sex friends?

If married, do I share more with my spouse than friends or parents?

Does personal sharing make me feel closer to my friends?

6. *Intimacy and growth.* Select one of your close friendships or a love relationship. Then jot down your answers to the questions about intimacy and growth at the end of the chapter. To what extent does this relationship encourage each of you to grow as a person?

Male
and Female

4

SEX ROLES
      Sex-role stereotypes
      Changing sex roles
      Sex roles and sexuality

SEXUAL BEHAVIOR
      Masturbation
      Sexual intercourse
      Problem behaviors

CHANGING ATTITUDES TOWARD SEX
      Freedom and fulfilment
      Caution and commitment
      Love and sex

SUMMARY

SELF-TEST

EXERCISES

Kathy and Bob are a married couple in their early thirties. It is evening and they are relaxing in their living-room after dinner. While pouring coffee, Kathy asks, "Have you heard the news about Frank and Elaine?"

"What news?" asks Bob.

"Frank is playing around with another woman."

"Oh, that," replies Bob. "Yeah, I head something about it. It's probably idle gossip. Anyway, it's no big deal. A lot of guys play around."

"No big deal, eh," Kathy says in a raised voice. "That's easy for you to say. Elaine is trapped at home with a two-year-old and expecting another child. And you say, 'It's no big deal.'"

"Well, maybe he's missing something at home. I mean, look at me. I'm not playing around," laughs Bob. "But then I've got such a loving wife."

"It's not funny," Kathy continues. "Besides, why is it always the woman's fault if her husband strays? If you ask me, men have sex on the brain. Just the other day I read in Ann Lander's column about this woman who said she and her husband had sex four times a week, and still he wants more. My God, what an animal!"

"Well, you can't blame the guy for trying," Bob says as he laughs softly.

"You're just like all the rest of them," laments Kathy. "All you can think of is sex."

"Oh, I see," says Bob in a mocking voice. "Women are never interested in sex. Ginny Black's affair with that tennis pro was just a little romantic interlude. It didn't have anything to do with sex, right?"

"Well, not exactly," admits Kathy. "With such a cold fish for a husband, I can't much blame her. She was just starved for affection. She's not that interested in sex."

"In other words," growls Bob, "when a woman goes outside the marriage, it's really her husband's fault. But when a man does it, it's his own fault, because men are just 'sexual animals.' "

"It's not quite that simple, I realize. But I still say women are more interested in love than sex," asserts Kathy, as she walks toward the ringing telephone.

SEX ROLES

Who do you most agree with, Kathy or Bob? Your answer apparently depends on your sex. When dating couples in college were asked why their partners might get involved with someone else, their responses echoed the views of Kathy and Bob. Women felt their men would be seeking sexual variety, confirming the view that women tend to see men as "sexual animals." Men worried that their partners would be seeking more commitment, confirming the idea that men regard women as more "marriage-oriented" than men.[1]

Such differences in opinion partly reflect the influence of sex roles—the social expectations regarding appropriate behavior for males and females. From the moment of birth, you and I are not only classified as male or female on the basis of our biological sex, we are also treated in a manner appropriate to our sex. The name you're given, the way you're dressed, and how you're reared depend largely on sex roles. Given such different treatment, it's no wonder that men and woman have difficulty understanding each other.

On the positive side, sex roles help you to act in an acceptable manner in society. By assimilating sex-role expectations throughout your formative years, you come to regard them as a natural part of your makeup. Boys consequently, strive to become breadwinners and pride themselves on protecting women and children. Similarly, girls seek to make themselves attractive and look forward to marrying and perhaps having children. At the same time, it is increasingly apparent that conventional sex roles have their disadvantages too.

[1]G.L. White, "Jealousy and Partner's Perceived Motives for Attraction to a Rival," *Social Psychology Quarterly* 44, 1 (1981): 24–30.

Sex-role stereotypes

Many of the disadvantages of sex roles are due to sex-role stereotypes—widely held generalizations about the characteristics of males and females. More unconscious than not, such generalizations tempt us to exaggerate the real differences between men and women. We're also likely to overlook the actual differences between individuals of both sexes. When we see people who closely resemble these stereotypes, we may say things like, "He's really a macho guy," or, "She's very feminine." Yet there are many people whose personalities don't correspond very well to these stereotypes. Think of all the men who don't enjoy traditionally male interests such as playing sports and making a lot of money. Think of all the women who downplay the traditionally female activities like housekeeping and child-rearing by pursuing a career, or perhaps by combining family and career responsibilities. In short, both sexes exhibit a wider range of appropriate behaviors than are implied in the sex-role stereotypes.

However, individuals who stray too far from the prescribed sex role risk being labeled negatively and suffering from lowered esteem. This is the case with Alan, a history teacher at a nearby community college. Many of Alan's personality characteristics result from his not having had a father. Alan's parents were killed in an automobile accident when he was six years old, and he grew up with an elderly grandmother. Alan enjoyed his studies, and was often teased for his bookish ways. His office at the college is filled with pictures and flowers, like the offices of his female colleagues. He serves as advisor to the student dramatics club. His gentle, somewhat emotional mannerisms in class and around the staff have earned him the nickname "Mr.

Figure 4-1

Nice Guy." Because his working hours are more flexible than his wife's, Alan takes care of their kids in the afternoon and regularly prepares the family dinner. Occasionally, Alan is angered by someone's suspicion that he is "gay." For the most part, his colleagues regard him as a regular person but a bit different, perhaps a "wimp." Alan tries not to let this bother him, but deep down it does.

Even those who identify strongly with their sex role may become vulnerable to self-doubts and unhappiness. Consider Lola, an attractive, very feminine, middle-aged homemaker. She grew up in an ethnic group which believed that the woman's place was in the home, and she has totally accepted that role. Lola is deeply dependent on Fred, her husband. Fred makes all the major decisions in the family and pays all the bills. Even when something happens like the washing machine breaking down, Lola calls Fred, who arranges for the repair. It's common knowledge among their friends that Lola has been unhappy with Fred for years, but she has remained married mostly for the kids' sakes. Also, Lola says, "It's too late to start doing something else like a job. Who wants a middle-aged woman?" Lola mostly stays home, keeps a neat house, fixes a nice dinner for Fred, and reads a great deal. She feels she ought to be happy. But she isn't. She has nagging doubts about her self-worth and is bothered by bouts of depression.

How Masculine or Feminine Are You?

To find out, complete the following. On a scale of 1 to 3 rate how often each of the following characteristics describes you: 1—usually not; 2—occasionally; 3—often or always.

___ ambitious	___ affectionate
___ assertive	___ compassionate
___ competitive	___ cooperative
___ self-reliant	___ loyal
___ willing to take risks	___ sensitive to others

Do the above exercise before reading further.

In determining your sex-role identity, you'll need to know that the characteristics in the left-hand column are associated with the masculine sex role and those in the right-hand column with the feminine sex role.

Now take the five characteristics on which you have the highest scores. Do you find that you have two or three characteristics from each sex-role? Or do you find that four or five of your characteristics are associated with the sex role for your sex? If so, you may have a more stereotyped masculine or feminine identity. In either case, remember this is an exercise, not a test.

What are some advantages and disadvantages of having a stereotyped sex-role identity? Can you also point out the advantages, and possibly some disadvantages, of having a mixture of desirable sex-role characteristics?

Men, as well as women, benefit from more flexible sex roles.

Changing sex roles

Fortunately, social forces like the changes of the 1960s and the women's libera-
tion movement have helped to bring about more flexible sex roles for both
men and women. At the least, our notions of *male* and *female* are less polarized
now, with the result that individuals feel freer to be themselves. Easygoing,
artistically inclined men need not prove their masculinity. Energetic, aggressive
women need not hide their native abilities. The greater flexibility in sex roles
may also encourage individuals of both sexes to develop those personal traits
needed for living in a complex, rapidly changing society. Sandra Bem has
proposed the term *androgyny* (*andros* for man plus gyne for woman) for the
ability to combine desirable traits from both sex roles. Thus in contrast to being
a stereotyped male or female, a psychologically androgynous person could be
forceful or gentle, angry or loving, as the situation demanded.[2]

  More flexible sex roles are especially evident among the young and the
college-educated, and among women, particularly single and divorced women.
More women are attending college, working outside the home, and combining
career and family responsibilities. They also feel freer to act assertively and
take the initiative in social and sexual relationships with men. It is increasingly
evident that men may also benefit from more flexible sex roles. Some men feel
less compelled to work primarily to support their families and are entering

[2]S. Bem, "Sex-role Adaptability: One Consequence of Psychological Androgyny." *Journal
of Personality and Social Psychology 31, 4, (1975) :634–643.*

traditionally female-dominated fields like nursing and elementary-school teaching. Men are also realizing the importance of close relationships and are sharing more fully in child rearing. The notion of androgyny does not mean that men and women must become alike. Indeed, biological differences remind us of the folly of such a goal. It means, rather, that we can stop trying to make men and women so different. Would you agree?

Dave and Cindy, a couple in their mid-thirties, exemplify many of these changes. Dave teaches biology in a small four-year college. Since most of his students are nurses, he's taking the required courses to get his R.N. too. Dave is well respected by students and faculty alike, and has served as president of the faculty senate. Cindy is a personnel manager for a large insurance company. She's attended several workshops on assertiveness training in order to handle better the tough decisions demanded by her job. Both contribute to the family income and share a joint checking account. They also share more equally in rearing their children than their parents did. Their individual lifestyles are more varied and relaxed than people of their parents' generation. Dave goes to a hair stylist; Cindy drives the tractor-mower to cut grass around the house. In short, with the emergence of the more flexible sex roles which they take for granted, both Dave and Cindy feel freer to be themselves.

Sex roles and sexuality

Sex role and biological makeup shape the way we perceive our own sexuality and that of the opposite sex. In part, of course, our maleness and femaleness reflect biological differences. For males, whether we're considering reproduction or pleasure seeking, sexuality revolves largely around genital sex. There is also a strong association between the male sex hormone, testosterone, and aggressiveness, providing a partial explanation of characteristic male behavior. However, female sexuality is more complex, because the areas of erotic stimulation are more varied in women than in men. Furthermore, female sexuality includes at least three types of sexual behavior involving two people: sexual intercourse, childbirth, and nursing. Hence the characteristically close association among women between sexuality and intimacy.

However, sex-role stereotypes have exaggerated the biological differences between men and women. As a result, men are widely regarded as "sexual animals," preoccupied with conquests of women as sexual objects. On the other hand, women are more apt to be viewed as "marriage-oriented," basically disinterested in sex but willing to engage in it for the sake of love and the security of marriage and family life. Sex-role differences may also be seen in the way men and women are sexually aroused. Ordinarily, men are readily aroused by erotic pictures like that of a nude female. Women are more likely to be aroused by a romantic story. Such differences also show up in the way men and women respond to pictures of a couple in a romantic setting. Men, socialized to think in abstract terms, tend to lift the woman out of the picture and fantasize about her privately, usually imagining themselves having sex with her. Women, socialized to think more in emotional and personal terms, tend to project themselves into the picture, imagining themselves in the woman's place. Consequently women are more readily aroused by a romantic story or a scene of tender expression between a man and a woman than by a picture of a nude male.

Fortunately, changing sex roles are helping men and women to see themselves and each other more realistically. Until recently it was thought that the sex drive peaked in men in the late teens, but not until the thirties in women. Today, women are experiencing peak sexual desire at increasingly earlier ages, suggesting that much of the disparity between men and women reflects sex-role influences. Also, there is no convincing evidence that women's sex drive is any less intense than men's. In some instances a woman's sexual responsiveness surpasses that of a man's, though this varies more widely among women than men, and within a particular woman at different times. Also, much of the difference in sexual arousal between men and women may have to do with social conditioning, especially social restraint. Women who affirm their sexuality and enjoy satisfying relationships with men, especially happily married women, are as readily aroused by erotic pictures as men are.

Similarly, men are anything but the sexual animals they're pictured to be. A significant minority of men experience relatively low levels of sexual desire and arousal, a condition referred to as *inhibited sexual desire*. It is mostly men who suffer from low self-esteem, and in some instances a sense of sexual inadequacy, who view women as sex objects. Men who feel good about themselves and are secure in their masculinity are apt to regard women in more humane terms like themselves. Nor are men necessarily insensitive to the relationship between love and sex. In one survey, one-third of the men thought that love was the most important thing in the world. Another one-third acknowledged that love was either essential for sex or made it better.[3]

SEXUAL BEHAVIOR

Some sexual behaviors are easily observable, like the affectionate hugging and kissing by young couples in school hallways and campuses. Other sexual behaviors occur in private and are difficult to observe, like masturbation and sexual intercourse. For these behaviors we must rely largely on individuals' self-reports. Unfortunately, a lot of information about sex comes from hearsay and "pop-sex" research and lends itself to exaggeration.

As an example, I cite a survey of sexual behavior in the author's own college. Results showed that about nine out of ten men and almost eight out of

[3]A. Pietropinto and J. Simenauer, *Beyond the Male Myth* (New York: Quandrangle Books, 1977), 208.

TABLE 4-1.   Primary Erogenous Zones Excluding Genitals.

Zone	Males, %	Females, %
Back	4.9	4.3
Breasts	4.9	36.5
Chest	4.6	0.24
Ears	7.0	8.1
Lips	10.0	6.0
Neck	4.6	6.5
Stomach	5.2	6.7
Thighs	31.5	14.2
Other	6.1	3.4

Although almost any portion of our bodies may become an erogenous zone, some parts are naturally more sensitive than others, resulting in a wide consensus as to our most erogenous zones, as shown above.

Source: Bernard Goldstein, *Human Sexuality* (New York: McGraw-Hill, 1976), 130.

ten women had engaged in sexual intercourse, a rather high figure compared to other surveys at the time. Furthermore, about three-fourths of both sexes rated their performances in bed as either excellent or good. Although an equal number of women rated their partner's performance in bed as good as their own, the men weren't so impressed. Only about one-fifth of the men thought their partners did as well as they did in bed. All these figures become less impressive however, when you discover they were based on only eighty-four anonymous responses to a questionnaire printed in the college newspaper. Do these eighty-four people represent a student population of over seven thousand students? It's extremely unlikely. Yet unsuspecting readers might easily draw the wrong conclusions, and exaggerate the extent of sexual activity among their peers.[4]

With such a caution in mind, let's take a look at some of the familiar sexual behaviors like masturbation and sexual intercourse, along with certain sexual problems.

Masturbation

One of the most widely practiced forms of sexual behavior is masturbation—self-manipulation of the sex organs to produce pleasure. Adolescents begin masturbating long before they engage in sexual intercourse. Almost all males and from one-half to two-thirds of females have masturbated to orgasm by late adolescence. Even among married couples in their twenties and thirties, a ma-

[4]*Montgazette,* Vol. 11, No. 14 February 1977, 7.

jority of men and women masturbate on occasion. Many of the elderly continue masturbating long after they have given up intercourse.[5]

People masturbate for many reasons. First, masturbation is a convenient way of experiencing the pleasure of arousal and orgasm. It is also a valuable means of self-exploration. Men may experiment with their response pattern as a way of achieving ejaculatory control. Women may masturbate as a way of learning to achieve orgasm more easily. Masturbation is also commonly used as a substitute when a sex partner is not available, especially among those in institutions. Individuals rely largely on their own imagination and fantasies to heighten sexual arousal during masturbation, and to a lesser extent on erotic pictures and stories. Although people experience less anxiety and guilt over masturbation than in the past, a few still worry that they masturbate too frequently. Even more have misgivings about achieving pleasure through self-stimulation. The most probable explanation of this is that masturbation lacks the stimulation and closeness of the love relationship that usually accompanies sexual intercourse.

Sexual intercourse

Perhaps the biggest change in sexual habits of the past few decades has been the marked increase in sexual intercourse among unmarried young adults, especially college-aged youth. This is especially true for women. Premarital sex among college-aged women more than doubled between the 1930s and the late 1970s, though it has levelled off somewhat since then, with about 50 to 60 percent of college women now sexually active. There have been modest increases in sexual activity among college-aged men during the same period. Naturally, the exact percentages of sexually active individuals vary from one campus to another and over time. Also, the increase in sexual activity has been greatest among those in the large middle class—traditionally the bearers of prevailing social morality. Working-class men have always been more sexually active than their middle-class counterparts. So have highly educated, affluent women. In recent years, middle-class youth, especially young women, have become more sexually active.[6]

Many influences have helped to bring about the increase in sexual intercourse among unmarried youth. A major factor is the growing acceptance of premarital sex, initially among the college-aged but now among many adults as well. The availability of contraceptives along with the legalization of abortion have also helped to diminish the fear of unwanted pregnancy. Also, the baby boom following World War II has led to an increase in the numbers of college-aged youth and young adults, usually the most sexually active group. The exploitation of sex in advertising, the mass media, movies, and books has also

[5]E. Atwater, *Psychology of Adjustment*, 2nd ed. (Englewood Cliffs, N.J.: Prentice-Hall, Inc., 1983), 170–171.

[6]J. Leo, "The Sexual Revolution is Over," *Time* (April 9, 1984) : 77.

helped to make sex more acceptable. As a result, the social pressure toward conformity has shifted in favor of permarital sex. One girl said, "My older sister says she used to lie to her friends and say she was a virgin to protect her reputation. It is just the opposite for me. I lie to my friends claiming I'm not a virgin."[7]

Most couples either feel they are in love or are going steady before they engage in sexual intercourse. Of course, there are some individuals who sleep around with different partners. Others have sex on their first date, and sometimes "one-night stands." But as one young woman put it, "I think a lot of women who engage in those 'one-night stands' are secretly hoping it will lead to something more." Even those who sleep around like to feel they are in love or may stay together for several months. For the most part, sexual intimacy strengthens the bond between a man and a woman. In one survey, college

For most people, love and sex go together.

[7]R. Crooks and K. Baur, *Our Sexuality* (Menlo Park, CA: The Benjamin/Cummings Publishing Company, Inc., 1983), 421.

women felt greater love for their boyfriends if they had engaged in sex, especially if their first sexual experience was with their current boyfriend. The relationship between love and sex was somewhat weaker for men. Yet sexual intercourse had no lasting effect on the couple's future relationship. Couples who had sex were no more or less likely to stay together than couples who had not had sex. Factors like shared interests and mutual emotional involvement played a greater role in the couple's staying together or breaking up.[8]

Problem behaviors

Two of the most common sexual problems for men are premature ejaculation and the inability to sustain an erection. The first usually results from previous conditioning, especially having one's early sexual experiences in semiprivate conditions which encourage a quick ejaculation. Until recently it was sometimes believed that virile men would ejaculate quickly. But now that the average time for intercourse has increased to about ten minutes, more men delay ejaculation in order to help their partners reach orgasm. Hence, premature ejaculation may be a problem even for "virile" men. There are a variety of techniques designed to help men learn how to delay ejaculation.

Inability to achieve or to sustain an erection, formerly called impotency, tends to become more of a problem for men as they reach their fifties. But more young men are now reporting this problem. One reason may be the man's heightened anxiety over performing well in bed. Another reason has to do with boredom from having sex with the same partner, which may be alleviated by using more variety in one's lovemaking techniques. Temporary failure of an erection often results from fatigue and excessive use of alcohol and drugs.

The most common complaints for women are slowness of arousal and difficulty in reaching orgasm. While such problems may come from fatigue and excessive use of alcohol and drugs, psychological factors often play a significant part here. A woman may feel apprehensive or guilty about her sexual desires. Or she may harbor hostility or resentment toward her partner for something he has said or done. When she becomes overconcerned about reaching orgasm, she unwittingly delays it. Also, a man's insensitivity or poor lovemaking techniques may inhibit a woman's sexual arousal. Better understanding of the sexual response cycle, i.e., arousal, plateau, orgasm, and resolution, as well as more varied lovemaking techniques may help. Most helpful of all is an attitude of love and sensitivity allied with a healthy acceptance of sexuality on the part of both partners.

Another problem area in sex concerns the failure to use contraceptives or a birth control method. In one campus survey, only one-third of the sexually active women reported using contraceptives regularly. Another one-third said

---

[8]L.A. Peplau, Z. Rubin, and C.T. Hill, "Sexual Intimacy in Dating Relationships," *Journal of Social Issues* 33 (1977): 86–109.

they never did. Contraceptives were least likely to be used the first time a couple engaged in sexual intercourse. However, individuals of both sexes were more likely to use some method of birth control in their subsequent sexual activity.

People fail to use contraceptives for a variety of reasons. Often, partners don't want to spoil the spontaneity of sex by bringing up the subject. Some people fail to take precautions because of negative or ambivalent feelings about sex. Using a contraceptive means admitting to yourself that you may have sex. Consequently, sex education involves more than simply providing relevant information about birth control methods. It must also help people deal with their negative and ambivalent attitudes toward sex, and change their birth control habits.[9]

Fortunately, two-thirds of the women who use contraceptives regularly are protected by the most effective methods available, sterilization, the pill, and the intrauterine device (IUD), as shown in Table 4–2. Younger women rely more heavily on the pill or their partner's use of the condom. Women over thirty tend to favor tubal sterilization or a vasectomy for their partner. Although only a small number of women do not practice any method of birth control, they account for about four out of every ten unintended pregnancies and obtain 27 percent of the abortions in the United States.[10]

TABLE 4-2. Percentage of U.S. Women Using Various Contraceptive Methods, According to Age-groups.

		AGE-GROUP					
Method	Total	15-19	20-24	25-29	30-34	35-39	40-44
Sterilization	32	*	6	25	43	62	61
Tubal	(19)	(*)	(4)	(15)	(25)	(36)	(35)
Vasectomy	(13)	(*)	(2)	(10)	(17)	(26)	(26)
Pill	27	44	50	34	17	8	5
IUD	6	3	6	8	9	6	4
Condom	12	21	13	12	12	8	11
Spermicides	4	7	3	3	4	3	5
Diaphragm	5	1	7	7	7	3	3
Withdrawal	3	5	3	3	2	2	2
Rhythm	2	*	1	1	1	3	2
Other	*	2	*	*	1	*	*
None	8	18	11	6	5	6	8
Total	100	100	100	100	100	100	100

*Less than 0.5 percent.

Source: Jacqueline Barroch Forrest and Stanley K. Henshaw, "What U.S. Women Think and Do about Contraception," *Family Planning Perspectives,* 15, 4 (July/August 1983): 163.

[9]M. Zelnik and J.F. Kantner, "Sexual Activity, Contraceptive Use and Pregnancy among Metropolitan-area Teenagers; 1971–1979," *Family Planning Perspectives,* 12 (1980) 5 :230–237.

[10]J.D. Forrest and S. K. Henshaw, "What U.S. Women Think and Do about Contraception," *Family Planning Perspectives,* 15, 4 (July/August, 1983): 163.

Another problem is the risk of getting a *sexually transmitted disease,* normally abbreviated *STD,* and formerly called *venereal disease, VD,* after Venus, the goddess of love. The increase in sexual activity among unmarried people in recent decades has brought about a marked rise in sexually transmitted diseases. Not surprisingly, the incidence of these diseases is highest among those in the twenty- to twenty-four-year-old group, with the next highest incidence among those in the fifteen- to nineteen-year-old group.[11]

Gonorrhea is one of the most common sexually transmitted diseases. The incidence of gonorrhea tripled between 1965 and 1975, though it has leveled off somewhat since.[12] A big reason has been the increased use of the contraceptive pill, allowing more genital contact between the sexes. Use of the condom may help prevent gonorrhea during intercourse, but it does not guarantee immunity. Many people, especially women, fail to seek treatment because they have so few symptoms that they do not realize they are infected. Women with untreated gonorrhea may suffer from inflammation of the Fallopian tubes, infertility, birth malformations, or menstrual disorders. Also, untreated gonorrhea is the single most common cause of sterility among males.

Syphilis is much less common than gonorrhea but is a far more serious disease. There are about 100,000 new cases of syphilis reported annually, adding to a pool of untreated patients estimated to number more than 350,000. Syphilis usually shows up in three stages. First, from a week to several months after contact with an infected person, a sore appears at the place of contact. Although the sore usually disappears within a month or two, other signs may appear, such as rashes and sores on other parts of the body. These symptoms eventually disappear, but if the disease is left untreated it may continue to an advanced stage where it can cause damage as serious as blindness, heart disease, or paralysis.

Genital herpes is another sexually transmitted disease that has become prominent in recent years. It is estimated that about 20 million Americans currently suffer from this disease.[13] In addition to the periodic discomfort, genital herpes can lead to serious complications. Pregnant women may require a Cesarean section if active herpes is present in the birth canal at the time of delivery. Also, women infected with genital herpes are eight times more likely to contract cervical cancer than other women.[14] The difficulty of treating this disease along with the complications for one's lifestyle has led to the formation of support groups among genital herpes sufferers. Some herpes carriers now identify themselves as such when seeking romantic and sexual partners in

[11]NIAID Study Group, *Sexually Transmitted Diseases: 1980 Status Report.* Washington, D.C.: U.S. Government Printing Office (NIH Publications No. 81-2213), 1981.

[12]U.S. Bureau of the Census. *Statistical Abstract of the United States: 1980.* Washington, D.C.: Government Printing Office, 1980, 126.

[13]*Time* (April 9, 1984) : 77.

[14]*The Harvard Medical School Health Letter* (Cambridge, MA.: Department of Continuing Education. Harvard Medical School, April 1981) p. 2.

classified personal ads. Occasionally one partner has sued another when genital herpes has been transmitted without prior warning.

CHANGING ATTITUDES TOWARD SEX

There is now more openness and honesty about sex than there was in the past. These changed attitudes have been brought about largely by a group of social changes collectively labeled *the sexual revolution*. Those who chart social trends point out that such changes began much earlier than the experimentation of the 60s and 70s, and are leveling off somewhat now. Let's take a look at a few of the prevailing attitudes toward sex that have resulted from such changes, along with the more recent shift back toward traditional sexual values.

Freedom and fulfilment

Most people take their personal sexual freedom largely for granted, and place a high value on it. They question definitions of sexual morality made in conformity to set standards, whether those of the church, society, or their own parents. But increased sexual freedom has both advantages and disadvantages. On the plus side, greater personal freedom may help individuals to develop their own sense of values in sexual matters, and make them more accountable for their sexual behavior. On the minus side, such freedom also makes tremendous demands on an individual's personal maturity. It exposes them to the risk of engaging in sex before they are emotionally ready, for example, or failing to use birth control methods. Another disadvantage is the uncertainty about sexual morality. In one national survey, more than two-thirds of those under twenty-five years of age reported being uncertain or confused about right and wrong in sexual matters.[15]

Another major change has been the acceptance of sex as long as the partners are in love—sometimes known as the "love ethic." Now it is the state of being in love, rather than marriage, that makes sex acceptable, and this encourages a greater incidence of premarital and extramarital sex. On the one hand, this approach makes the motives and consequences of sex as important as the act itself. Partners may now ask themselves: "Is the desire for sex mutual? Does sex enrich or weaken our relationship? Will it harm either of us in any way?" On the other hand, such questions cannot be answered authoritatively. They must be answered by the partners themselves. There is thus the risk that either or both of them will act on impulse, later justifying their behavior in the name of love.

We've also seen an increased emphasis on sexual fulfilment. Sex isn't

[15]*Time* (November 21, 1977) : 112.

just for procreation anymore. It's also a source of intense pleasure and a means of expressing one's love. Such a view has brought several positive changes. Unmarried couples may engage in sex as a means of mutual pleasure, or as an expression of love, without rushing into marriage. Married couples feel less obligated to have children to justify their marriage. People feel freer to engage in a wider variety of sexual practices without feeling they are doing something wrong. More and more, healthy sexuality depends on the mutual satisfaction of the participants and less on the particular act itself. However, the pursuit of sexual fulfilment has sometimes resulted in undue anxiety over sexual performance. Men may become so preoccupied with their performance in bed that they turn into worried spectators rather than joyful participants. Women may become so concerned about reaching orgasm that they unwittingly make it all the harder to achieve. In short, the obsession with sexual fulfilment can give rise to new anxieties over sex, or even produce mechanical, joyless sex.

Caution and commitment

Here and there one sees signs that the obsession with sex is subsiding. More people are becoming disenchanted with singles bars and casual sex. Typical is one young man's comment: "In the first six months after my divorce, I slept around with several women. But now I want something more." Other people are joining the move toward intimacy, commitment, and lasting relationships. Marriage and birthrates are up; divorces are down somewhat.

The new caution in sexual matters reflects a number of influences. The fear of herpes is a major factor. With something like 20 million Americans afflicted with genital herpes, people are understandably cautious in their selection of sex partners. Age too is an important factor. The large population of "baby boomers" are now reaching their middle years and are settling down, marrying, having families, and devoting more energy to their careers. There is

Figure 4-2 Sex isn't just for procreation anymore.

also a growing sophistication about sex. Many of those who've experimented with casual sex have had their share of heartbreaks and are looking for more satisfying relationships. Lastly, the new conservatism in sex may be part of the new conservatism in society. People are tired of hearing about the sexual revolution. They are more concerned about things like economic security.

What Is Your Attitude Toward Homosexuals?

Ask yourself these questions: Do you think a homosexual would make a good president of our country? How do you feel about having a homosexual teacher? Would you get upset if a recognized homosexual sat next to you in class? How would you feel if your child adopted a homosexual lifestyle? Honest answers to such questions reveal a lot about your attitudes toward homosexuals.

Are you aware that not everyone who engages in homosexual behavior is a homosexual? Homosexual experimentation in adolescence is usually a passing phase of sexual development. In most cases it doesn't lead to a lifelong preference for homosexuality.

Have you ever suspected a man might be a homosexual because of his effeminate mannerisms? The truth is that people who exhibit strong homosexual tendencies do not necessarily conform to the popular stereotypes of the effeminate male or the "butch" female. Actually, homosexuals of both sexes resemble their heterosexual counterparts more than they do each other. That is, women homosexuals (often called *lesbians*) tend to value the emotional rather than the sexual aspect of their relationship with women, while men are more apt to put the emphasis on genital activity. Many homosexuals also marry and have children.

The changes brought about by the sexual revolution have not been rejected however; rather, they have been absorbed into the mainstream of society. Practices that were shocking a generation ago, like living together or oral sex, have become more widely accepted. People are more relaxed about sex. They are more apt to put sex into its proper perspective.[16]

Love and sex

There is a return to the view that the major function of sex is a bodily expression of love. Obviously, sex continues to be a means of reproduction and a source of pleasure. But sex for the sake of pleasure has become less alluring, especially for seasoned individuals. People are rediscovering the traditional values of love, commitment, and fidelity.

It has long been known that couples who engage in sexual intercourse tend to have stronger feelings of love than couples who don't have sex. It works the other way too. That is, many men as well as women believe that love makes sex even more enjoyable. This is especially true in long-term relationships like marriage. The satisfaction and commitment a couple enjoys in their relationship may actually strengthen their overall pleasure, helping to compensate

[16]*Time* (April 9, 1984) : 83.

somewhat for the loss of sensual excitement that normally occurs in marriage over the years. George Leonard emphasizes this point in *The End of Sex.*[17] He feels that the widespread preoccupation with sex has led to manipulative relationships which eventually undermine sexual enjoyment. Consequently, his theme is: "sex is dead—long live love." But it is erotic love that he advocates. Erotic love incorporates a healthy sensuality and acceptance of sex as a part of love itself. Erotic love not only strengthens romantic love, but also improves sex. Perhaps it's no accident that couples have long referred to sexual intercourse as "making love," suggesting that sex and love belong together.

SUMMARY

1. The popular view of men as "sexual animals" and women as "marriage-oriented" reflects the influence of sex-role stereotypes. The move toward more flexible sex roles in recent years along with a better understanding of human sexuality is helping to bring about a more realistic and satisfying relationship between men and women.

2. There has been a marked increase in sexual intercourse among youth and unmarried young adults in recent decades. Problem sexual behaviors discussed were: common sexual dysfunctions among men and women, the failure to use contraceptives, and the increased risk of venereal disease.

3. Greater openness and honesty about sex is only one of the many changes in attitude brought about by the sexual revolution. Other attitudes discussed were greater personal freedom in sex, wider acceptance of premarital and extramarital sex, and an emphasis on sexual fulfilment. We also pointed out a recent shift toward caution and commitment in sexual matters, along with a greater appreciation that love and sex belong together.

SELF-TEST

1. _____ exaggerate the real differences between the sexes and minimize individual differences within each sex.
   a. sex hormones   c. homosexuals
   b. sex-role stereotypes d. all of the above

2. A person who possesses an equal number of desirable male and female sex-role characteristics is:
   a. bisexual   c. androgynous
   b. a split personality d. schizophrenic

[17]G. Leonard, *The End of Sex* (Los Angeles, CA: J.P. Tarcher, 1983).

3. In contrast to men, sexual arousal for women is more intimately bound up with:
   a. genital stimulation   c. sex hormones
   b. loving relationships   d. viewing erotic pictures

4. The most widely practiced type of sexual behavior is:
   a. sexual intercourse   c. oral sex
   b. homosexual behavior   d. masturbation

5. Most sexual intercourse among college-aged individuals occurs among:
   a. couples going steady   c. jock-type males
   b. promiscuous females   d. couples seeking recreational sex

6. The incidence of unwanted pregnancy depends directly on an individual's:
   a. marital status   c. educational level
   b. use of contraceptives   d. IQ

7. One of the most common sexually transmitted diseases is:
   a. gonorrhea   c. syphilis
   b. genital herpes   d. cystitis

8. Because of greater personal choice in sexual matters people may:
   a. feel more accountable for their behavior
   b. engage in sex before they are ready
   c. fail to use birth control devices
   d. all of the above

9. A major factor in the shift toward more conservative sexual attitudes and practices is the:
   a. church   c. fear of herpes
   b. reaction to pornography   d. women's lib movement

10. More and more people agree that:
    a. most career women are lesbians
    b. love and sex belong together
    c. men have stronger sex drives than women
    d. recreational sex is okay

EXERCISES

1. *How "male" or "female" are you?* If you didn't do this exercise earlier in the chapter, you might want to do it now. Do you find your top five categories contain a mixture of sex-role characteristics? Or do you have a more stereotyped masculine or feminine identity? How would you account for your sex-role identity? In what ways would you like to modify it?

2. *What "turns you on" sexually?* Do you know? If you're sexually involved

with someone else, is your partner aware of what arouses you sexually? What type of dress or behavior on the part of the opposite sex excites you sexually? Which parts of your body are most responsive to your partner's touch? You might compare your reactions with those recorded in Figure 4-1. Have you shared your feelings with your partner?

3. *What was your most enjoyable sexual experience?* Was it something like a nude embrace on a moonlit beach? Or was it an act of lovemaking that had special meaning for you? What made this experience so enjoyable for you? Was it mutually enjoyable for your partner?

4. *Which birth-control method do you prefer?* Do you prefer the pill, foam, condom or some other method? Or do you prefer one of the "natural" methods like the rhythm method (abstaining from intercourse during a woman's fertile period), or withdrawal of the penis before orgasm? Do you and your partner consult about this before engaging in intercourse? Or does one of you simply take the initiative to use a contraceptive on his or her own?

5. *Sharing your sexual fantasies.* Almost everyone entertains sexual fantasies. Yet we rarely share them for fear we'll be ridiculed. If you're married or sexually active with someone, try mutually sharing your sexual fantasies. It's better to begin sharing the milder fantasies. In this way, you can ease the fears and embarrassment and judge the impact of your fantasies on your partner. Avoid sharing fantasies that would shock your partner or threaten the relationship.

6. *Should people wait until they're in love to have sex?* Write a brief paragraph explaining your views. Does it depend on the individual and his or her present circumstances? If you feel it's okay to have sex without being in love, under what conditions?

Love
and Marriage

5

LOVE
    Romantic love
    Styles of loving
    Mature love

MATE SELECTION
    A filtering process
    Compatibility
    A rational or emotional choice?

THE MARRIAGE RELATIONSHIP
    Why people marry
    Types of marriage relationships
    Happiness is a satisfying
      relationship

SUMMARY

SELF-TEST

EXERCISES

Mike and Wendy are returning from a party. They've had an enjoyable evening, including a lively conversation on the way home. Mike turns the car into the driveway and brings it to a stop, leaving the motor running.

Almost on cue, Wendy says, "I've had a wonderful evening."

"Me too," says Mike.

After a short pause, Mike adds, "If you're really interested in going to the game with us next Friday, I'll see if I can get an extra ticket."

"I'd like that," replies Wendy, smiling at him as she gropes for the door with her hand.

Mike leans over and kisses her goodnight, tenderly but without much feeling.

"Goodnight," Wendy says softly.

"Goodnight."

As Wendy closes the car door, she feels vaguely disappointed. "It's strange," she thinks to herself, "that I couldn't tell Mike how much I love him. Why didn't I just put my arms around him and say so? On the other hand, he might have thought that I was giving him the 'come-on' for sex. Oh, well," she sighs and walks toward her house.

Driving home, Mike, too, feels disappointed. He was half hoping Wendy would invite him inside for a while. "Why didn't I suggest we go inside?" he asks himself. "Of course, if she had rejected the idea, I would have felt foolish. She might have misunderstood me, thinking I was pushing for sex. I really just wanted to be close with her."

As he drives he finds himself thinking about their relationship. They have been seeing each other for over three months. "Yet I don't think Wendy realizes how deeply I feel about her," he says to himself. "How could she? I've never come right out and said so." He smiles as he thinks about the affectionate hugging and kissing they enjoy on occasion. Sure, he has told her how good she feels to him. "But," he muses to himself, "I've never said 'I love you.'" Heaving a sigh, he says to himself, "Maybe the next time it seems right I'll tell her." But deep down he isn't so sure.

LOVE

Why do such experiences occur? It appears that love frightens us. As satisfying as love can be, it also makes us vulnerable. When we open ourselves and tell someone, "I love you," we risk being hurt. Recalling earlier hurts, perhaps more unconsciously than not, this risk becomes frightening. Then at the critical moments when we feel like sharing our feelings of love, we may back off, as Wendy and Mike did. We become wary of getting too close to those we love.

You'd think that love ebbed and flowed like the ocean. Yet love isn't that unstable. It's just that our momentary experiences and expressions of love come and go. One moment we're overflowing with positive feelings, giving and receiving love. The next minute we may find ourselves holding back our affection because of the fear of getting hurt. Although the Bible assures us that "perfect love casts out fear," for most of us the experience of love is less stable.[1]

Romantic love

One reason for the "here today, gone tomorrow" image of love is that for many people love means romantic love—a strong emotional attachment to someone of the opposite sex. Romantic love consists of a strong desire to be close to your loved one and a marked sexual attraction to that person. Partners in love are apt to express their affection by physically touching and hugging each other and gazing into each other's eyes.

[1]Marshal B. Hodge, "Our Fear of Love," in *Psychology and Personal Growth,* 2nd. ed., Abe Arkoff, ed. (Boston: Allyn and Bacon, 1980), 414–418.

Most of us have little difficulty recognizing when we're in love because of the widespread folklore about romantic love in songs, stories, and movies. Love is something you feel within, a kind of warm glow. Yet it's not completely under your control. People "fall in love," sometimes madly so. Furthermore, you tend to idealize your loved one. He or she can do no wrong. Love is also "blind," leading you to overlook your beloved's faults, including those that are perfectly obvious to everyone else. Romantic love is also possessive. You want this person all to yourself. Jealousy comes naturally. Under the spell of romantic love, lovers do sentimental, foolish things, such as printing a marriage proposal on a public billboard or running away on impulse to get married. There's also ambivalence and suffering in romantic love—expressed in such clichés as, "It's too good to last," or, "True love never runs smooth." One of the questions asked psychologists is, "Can you love and hate the same person?" If it's romantic, passionate love, apparently so.

Psychologists explain the intensity and irrationality of romantic love in various ways. Some say romantic love taps deep, unconscious aspects of our experience, like awakening a mother- or father-image. Others point out that romantic love flourishes in the soil of unfulfilled needs and dissatisfaction within oneself. Dependent, insecure, and lonely people are especially likely to fall in love. In one study, psychologists devised scales to measure love and dependency. They found that the more dependent someone was, the more "in love" that person was with his or her partner. Those who were the most "in love" were the most dependent; those who "didn't know" whether they were in love or not were less dependent on their partners.[2]

Then too, individuals entering into a romantic relationship make a commitment that involves giving up similar relationships, thus heightening their expectations from each other. As a result, love relationships have even a greater impact on both the satisfactions and frustrations of each person's basic needs than good friendships have. This was brought out in a study that included college students and community members, both single and married. In this group, love relationships differed from friendships in several ways. Those in love exhibited higher levels of preoccupation with their partners, exclusiveness and sexual desire, greater depth of caring, and a greater potential for enjoyment and other positive emotions. However, love relationships also manifested a greater potential for ambivalence, conflict, distress, and mutual criticism.[3]

Styles of loving

One of the hardest lessons to learn is that each person experiences and expresses love somewhat differently. Some people plunge into new relationships

---

[2]E. Berscheid and E.H. Walster, *Interpersonal Attraction,* 2nd. ed. (Reading, MA: Addison-Wesley, 1978), 157.

[3]Keith E. Davis, "Near and Dear: Friendship and love compared," *Psychology Today* (February 1985), 22–30.

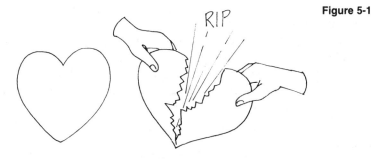

Figure 5-1

with emotional intensity. Others like to let love grow more gradually. Some people readily put their feelings into words; others prefer to demonstrate their affection in deeds. As a result, each of us has a different style of loving. Using literary descriptions of romantic love, one sociologist characterized several *love-styles*. Then he asked many different kinds of men and women to relate their own love affairs to these lovestyles. He found the six most common lovestyles are as follows:

1. *Eros* is the lovestyle in which you search for someone who embodies an image in your mind, like a "physical type." Love is instant and intense. The erotic lover is eager for rapid self-disclosure and wants an intense relationship, including sexual intimacy.

2. *Ludus,* the poet Ovid's term for playful love, is a more permissive style. Ludic lovers carefully control their emotional involvement, enjoying multiple relationships, most relatively short-lived. The ludic lover feels little jealousy and expects the same from his or her partner. Sexual intimacy is enjoyed as fun rather than as an expression of a serious emotional commitment.

3. *Storge* is a style in which there occurs a slow development of affection and companionship, with an avoidance of extreme emotions. Attraction is based more on shared interests than on strong personal feelings. Sexual intimacy comes only gradually and usually late in the relationship.

4. *Mania* is an emotionally intense style in which you become preoccupied with your lover. The typical manic shows the same intensity of love as the erotic lover, yet the same desire to hold back commitment as the ludic lover. The contradiction leads to an ambivalent, insecure love relationship. The manic lover often falls in love with someone he or she initially dislikes, ignores all warnings, and yet senses all along that "it won't last."

5. *Pragma* is the characteristic style of the "practical lover." Such vital statistics as the beloved's physical assets, age, education, and religion are taken into account in the search for a sensible match. This style is

seen in the long tradition of arranged marriages as well as in the more recent attempts at computer matchmaking.

6. *Agape,* or altruistic love, is characteristic of those who aspire to give love without necessarily expecting love in return. It is a gentle, caring love, guided more by reason than emotion. Although this lovestyle is an ideal rather than an achievable relationship, it is seen more frequently in older, more mature lovers.[4]

Your Lovestyle

Which lovestyle most resembles your own?

Admittedly, nobody falls neatly into any one lovestyle. But our individual styles of loving are more like some lovestyles than others.

Do you and your partner share similar lovestyles? Or has the difference in lovestyles become a problem for you? In what ways?

Mature love

When love quickly fades, we say the lovers were merely infatuated with each other. Infatuation is a highly emotional, often physical love that is short-lived. When you are in the throes of love, it's hard to know whether it's love or infatuation. If your love affair was short-lived, chances are it was infatuation.

Whenever romantic love matures into a deeper, lasting love, certain characteristics are present. First and foremost, the partners accept each other as they are. Fantasy and idealization gradually give way to reality. One of the strongest needs each of us has is to be "accepted for what I am" rather than being pressured to fit our partner's idealized image of us. Genuine love includes acceptance. Such acceptance allows individuals to be themselves, so that their love fosters growth and individuality rather than possessiveness.

Second, genuine love grows out of self-acceptance, or self-love, rather than personal inadequacies. When you accept yourself, you can more readily accept others. But when you can't accept some trait in yourself, often unconsciously, it becomes all the more difficult to tolerate this trait in others. Self-love is the opposite of selfishness. The selfish person, driven by self-hate, becomes preoccupied with herself and her desires in a way that alienates the people whose love she seeks. In contrast, those who love themselves are emancipated from defensiveness and self-adulation. They can reach out and give themselves to others in a way that makes them all the more lovable.

Third, mature love grows stronger with time. There is less of the

---

[4]J. Lee, "Styles of Loving," *Psychology Today,* Oct. 1974, 44–51. Reprinted from *Psychology Today Magazine.* Copyright © 1974 American Psychological Association.

love-hate conflict so characteristic of romantic love. Not that all is peace and harmony; people who love each other in a mature way still experience problems in their relationship. But their trust and respect for each other help them to manage such problems in a positive way. The shared struggles and the resolution of conflicts may actually strengthen their love for each other. In short, mature love has to do with a warm, caring attachment that grows stronger with time and experience.

How do you know you're loved? How do you know you really love someone else? It's not easy to put into words. But Sterling Ellsworth asked many people, both young and old, to describe the ways in which they "know" they are loved. Here's a summary of what they told him:

The Love List

1. The person giving the love does not need or want anything back from me.
2. The loving person is firm with me. He does not "please me" or do whatever I ask. He does not go against his *own* guts or deep feelings in order "not to hurt my feelings." He is *true* to himself.
3. I know I am loved because he listens and *understands* me when I talk or relate to him. He *takes turns* listening and talking and doesn't tell me what to do or what *he* thinks until I ask—and I often ask. He doesn't argue, he cares what *I* think and feel.
4. He hugs me. He holds me. He takes my hand or arm. He is not afraid of physical affection. He doesn't *use* this for some *deficiency* of his. It's never anything to do with sex. It's brother-sister love, human family love.
5. He trusts me, has faith and confidence in me, gives me jobs to do; and he separates my inner self from my outside performance.
6. The loving person respects *me*. He makes me feel there is something inside me that "turns him on." It's a non-verbal thing; a certain "soft" look in his face, a certain tone in his voice, the way he sits or moves—it's all right there.
7. His love is permanent and sure because it's based on his feelings *for himself*. The self he loves in him is the one he loves in me! It's guaranteed he'll always like me, since he'd have to stop loving his own inside self to stop loving mine.
8. He wants to be with me. The loving person is happy when I'm near. He loves to be alone, too. He *loves* me more than he *needs* me.
9. I know I am loved because he *tells* me. The person who loves me is not afraid to say it. He usually tells it like it is; good *or* bad, you know he'll tell you "where it's at," because he likes the truth better than pleasing or displeasing you.[5]

[5]S.G. Ellsworth, "Human Love Supplies vs. Cheap Substitutes," *College Student Survey* 5, 1 (1971):34–37. in *Psychology and Personal Growth*, 2nd. ed., Abe Arkoff ed. (Boston: Allyn and Bacon, 1980), 413.

Mature love means sharing the struggles as well as the joys.

MATE SELECTION

In counseling couples with marital difficulties, at some point I usually ask, "What attracted you to each other?" Rarely do I get a ready answer. After a few moments of thought, they come up with something like, "We enjoyed a lot of the same things," or, "He was very thoughtful and nice to me." Frankly, at that point in their relationship, many of these people can't imagine what could possibly have attracted them to each other. Happily married couples seem to have better recall.

Experts in the field have a variety of explanations for why people fall in love or select a particular marriage partner. Some point to the similarity of social characteristics like education, class, race, and religion. Others stress the importance of similar or complementary personal traits. If the truth were known, most partners are attracted to each other for a variety of reasons, many of them not even clear to themselves. Furthermore, their relationship soon takes on a life of its own, which helps to explain why some couples progress toward marriage sooner than others and with fewer ups and downs.

Actually, no one theory fully explains why you love or marry a particular person. Mate selection is a highly complex process. Fortunately, and contrary to the myths of romantic love, there isn't just *one* right person for you. There are a number of potential partners you could love and be happy with. The challenge is finding one of these persons at the right time in your life.

A filtering process

It may be helpful to see mate selection as a filtering process in which the field of potential partners is successively narrowed until a final choice is made. Different influences, mostly unconscious, play a dominant role at each stage of the selection process.

Initially, where you live and work and who you meet are very important. That is, nearness facilitates interaction, and greater interaction usually leads to greater liking. Accordingly, you're usually attracted to people you mingle with at school, work, or in your neighborhood. For a variety of reasons, you're initially more attracted to some people more than others. First impressions play an important role here, and so does physical attraction, as we explained in an earlier chapter.

Once you've begun getting to know someone, social characteristics narrow the field some more. That is, you tend to associate with people with whom you have more in common. Educational level, social class, ethnic background, race, and religion play a dominant role at this stage, as do similarity of interests and values. Also, we live in such a mobile society that people are making friends and marrying people from a wider circle of acquaintances than formerly. As a result, there are more "mixed" marriages in terms of social characteristics. This trend is further accentuated by marriage among college students. Apparently when you go away to school you meet a greater variety of people than you would in your home neighborhood.

Personal traits further narrow the field of potential partners, though experts disagree on the importance of similarity. Some stress the importance of marriage partners having similar personalities. There is some evidence that couples who are similar in, for example, physical attractiveness, self-esteem, sex drive, and neurotic tendencies move toward marriage faster than other couples do. At the same time, proponents of the "complementary need" theory stress that you're attracted to someone whose need patterns complement your own, at least in some important respects. Accordingly, a socially "out-going" woman might be especially attracted to a "strong, silent" man.

The ultimate test in mate selection is compatibility. What difference does it make whether two people have like or opposite personalities as long as they get along well? But compatibility reflects many factors in addition to personality. Role expectations are especially important in marriage. That is, how does each partner view their respective roles as husband and wife? Basic differences here can make or break a relationship. Charles and Ginny began dating steadily after they met in class. The more they got to know each other, the more in common they felt they had—at least, up to a point. But as they began considering marriage basic differences emerged. Soon their relationship cooled off. When asked why, Ginny put it this way: "We had a lot of superficial things in common. But when it came to marriage, we were worlds apart. He not only resented me having men friends but girlfriends too. He had this picture of me waiting for him when he got home after work. But I want a career as well as a family. We both realized it wouldn't have worked out."

Compatibility

Compatibility, or the ability to get along harmoniously, becomes even more crucial in long-term relationships like marriage. Without it, two otherwise mature individuals may experience frustration and alienation in their relationship. With compatibility, even somewhat immature partners may find satisfaction and companionship in their marriage.

Compatibility depends heavily on the fit between the partner's personalities, especially the mix of like and complementary traits. This can be seen in an inventory routinely given by the author to couples coming for marriage counseling. Both partners are scored on nine categories, depending on how they perceive themselves on various traits. The partners' matched profiles are then drawn on a graph. Most couples exhibit a mixed profile in which both partners are alike on many traits and complementary on others. How well they get along is usually associated with the particular combination of similarities and differences, and their ability to change and adapt to each other's needs.

Frank and Joyce are rather similar on most traits, though markedly

Figure 5-2   The better the fit. . . .

different on a few. Frank is rather shy and emotionally inhibited, while Joyce is more outgoing and expressive of her feelings. However, they have grown to appreciate and adapt to each other's differences, so that they get along well as a couple. In contrast, John and Mary Ann present a more polarized profile. John is extremely dominant, outgoing, and self-disciplined; Mary Ann is very submissive, inhibited, and impulsive. After an argument in which John told Mary Ann, "Either grow up or get out," she moved into her own apartment and took a lover. During the counseling session, I pointed out how their extreme differences in personality aggravated each other. That is, the more John tried to "control" Mary Ann, the more she acted out impulsively. The more she "misbehaved," the more he tried to correct her. Since both refused to change, their separation was probably inevitable.

The emotional involvement and commitment to the relationship vitally affects a couple's compatibility. In many cases, one partner is more emotionally involved than the other. The more involved partner, often the woman, may feel dependent and exploited; the less involved partner may feel trapped and guilty. Not surprisingly, the less mutual the involvement, the greater the chances a couple will eventually break up. In the survey of dating couples cited earlier, when one partner was more involved, over one-half of the couples broke up. Among those who were equally involved in the relationship, only one-fourth broke up.[6]

A rational or emotional choice?

Because romantic love is such an unpredictable guide to marital success, some authorities suggest that couples examine their compatibility by more rational means. One example is a computerized aid in mate selection. Gerald Smith and Jerry Debenham developed a computerized service as a teaching aid in classes on marriage and the family, and they feel this approach can be helpful for prospective couples who are unsure of their compatibility, as well as for those who are already having marital troubles.

Here's how it works. Each candidate completes a written questionnaire covering up to 180 categories, including such items as attitudes, interests, habits, and sex preferences. For each category, test-takers respond to questions about themselves, their ideal mates, and an actual prospective partner. The computer then compares the test-taker's answers with the judgment of a panel of experts, including a sociologist and two marriage counselors, on the significance of the similarities and differences in each category. The computer also rates the prospective partner in relation to the test-taker, the test-taker's ideal partner, and the experts' ideal partner for the profile of someone taking the test. On the basis of this information the computer predicts areas of potential

[6]L.A. Peplau, Z. Rubin, and C.T. Hill, "Sexual Intimacy in Dating Relationships," *Journal of Social Issues*, 33 (1977) :86–109.

difficulty and satisfaction in the prospective marriage and suggests areas of self-improvement on the test-taker's part. What are some of the strengths and weaknesses of this approach? How would you feel about using it?[7]

Notice I asked, "How would you *feel* about using it?" The reason is that our feelings play a vital part in making important decisions. For example, there is the incident in which Theodore Reik met Sigmund Freud on the street, at a time when Reik was trying to decide whether to get a Ph.D. in psychology or go to medical school and become a psychiatrist. Reik asked Freud, "What shall I do?" Freud replied, "Anything that important, don't think about, do what you feel like doing."[8] Freud realized that our emotions are an intuitive guide to what is important to us. Consequently, it would be just as much a mistake to ignore feelings as to rely on feelings alone. When it comes to important decisions like marriage, we need to choose with our hearts as well as our heads.

THE MARRIAGE RELATIONSHIP

"Love and marriage," say the lyrics of a popular song, "go together like a horse and carriage." People who're in love want to be together. They're eager to share their everyday lives, their goals and dreams. Some couples simply start living together and, as we'll discuss shortly, many of these couples eventually marry. But the majority of couples marry first. Despite all the pessimism about marriage today, Americans still hold marriage in high regard. More than nine out of ten men and women eventually marry, most of them during their twenties. The high rate of divorce can be seen to indirectly reflect people's high expectations of marriage.

Why people marry

Few of us can be certain why we marry. We certainly *choose* to marry. But we do so out of mixed motives, many of them not even clear to ourselves. Sometimes, friends who aren't so emotionally involved are more perceptive than we are, which is why we shouldn't take their reactions too lightly. Nevertheless, when people are asked why they married, their responses are suggestive.

The main reason people give for getting married is that they are in love. Now that marriage is no longer necessary for economic survival or the satisfaction of sexual needs, love has become the main rationale for getting married and staying married. Even upper-class couples and royalty, who frequently marry as much for social reasons as personal motives, prefer marriages based on love. In the *Redbook* questionnaire on marriage, 75,000 wives said that love is the major reason for getting married or remaining in a marriage. Most of them felt love was the important factor in their marriages. But love meant more than an emotional,

[7]G. Smith and J. Debenham, "Computer Automated Marriage Analysis," *American Journal of Family Therapy* 7, 1(1979) :16–31.

[8]H. Greenwald, *Direct Decision Therapy* (San Diego, CA: Edits Publishers, 1973), 290.

Figure 5-3

romantic feeling. Love implied a commitment to the relationship and a sharing of two lives, including management of disagreements between them.[9]

Companionship and fulfilment ranked just behind love as the reason for marrying and staying married among the wives in the *Redbook* survey. Companionship takes on many qualities of an intimate friendship, with the partners sharing their joys and problems. In fact, most wives felt their husbands were their best friends. Marriage is also expected to fulfil a variety of psychological needs, such as intimacy, security, and growth, reflecting the increasing importance of "growth needs" over "maintenance needs" in our society.

Marriage also remains the most acceptable basis for sexual intimacy. Although more people are having sex outside marriage, the image of the "swinging singles" has been exaggerated. As a group, married people consistently say they are happier than single people.[10] The commitment and intimacy of marriage may actually enhance sexual satisfaction among married people, as we discussed earlier.

People also marry to have a family. Yet childless marriages have become much more acceptable in recent years. Furthermore, more couples are waiting later to have their first child, and are having fewer children.

[9]C. Tavris and T.E. Jayaratne, "How Happy Is Your Marriage: What 75,000 Wives Say About Their Most Intimate Relationship," *Redbook Magazine.* (June 1976) :90–92.
[10]P. Shaver and J. Freedman, "Your Pursuit of Happiness," *Psychology Today* (August 1976) : 26–32.

What about the couples who "have to get married" because of pregnancy? This is more likely to happen when the girl is in her teens. The older she is, the more open she is to other options for handling premarital pregnancy. Interestingly, couples who marry because the woman is pregnant do not have a significantly higher divorce rate than other couples, especially when both of them are in their twenties. However, couples who marry after having a baby out of wedlock are much more likely to divorce eventually. Perhaps many of the same factors that delayed their marriage play a role in their divorce.[11]

Other motives play a role in getting married. Economic security is still important, though less of an influence than it used to be. More women are now working outside the home before and during marriage. Social acceptance is another factor, though couples are not likely to mention this. Remaining single is much more acceptable than it used to be.

Living Together

The number of unmarried couples living together has more than tripled since 1970, resulting in about 2 million unmarried households by the mid-1980s. The majority of these people are under thirty-five years of age and have never been married or divorced.

Couples who live together tend to drift into such an arrangement, usually after going together for a while. College students who live together frequently maintain places of their own as well. This affords them occasional privacy and avoids unpleasant confrontations with parents. Such couples are only slightly less inclined to marry than other couples. Yet once married, their chances of being happy and staying married are about as good as those of couples who have not lived together before marriage.[12]

Tom and Lisa are typical of many young couples living together. They report greater satisfaction and intimacy in their relationship than other dating couples they know. Yet they have some of the same problems as married people. Lisa complains that Tom tries to dominate her too much, and Tom wishes Lisa would agree to have sex more frequently. Despite such problems, though, Tom and Lisa enjoy living together and plan to marry. But they don't want all the customary rituals, like a honeymoon.

Types of marriage relationships

Marriages are not all alike, even the happy ones. There are, rather, many types of married relationships. Some of the most common ones are reported in a survey by Cuber and Haroff (1980). These authors interviewed over one hundred couples who had been married for at least ten years and had never seriously considered divorce. Couples were asked how they felt about their

[11]W.H. Grabill, *Premarital Fertility*. Washington, D.C.: U.S. Bureau of the Census, Current Population Reports, Series P-23, No. 63, August 1976.
[12]B. Risman et al., "Living Together in College: Implications for Courtship," *Journal of Marriage and the Family*, 43, 1 (1981) 77–83.

marriage and what made it work. Drawing on their answers, Cuber and Haroff distinguished five types of marriage relationships.[13]

The *conflict-habituated marriage* is one in which disagreement and quarreling have become a way of life. Much of the quarreling is done in private, so that only a few close relatives or friends are fully aware of the never-ending conflict between the partners. Yet both partners seem to thrive on the stimulation of their differences. Amy readily admitted having this kind of marriage, saying, "I think we've been fussing and nagging each other ever since we met. Most of the time I can't even tell you what we're quarreling about. But it keeps us on our toes. This way, I know Bob cares about me. Yet we do spend an awful lot of energy picking at each other."

The *devitalized marriage* is characteristic of couples who have been in love but have drifted into an "empty" marriage. They stay together mostly for the sake of their children and community standing. Strangely enough, many of these couples do not feel especially unhappy, believing it is natural for married life to be dull after the excitement of the earlier years has passed. Unfortunately, this is the most common type of marriage. One husband described his marriage this way: "Right after we married, Nancy and I really enjoyed doing things together. But lately we go our own ways. I'm busy at work. Nancy takes care of the kids and spends a lot of time with her college courses. Oh sure, we do some things together. But we don't really have much in common anymore. I think we're in a rut. We probably stay married out of 'inertia.' "

The *passive-congenial marriage* is similar to the devitalized marriage, except the couple has always had this kind of relationship. Frequently, couples drift into this sort of arrangement because it allows each of them to direct their energies and involvement elsewhere. Yet they have enough in common and feel sufficiently comfortable to maintain the marriage. Jean says of her marriage, "I don't feel every couple has to be passionately in love. Tom and I each have a full life. He's busy with his patients and going to conferences. I'm busy at the store and my church work. We do have our evening meal together. But we don't go in for all that 'togetherness' stuff."

Cuber and Haroff point out that these three types of marriage are different forms of the utilitarian marriage, in which the practical roles of marriage are more important than the marriage relationship itself. In contrast, the last two types of marriage are forms of the intrinsic marriage, in which the relationship itself is central to the marriage.

Couples with a *vital marriage* enjoy an intimate personal relationship with each other. They are friends and lovers as well as husband and wife. Much of the satisfaction comes from sharing, whether it be their children, hobbies, or jobs. Yet each partner maintains a strong personal identity. Communication tends to be honest and open, with conflicts being settled rather quickly. This is

[13]J. Cuber and P. Haroff, "Five Types of Marriage," in *Marriage and Family in a Changing Society*, ed. J. Henslin (New York: Free Press, 1980), 204–213.

Happily married couples, like lovers, enjoy doing things together.

the most satisfying type of marriage, but also the least common. Doug who feels fortunate in his marriage, says, "Pat and I just enjoy being with each other. We always have. It isn't that we have any high-powered social life. We're really homebodies. We enjoy doing things together, whether it's painting the children's room or having a glass of wine and listening to music. My wife is my best friend. And she feels the same way about me."

The *total marriage* is like the vital marriage, except more so. The couple engages in total togetherness. Ann and Charlie went through a lot of rough times before developing a close relationship. She says, "People wonder what it's like working with my husband all day. 'How does that affect your marriage?' they say. And I say, 'Charlie isn't just my husband. He's my life partner. We do everything together. We never make a decision without consulting the other. Everything is a family affair.' "

Happiness is a satisfying relationship

No sooner were Jim and Laura married, than Jim had to relocate because of his new job. The following year, they suffered another disappointment when Laura had a miscarriage. Yet Jim and Laura are relatively happy because they have a very satisfying marriage. On the other hand, Mark and Cynthia are already disenchanted with married life, despite Mark's successful career and Cynthia's fulfilment in school. They feel something is "missing" in their marriage.

The contrast between these two couples illustrates that marital happiness depends largely on how satisfied couples are in the *relationship* aspects of their marriage. This point was brought out in a landmark survey of mental health among Americans, showing that couples who are the happiest in marriage attribute their happiness to the marriage relationship itself. Those who are less happy put more emphasis on other aspects of marriage. It all adds up to this: when you are happy with your partner, you're happy in the marriage despite the disappointments in other areas of life; when you're not so happy with your partner, you look for happiness in other things, like your career, children, or outside interests.[14]

Traditionally, women have valued the relationship aspects of marriage more highly than men. As a result, women tend to become more emotionally involved in their marriages. But by the same token, when things aren't going well in the marriage, women are more apt to complain of marital unhappiness than their partners are. Men are generally more wrapped up in their careers. Today, however, both men and women are more inclined to judge marital happiness by the same standards, especially by the importance of their personal relationship. Fortunately, more couples are reporting greater satisfaction in their marriages. One reason is the increased emphasis on companionship, communication, and fulfilment in marriage, all integral parts of the relationship itself. Another reason is the growing tendency for dissatisfied couples to divorce, as we'll explore in the next chapter.

SUMMARY

1. Much of what we call love includes romantic love—a strong emotional attachment to someone of the opposite sex. Although the ups and downs of romantic love can be partially explained in terms of fantasy and unfulfilled needs, most people say their experiences of romantic love have made them happier. As love matures, fantasy gives way to reality, so that partners accept each other more as they are.

2. We described mate selection as a filtering process in which different influences play the dominant role at successive stages. Nearness, physical attraction, and social characteristics obviously influence people's attraction to each other. But eventually their compatibility becomes a crucial factor. Consequently, the decision to marry someone includes both rational and emotional considerations.

[14]J. Veroff, R.A. Kulka, and E. Douvan, *Mental Health In America* (New York: Basic Books, 1981), 162.

3. People frequently say they marry for love and companionship. Yet relatively few couples achieve a vital marriage relationship. Most couples end up with a utilitarian, role-centered marriage. The couples who are happiest in their marriage, however, are happy in their relationship with each other.

SELF-TEST

1. The folklore of romantic love suggests that:
   a. people fall in love
   b. love is blind
   c. true love never runs smooth
   d. all of the above

2. _____ love is the lovestyle characteristic of people who give love without necessarily expecting love in return.
   a. altruistic
   b. playful
   c. erotic
   d. practical

3. In contrast to romantic love, mature love:
   a. is based on self-rejection
   b. becomes stronger with time
   c. includes strong dependency needs
   d. all of the above

4. We tend to choose marriage partners from people who:
   a. live or work near us
   b. have similar social characteristics as ourselves
   c. are sexually attractive to us
   d. all of the above

5. In selecting a marriage partner, the ultimate test is:
   a. sex appeal
   b. religion
   c. compatibility
   d. physical attraction

6. Ideally, the selection of a marriage partner should be a _____ choice.
   a. emotional
   b. rational and emotional
   c. computerized
   d. rational

7. Compared to other dating couples. unmarried couples who live together:
   a. are more inclined to get married
   b. have more sexual problems
   c. enjoy greater intimacy
   d. are much less inclined to marry

8. According to the *Redbook* survey on marriage, the major reason for getting married or staying married is:
   a. fulfilment
   b. love
   c. security
   d. growth

9. The most common type of marriage is the _____ marriage.
   a. passive-congenial
   c. conflict-habituated
   b. vital
   d. devitalized
10. The happiest married couples tend to emphasize the _____
    aspects of marriage.
    a. relationship
    c. parent and children
    b. security
    d. sexual

EXERCISES

1. *Describe your experience of romantic love.* Select a love affair, past or present, and describe it in a few paragraphs. What attracted you to each other? What was it like being in love? Has being in love made you a happier person? Or has your experience made you more cautious about such relationships? How could you tell the difference between love and infatuation?

2. *Your lovestyle.* Reread the section on lovestyles. Which of these lovestyles most resembles your own style of loving? If you're married or going steady with someone, both of you might want to do this exercise. Do you and your partner share the same lovestyle? Or has the difference in lovestyles become a problem for you?

3. *What are you looking for in a mate?* Jot down half-a-dozen personal qualities you would like in a marriage partner. Then check the three most important ones. Now do the same for those qualities you would *not* like in a partner. Write a paragraph explaining why these personal qualities are so important to you.

4. *What do you have to offer a prospective mate?* Make a list of personal strengths and weaknesses you would bring to a marriage. Include an equal number of strengths and weaknesses. What are your most desirable qualities? What are your main shortcomings? If you're married or going steady with someone, ask your partner to comment on your list.

5. *What kind of marriage or love relationship do you have?* Which of Cuber and Haroff's types of marriage relationships does your marriage most resemble? If you're unmarried but going steady or living with someone, apply the same material to your present opposite-sex relationship. Do you and your partner agree on which type of marriage your relationship most resembles?

6. *How satisfying is the "relationship" aspect of your marriage or love relationship?* Do you and your partner feel very compatible with each other? Would you consider your partner your best friend? Or do you find more fulfilment in the other aspects of your relationship, like shared interests, sexual intimacy, children, or family activities? Would you agree that marital happiness depends largely on the personal relationship the partners enjoy?

Marital
Adjustment

6

HUSBAND AND WIFE
      Husband and wife roles
      Who's in charge?
      Marital conflict
      Changes in marriage over time

SEX IN MARRIAGE
      Sexual compatibility
      Common problems
      Starting a family

DIVORCE AND REMARRIAGE
      Causes of divorce
      The divorce experience
      Single-parent families
      Remarriage

SUMMARY

SELF-TEST

EXERCISES

Bruce and Becky are planning a June wedding. In the beginning, they agreed on a small, informal wedding with mostly their families and friends. But the nearer it got to June, the more elaborate the wedding plans became.

"All we ever talk about is the wedding," Bruce complains. "You know, who gets an invitation, what the bridal party wears, and all that."

"I know," sighs Becky. "It's so time-consuming."

"I thought we agreed this wasn't going to be one of those formal, superficial affairs."

"My mother has other ideas," says Becky. "She says 'You only get married once, it's a very special time in your life.' "

"Yeah, I know, but who's getting married?" asks Bruce.

"Is it that bad?"

"It's like it's their show," Bruce says, throwing up his arms in resignation.

"Not really," consoles Becky. "It's just that they're so pleased their little girl is getting married they get carried away with their feelings. I think we can reason with them."

"Like the way we did about our apartment?" asks Bruce sarcastically.

"That was different," protests Becky. "You know how Dad feels about wasting money on rent. Besides, it was thoughtful of him to loan us money for a down payment on our house."

"I don't like it," growls Bruce. "The more your parents do for us, the more dependent on them we become."

"I *am* their daughter," reminds Becky. "They're just trying to help us."

"I don't see it that way," says Bruce in a sullen voice. "If you start out pleasing your parents, what's it going to be like five years from now?"

Heaving a sigh, Becky says, "Oh, I guess you have a point. Sometimes I get the feeling they're afraid of losing me. It's silly. I'll always love them."

"Why don't you tell them to let go?" suggests Bruce. "Remind them it's *our* wedding, not theirs."

"I'll talk to Mom about it," reassures Becky. "She's the one pushing for the big wedding."

HUSBAND AND WIFE

Like many young couples, Bruce and Becky are spending a lot of time planning their wedding and little time preparing for their married life afterwards. Weddings are so involved it's easy to get wrapped up in the details of the ceremony and the reception, not to mention the many other things that have to be done. As a result, couples slip into a kind of "moratorium" about their married life until after the wedding.

Actually, the engagement period may be seen as a "testing ground" for the marriage that follows. There are so many decisions to be made. Does the couple defer to their parents, especially the bride's parents, who traditionally pay many of the wedding expenses? Or is there a mutual give-and-take between the couple and their parents? How well does the couple work together? Do both share in the decisions? Or does one insist on having his or her way much of the time? How well people like Bruce and Becky handle such matters sets the tone for their married life.

Husband and wife roles

Much of the adjustment during the early years of marriage revolves around the partners' respective roles as husband and wife. The man may regard himself as a good husband because he works hard and provides for his family. Yet he may fail to appreciate his wife's desire for more emotional support and help with the children. Similarly, the woman may see herself as a good wife because she

Role reversal can be satisfying to both spouses.

serves well-cooked meals and runs the home efficiently. She may not realize her husband cares more about having someone who is responsive to his emotional and sexual needs. Unfortunately, such expectations are rarely verbalized early in the marriage. In due time, mostly through disappointments and arguments, married couples become acutely aware of the gap between their expectations of each other and their respective behaviors. How well they adjust in the marriage depends a lot on their flexibility and willingness to adapt to each other's expectations.

Couples are also adapting to new roles in marriage. A major change is greater sharing in decision making, especially on important matters affecting married life. A wise husband will consult with his wife before taking a promotion at work that involves a move out of town. Similarly, a considerate wife will ask her husband's opinions before redecorating their home. Another important change is greater flexibility in marital roles. More wives are working outside the home. More husbands are taking an active role in rearing the children. When the husband travels in his job, his wife may take on additional responsibilities previously reserved for men, such as paying the bills. Similarly, when the wife works outside the home, her husband may help with housework. But the evidence so far is not impressive. See Figure 6.1.

Expanded roles for husbands and wives may also lead to misunderstanding, with each partner expecting greater rewards at no additional cost. For example, Bill may be glad to hear that Joanne wants to work outside the home. Yet he may expect her to continue handling all the family responsibilities, as before. Or Joanne might be planning to keep most of the money she

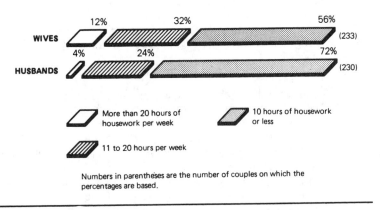

Figure 6-1. Time Spent in Housework Among Married Couples When Both
Partners Are Employed Full Time and Agree Housework Should Be
Shared.
Although working wives do less housework than homemakers do,
they still do most of the house chores. Husbands of working wives
help out around the house more than husbands of homemakers do.
But their contribution is not overly impressive. Even an unemployed
husband does less housework than a wife who puts in a forty-hour
workweek.
From *American Couples* by Philip Blumstein, Ph.D. and Pepper
Schwartz, Ph.D. Copyright © 1983 by Philip Blumstein and Pepper
W. Schwartz. By permission of William Morrow & Company, 145.

earns, while expecting Bill to help more with the children and the house. To avoid misunderstanding, both Bill and Joanne must modify their roles in a more realistic, mutually satisfying way.

Many couples continue to identify with conventional marital roles. This is especially true among those with less education who maintain strong kinship ties. Such couples tend to report less satisfaction in the companionship aspects of their marriage as well as less mutual satisfaction with their sex life. Of course, there are advantages as well as disadvantages to this type of marriage. A major advantage is that both partners have a clear understanding of what is expected of themselves and each other in the marriage. Individuals who have grown up in this type of home may feel especially comfortable with such a marriage. Probably the biggest disadvantage is that the partners will become trapped in rigid sex roles that ignore their personal strengths and weaknesses.

What's Your Mate's Most Irritating Habit?

Individuals getting a divorce often cite their spouse's irritating habits, such as sloppiness around the house or TV habits. As petty as it may sound, such annoying habits are a significant cause of marital unhappiness.

Some typical examples cited by *wives* are:

"My husband never picks up his clothes or cleans the bathroom after taking a shower. He expects me to be his 'mummy.' "

- "He never says 'I'm sorry.' He just can't admit he's made a mistake. It infuriates me."
- "Marvin will switch off the TV and say, 'Let's go to bed,' just like that. There's no courting, no warm-up; just instant sex."

Common examples cited by *husbands* include:
- "She's always nagging me to do something around the house. It's as if my main job is to be 'Mr. Fixit.' "
- "If I had a nickel for every time she has a 'headache,' I'd be a millionaire. Getting her to have sex is an exercise in frustration."
- "Every time we go out, I've got to wait on her to fix her hair, adjust her dress or the like. It's a pain in the you-know-what."

If you're married or going steady, perhaps your partner has some habit that especially irritates you. What's your partner's most annoying habit? How do you cope with it?

Who's in charge?

Another area of marital adjustment has to do with the balance of power between the husband and wife. This too is changing. One young man said, "When I was growing up, my father ran the show. Whatever he said, that was it. My relationship with Jill is different. We try to talk things out until we reach a consensus. That's the way I think it should be."

How well such changing attitudes work out in practice can be seen in a survey of 231 dating couples, most of them college students. Almost half were Catholic, with about one-quarter Protestant and one-quarter Jewish. When asked about their attitudes toward power in man-woman relationships, these young people overwhelmingly favored equality. About nine out of ten of both sexes said that the man and woman should have "equal say" about things pertaining to their relationship. However, when asked who actually had more say in the relationship, their answers were dramatically different. Only about half the men and women felt both partners had equal say. Among the rest, the majority felt that the man had more say. This held true in all areas of the relationship examined in the survey, though the pattern varied somewhat from one area to another. Men were least dominant in recreation, including "what you do and where you go in your free time." Equality was greatest in matters of conversation, such as "what you talk about and what you don't talk about." The balance of power was more complex in sex. Men usually had more say about the type and frequency of sex. Women took the lead in the use of contraceptives.[1]

Men have traditionally been regarded as the head of the home. At least, men have asserted their power more directly, women more subtly. Women who run their homes have usually exerted their power in a way that doesn't show. This pattern of male domination continues among many working-class couples with only a high-school education. But with successive levels of higher education, a higher percentage of men and women report having equal power in their relationship. In the survey cited above, male-dominated couples, female-dominated couples, and those who share power equally stayed together or broke up in equal numbers. Yet men and women were more satisfied when both partners had equal power, or when the man had more to say, than in female-dominated relationships. Apparently it is easier for couples to follow the traditional pattern or the currently accepted democratic pattern.[2]

Marital conflict

Some conflicts are inevitable in a close relationship like marriage. The most common areas of marital conflict are, in descending order: breakdown in communication; loss of shared goals; sexual incompatibility; infidelity; lack of excitement in the marriage; money; conflicts about the children; alcohol or drug abuse; and inlaws.

In my own work with couples, I practically always find that a breakdown in communication, or in many instances the failure to develop good communication, exaggerates the conflict between spouses. When one husband complained that his wife had been cool to his sexual advances the past weekend, he was surprised at her response in the counseling session. "Actually, I was kind of horny myself," she said. "Why didn't you tell me?" he asked. "If I have to ask you for sex, it's no good," she replied. "You ought to be able to tell." "Ugh," moaned the husband, throwing up his arms. "What am I supposed to be, a mind reader?" As you might suspect, we spent the rest of that session improving their communication about such matters.

The crucial factor is how a couple handles its conflicts. All too often, individuals unconsciously handle conflicts the way their parents did. In some instances the partners may try to ignore their differences, or gloss over them superficially. The basic conflict remains hidden, surfacing here and there in symptoms. The partners may become bored with each other. Or they may

---

[1]L.A. Peplau, Z. Rubin, and C.T. Hill, "The Sexual Balance of Power," *Psychology Today* (November 1976): 142–147, 151.

[2]Ibid. : 147, 151.

Breakdown in communication is the most common problem in marriage.

criticize or nag each other at the slightest provocation. When couples put off dealing with their conflicts, the dissatisfaction may mount until it erupts in an emotional and explosive fight. In other cases, couples fight more openly, but they don't know how to deal with conflict constructively. They bring up irrelevant incidents from the past to prove a point. Or they make sarcastic remarks that hurt their spouse. In short, they fight "dirty" in a way that further alienates them from each other. They may also act childishly. The husband may pick up his pillow and move into the guest room for a week. Or the wife may give her husband the "silent treatment" for several days.

Happily married couples also experience conflicts. But they know how to manage conflicts in a positive way. They tend to focus on the issues at hand, with less dredging up of things from the past. They try to listen to each other, acknowledging their spouse's criticisms when well taken. They also try to express their views and feelings in nonjudgmental ways, as we'll discuss in the chapter on effective communication. In short, they "fight fair" in a way that promotes intimacy. As one woman said, "A good fight sometimes clears the air, bringing us closer together than before." We'll explore some of the principles of conflict management in a later chapter on this subject.

How Well Do You Manage Money?

Money has increasingly become a source of marital conflicts in recent years. Here's a do-it-yourself test to help couples discover their attitudes toward money. After each of you completes the following statements, compare notes and work out mutually acceptable solutions.

What most bothers me is not having money for. . .
I hate to see money spent on. . .
Each year I'd like to save at least. . .
I feel most major money decisions are made by. . .
Our biggest problem in money management is. . .
I'd like to splurge on. . .

Changes in marriage over time

A young couple enters the room holding hands. They are dressed alike. Someone comments, "They look like twins." When approached by the host, both ask for the same drink. "I'll bet *they* haven't been married long," quipped one man. "That's right, dear," said his wife. "I think they were married last month."

Such marital bliss is characteristic of the first few months of marriage, sometimes known as the "honeymoon" phase. After that, many marriages follow this common pattern. There is a high degree of marital satisfaction in the first two years, followed by a marked decline. The ebb and flow of marital satisfaction continues, reaching a low point just before the end of the second decade. Perhaps there are too many teenagers in the house. Once the children leave home, couples tend to enjoy their marriage more. In fact, couples who celebrate their fiftieth anniversary generally report greater happiness in their marriage then than in their earlier years.[3]

Marriages also tend to become devitalized over time, with less emotional involvement between the partners. Spouses talk with each other less frequently, disclose less about themselves, and are more apt to misunderstand each other. They're also more prone to fault finding. There is less love expressed between the partners, but there are also fewer problems. The truth is: the couple simply grows apart. Husbands become preoccupied with their careers. Once the children start leaving the nest, wives look for fulfilment outside

---

[3]A.M. Greeley, "The State of the Nation's Happiness," *Psychology Today* (January 1981).

Figure 6-2

the home. Some return to school; others may take a job or become become more active in commmunity affairs.

Fortunately, there are many exceptions to this pattern. Couples who enjoy their marriage and keep in good touch with each other grow closer over the years. Even couples with a less than desirable relationship may mellow in their marriage as they enter the "empty nest" stage. Having more time for themselves can seem like a second honeymoon. If you're married, how has your marriage changed over the years? What would you say about other couples you know, including your parents?

SEX IN MARRIAGE

During a classroom discussion of marriage, a woman blurted out, "I don't think a couple can have a happy marriage without a good sex life." Then she paused, waiting for someone to object, but nobody did. Actually, her point is well taken because there is a strong positive association between marital happiness and sexual satisfaction. Couples who are happy in their marriage tend to be active sexually. But it can work the other way too. During the latter stages of marriage counseling, I'll sometimes notice a couple is getting along much better without any obvious reason. When I comment on this, a typical response is, "We're making love more often now." It shows in the way they treat each other there in my office.

Sexual compatibility

The relationship between marital happiness and sexual fulfilment is especially evident in the early stage of a marriage. The couple's closeness during their courtship and honeymoon spills over into their sex life. Newly married couples may be seen gazing at each other, hugging and touching each other, in short, expressing their love through physical intimacy. Such physical intimacy also strengthens their relationship. Such closeness unfortunately tends to wane over time. Couples become bogged down in daily routines. Differences and conflicts emerge. Sex becomes more routine and less exciting. As a result, the longer a couple has been married, the less frequently will the partners engage in sexual intercourse. Although this usually leads to diminished sexual satisfaction, the decline is not necessarily dramatic. In one survey, two-thirds of the couples married ten years or longer described their sex life as "very good" or "good," conpared to 82 percent of newly married couples. Much depends on the particular couple. Marriages that have been

Figure 6-3.

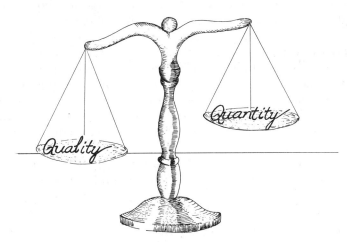

sexually satisfying tend to remain that way, though sexually lukewarm marriages may get even cooler.[4]

Couples who have been married a long time readily admit the quality of sex becomes more important that its frequency. What counts most is how mutually satisfying sex becomes. There appears to be more mutual satisfaction in sex among better educated, affluent couples. But again, much depends on the particular couple, especially their willingness to learn and grow together. A very important factor is each partner's understanding and competence in sex. It also helps to have some understanding of the sexual response cycle, including the excitement, plateau, orgasm, and resolution phases of intercourse. Husbands may arouse their wives more readily by encouraging them to express their own preferences and being sensitive to their desires. Wives may enjoy sex more by incorporating genital stimulation into their love lives and becoming more active during sexual intercourse. Variations in lovemaking may also help. Husbands may become more adept in clitoral stimulation as well as vaginal thrusting. Partners may learn to pace their own arousal such that the partner with the slower arousal may catch up before the other reaches orgasm. The experience of simultaneous orgasm becomes less important than mutual orgasm. Furthermore, couples report enjoying the emotional closeness and security accompanying sex despite occasions when one partner fails to reach orgasm.

Common problems

The most frequently encountered problem in sex is the discrepancy between the partners' desire for sexual intercourse. In many cases, husbands desire sex more often than wives and experience orgasm more regularly than wives. Such discrepancy stems partly from the greater emphasis on genital sex among men as well as the slowness of arousal and difficulty reaching orgasm among some women mentioned earlier. The latter may be accounted for partly by the greater complexity of women's sexual makeup as well as the emotional inhibition of sex associated with the conventional female sex role. But as we noted earlier, both the desire for sex, and the satisfaction gained, vary more widely among women than men, and within any particular woman it may vary over time. Furthermore, the more frequently intercourse leads to orgasm for the woman, the more likely she is to enjoy sex and want to engage in it. Or as one woman said, exaggerating to make the point, "There are no sexually unresponsive women, only inept lovers."

Two common problems for men, difficulty in achieving an erection and premature ejaculation, have already been discussed in the chapter on sex. Curiously as men reach middle age, difficulty in achieving an erection becomes

[4]R.J. Levin and A. Levin, "Sexual Pleasure: The Surprising Preferences of 100,000 Women," *Redbook Magazine* (September 1975): 51–58.

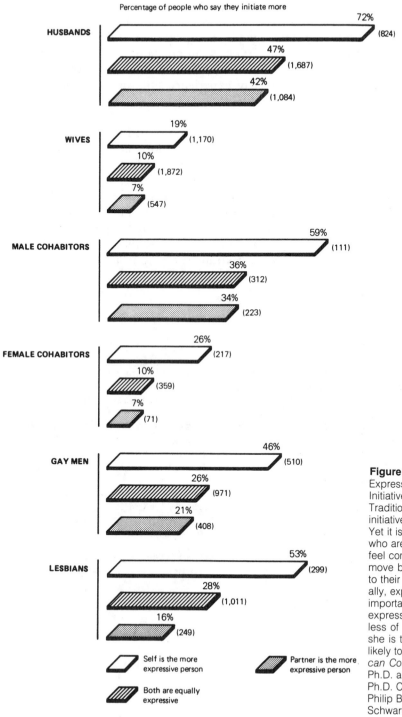

Percentage of people who say they initiate more

HUSBANDS
72% (824)
47% (1,687)
42% (1,084)

WIVES
19% (1,170)
10% (1,872)
7% (547)

MALE COHABITORS
59% (111)
36% (312)
34% (223)

FEMALE COHABITORS
26% (217)
10% (359)
7% (71)

GAY MEN
46% (510)
26% (971)
21% (408)

LESBIANS
53% (299)
28% (1,011)
16% (249)

☐ Self is the more expressive person

▨ Partner is the more expressive person

▥ Both are equally expressive

Numbers in parentheses are the number of people on which the percentages are based.

Figure 6-4
Expressiveness and Taking the Initiative in Sex.
Traditionally, men have taken the initiative in sexual intercourse. Yet it is also true that women who are emotionally expressive feel comfortable making the first move because they are sensitive to their partner's feelings. Actually, expressiveness is such an important quality that the more expressive the partner, regardless of sex, the more likely he or she is to initiate sex and the less likely to refuse sex. From *American Couples* by Philip Blumstein, Ph.D. and Pepper Schwartz, Ph.D. Copyright © 1983 by Philip Blumstein and Pepper W. Schwartz. By permission of William Morrow & Company, 218.

more of a problem while premature ejaculation becomes less so. Such changes reflect the reduced vigor and the slowing down of bodily responses that accompany the aging process. Men in poor physical shape and under a lot of stress are most likely to have trouble in sustaining an erection, especially when they drink too much or abuse drugs. However, those who keep in good physical condition and are sexually active may experience little or no difficulty with these problems.

Marital infidelity, a perennial problem, is now on the increase. Extramarital affairs have traditionally been tolerated more in men, though this too is changing. Today, more wives are engaging in extramarital sex. Women who've engaged in sex before marriage and work outside the home are much more likely to have extramarital sex than other women. Why do people seek sex outside their marriage? The usual explanations are that men are seeking greater sexual variety and women are looking for love, as we discussed in the chapter on sex. Yet in many cases the reasons are more complex. Other possible motives for extramarital sex include dissatisfaction with the marriage, the need for outside stimulation, and in some instances the desire for retaliation.[5]

Inhibited Sexual Desire

A surprisingly common problem among men and women is a lack of sexual desire. This is referred to as *ISD*—inhibited sexual desire. About one out of every five men, single and married, suffers from this sexual dysfunction, with an even higher incidence among women.[6]

At times there is a general disinterest in sex. More often than not, a person no longer desires sex with his or her spouse. Women who lack a desire for sex generally feel no romance in their relationship or marriage, or say they do not return their partner's love. Men who lack sexual desire are more apt to be divorced or, if married, do not return their partner's love.

In a few cases, the lack of sexual desire is caused by hormone deficiencies or other physical problems. But in most instances, the lack of sexual desire stems from emotional factors. Boredom is a leading cause of low sexual desire. Close behind boredom comes anger, especially buried anger. Other factors are anxiety, guilt, low self-esteem, and fear of intimacy.

In all likelihood people have been plagued by this problem in every age. With the openness and honesty about sex that exists today, they are more likely to seek help.

---

[5]R.J. Levin, "The Redbook Report on Premarital and Extramarital Sex," *Redbook Magazine* (October 1975): 38–44, 190–192.

[6]John Leo, "The Revolution is Over," *Time* (April 9, 1984) : 83.

Starting a family

Until recently it was assumed that married people would have children. But that's no longer true. Now that couples are marrying more for companionship, *voluntary childlessness* has become quite acceptable. The decision not to have children usually occurs by default. The couple usually just postpones making a decision until the postponement becomes permanent.

More couples are waiting until their late twenties or early thirties to have their first child. In doing so, they have a chance to strengthen their marriage and advance their careers before adding to their family responsibilities. Jim and Cindy both wanted to work and save some money before having children. After their second child was born Jim said, "We waited so long to have children, we actually enjoy picking up the toys. Of course, we'll be ready for retirement before they're grown." On the other hand, couples who have their children early stress the value of growing up with their children and having a significant part of their mature years for themselves. Such is the case with Charlie and Sandy, who had three children before they reached their thirties. After their last child was born Sandy said, "I'm glad we had our kids early while we have the energy. Once the last child starts school, I'll have plenty of time for developing other interests."

More couples are waiting until later to have their first child.

Couples are also having fewer children than in the past, with the two-child family typical now. An obvious explanation is the increased expense of having children. An even more important reason has to do with the change that has occurred in attitudes, values, and lifestyles in the past few decades. Today, couples are less willing to sacrifice for their children. Although this may sound selfish, it also means couples are more likely to have children because they want to than out of a sense of obligation.

The presence of children can't help affecting a couple's marriage. On the one hand, young parents gain a sense of purpose and responsibility in their marriage. They also share a lot of affection and fun in family life. But rearing children can be expensive, especially as they reach college age. Couples with children also have difficulty balancing their work and family responsibilities, not to mention finding time for themselves. As a result, marital satisfaction usually decreases with the arrival of each subsequent child. Yet as the children grow up and leave home, many couples experience renewed levels of happiness, especially if they feel good about the way their kids have turned out.

DIVORCE AND REMARRIAGE

There has been a dramatic increase in the divorce rate in the United States throughout this century. In 1930, only one out of five marriages ended in divorce, compared to one out of three in 1960. Today, the divorce rate is two out of every three marriages, though the figures are leveling off somewhat. Keep in mind these figures don't tell the whole story. Not included are couples who separate without bothering to get a divorce, and unhappily married couples who stay together because of children, for example.

Also, many couples entertain the idea of divorce without acting on it. In one survey, about half the women admitted they had seriously considered divorce at one time or another.[7] In some cases, couples are under a lot of stress. After returning from an extended motor-home trip with four children, one woman said, "Our vacation was a nightmare. The kids fought most of the time. Our trailer broke down twice. Carl and I were at each other's throats constantly. We really considered divorce." Once they had returned home and the stress subsided, they knew better. In other instances, people act before thinking. An impulsive partner may call a lawyer or move out in a moment of anger, only to reconsider when his or her emotions have cooled.

Causes of divorce

People may seek a divorce for any number of reasons, ranging from the frivolous to basic incompatibility. Since divorce is a legal transaction, the "real"

---

[7]T. Schultz, "Does Marriage Give Today's Women What They Really Want?" *Ladies Home Journal* (June 1980): 89–91, 146–155.

reasons for a couple's breakup are often hidden behind the official grounds for divorce. But a survey of counseling records of six hundred couples seeking divorce is suggestive. Wives gave twice as many complaints as their husbands, probably reflecting their greater emotional investment in marriage. Wives complained of problems with money and drinking, as well as physical and mental cruelty. Husbands were more likely to mention sexual incompatibility, marital infidelity, neglect of the house, and cruelty. There were also social-class differences. Working-class couples were more likely to cite problems with money and physical behavior, while middle-class couples were more concerned about psychological and emotional satisfaction.[8]

The increasing divorce rate says as much about the changing expectations of marriage as it does marital instability. People expect more from their marriages today than they did in the past, especially regarding intimacy and psychological fulfilment. More and more, happily married couples say their spouse is their closest friend, and unhappily married couples complain of incompatibility and emptiness in their marriage. The greater acceptance of divorce, and the ease of getting one, are also contributing factors. No-fault divorce, streamlined legal procedures, the larger number of divorced people, and support groups for the formerly married, for example, all make divorce easier to obtain and adjust to.

The divorce experience

Since divorce is often regarded as a failure, many people going through one are plagued by feelings of self-blame, personal inadequacy, and depression. Yet the impact of divorce depends largely on the particular couple and specific factors such as the age and personality of each spouse, the duration and level of dissatisfaction of their marriage, the presence of children, and opportunities for remarriage.

Jill, an attractive woman in her late twenties, had no trouble getting a divorce. She was living in California at the time and saw an ad in the newspaper for a streamlined legal procedure for people like herself. It was designed for couples who had been married only a few years, with no children, and no significant property settlements. "It was so easy," she said. "We simply filled out a short form, mailed it in, and the divorce was final in ninety days."

For Doug and Debbie, a middle-aged couple with four children, it was a different matter. Unhappily married from the beginning, they stayed together largely because of the children, and partly because of Doug's career in a large corporation. As Debbie went through a midlife crisis, she became depressed and attempted suicide. Doug began drinking heavily and engaged in several extramarital affairs. Even though they sought marriage counseling,

---

[8]G. Levinger, "Sources of Marital Dissatisfaction among Applicants for Divorce," *American Journal of Orthopsychiatry* 36 (1966): 803–807.

they disagreed about a solution. He wanted to work things out; she wanted a divorce. Since she also wanted a significant financial settlement along with custody of their four children, it was a bitterly contested divorce. "I never felt so angry and bitter in my entire life," Doug said. "We both lost the respect of our kids, and my work suffered too."

Divorce is especially stressful because so much is happening at once. Bohannan has identified six overlapping experiences common to most people's experience of divorce.[9]

1. The *emotional divorce* usually occurs first. The partners withdraw emotionally from their relationship, or coexist in mutual antagonism. Either way, this may do more damage to the children than a legal divorce.

2. The *legal divorce* is necessary if the partners ever want to remarry. Although many states now provide no-fault divorces and divorce mediation is available, legal divorce is usually expensive and emotionally exhausting.

3. The *economic divorce* deals with finances and property settlement. This usually involves many painful decisions and leads to a lower standard of living for everyone involved.

4. The *coparental divorce* involves the custody of the children. Although the partner who is not given physical and legal custody is usually granted visitation rights, this partner, usually the father, tends to feel rejected and visits the children less frequently over time.

5. The *community divorce* has to do with the change of attitudes and status in the community. Although both spouses experience a loss of friends, and often community ties, the formation of support groups for divorced people helps to alleviate much of the loneliness and rejection that inevitably accompanies divorce.

6. The *psychic divorce* pertains to the separation of one's self from the influence of the ex-spouse. This is usually the last and most difficult part of divorce, but also potentially one of the most constructive because of the personal growth which often follows.

Children of divorcing parents usually experience a great deal of stress. Children of all ages feel intense anxiety, anger, loneliness, and sadness. Young children who are unable to understand what is happening tend to blame themselves for their parents' divorce. Adolescents are less likely to blame themselves, but they are especially vulnerable to being forced to take sides with one parent. Adolescents are also apt to hide their feelings, thus prolonging their adjustment to divorce. According to one study of broken families, at the end of a

[9]P. Bohannan, "The Six Stations of Divorce," in Paul Bohannan (ed), *Divorce and After.* Garden City, N.Y.: Doubleday and Co., Inc., Anchor edition, 1971, pp. 33–62.

year-and-a-half, one-quarter of the children and adolescents had successfully adapted to their new home situation. About half of them made a reasonable adjustment, though plagued by understandable problems, while the remaining quarter remained intensely dissatisfied.[10]

Single-parent families

The high rate of divorce has brought about a dramatic increase in the number of single-parent families. As you can see in Figure 6–5, the majority of single-parent families are headed by women, with the trend being especially marked among black women.

Single-parent families headed by women generally face economic hardship. Since women have traditionally been given custody of the children, boys are apt to suffer from the absence of a father. Boys tend to experience emotional and social problems, especially in matters like school grades and delinquency. Although girls usually suffer less from the absence of a father, they

Figure 6-5. Children under 18 by Race Living with Both Parents or a Single Parent: 1960, 1970, and 1978.
Note the trend toward a smaller proportion of children living with both parents and a larger proportion living in single-parent families, especially those headed by women.
Source: U.S. Department of Commerce, Bureau of the Census. *Social Indicators.* Washington, D.C.: Government Printing Office, 1980, p. 25

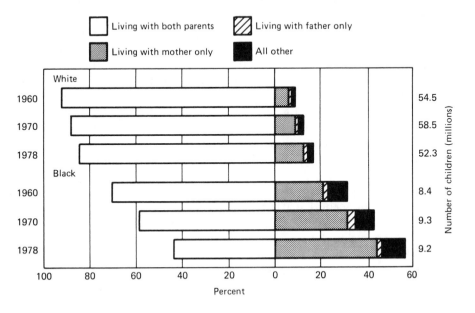

[10]J.S. Wallerstein and J.E. Kelly, *Surviving the Break-up* (New York: Basic Books, 1980), pp. 206–234.

may experience greater anxiety and difficulty relating to the opposite sex. Girls may be shy around males and begin dating at a later age. Or they may exhibit the opposite behavior, becoming flirtatious and dating at an earlier than average age.

More fathers have been granted custody of their children in recent years, with the number of single-parent families headed by men doubling during the 1970s. Adolescent boys are especially apt to benefit from living with their fathers. In at least one study, boys living with their fathers exhibited greater maturity, sociability, and independence than boys in mother-custody homes. A similar trend is evident among girls living with their mothers.[11]

On the other hand, the effect of having only one parent on children and adolescents varies considerably among families and from one individual to another. A lot depends on such matters as the child's attachment to the absent parent; the attitude, adjustment, and economic resources of the custodial parent; and the level of cooperation and conflict between the ex-spouses. Children and adolescents may also benefit from the influence of a variety of other people, like an older brother or sister, an interested teacher, or a special aunt, uncle, or grandparent.

Remarriage

More than three-quarters of divorced people remarry. Typically, both partners are in their thirties and marry within two to five years after their divorce. In most instances, a divorced person marries another divorced person. They may have met each other at one of many support groups for singles or the formerly married, such as Parents Without Partners.

How successful are second marriages? Frankly, this is a difficult question to answer because the record is mixed. Statistically, second marriages are even more likely to end in divorce than first marriages. We should hasten to add that there is a small number of "repeaters" who marry and divorce several times, thus exaggerating the overall figures. Another explanation is that people who have solved a difficult marital situation by obtaining a divorce are even less hesitant to do it again. They "know the ropes" and have the courage to act on their convictions.

However, such divorce figures are misleading. For one thing, the percentage of second marriages that end in divorce decreases as one ascends the socioeconomic ladder. The more affluent and educated people are not only more inclined to divorce when their marriages go sour, but they also work harder at their second marriages. Another reason is that many partners in a second marriage have benefited from their mistakes in their earlier marriages. They may realize all too well the value of give-and-take in marriage.

[11]John W. Santrock, *Adolescence*, 2nd. edition. Dubuque, Iowa: William C. Brown Publishers, 1984, 260–261.

They probably also have a more realistic understanding of marriage and the importance of good communication. Age and maturity also play a part, in that the older people are when they marry or remarry, the better their chances are for a happy marriage.

Probably the most important ingredient for a successful second marriage is each partner's awareness that it takes a mutual commitment to make it work. As long as individuals continue to blame their ex-spouses for the divorce, regardless of who carried more responsibility, they are not ready for remarriage. Only as the ex-partners realize the part each has played in a failed marriage, and has made a serious attempt at making the needed changes in himself or herself, are they ready for another marriage. I became acutely aware of this at a social gathering I attended. Looking around the room, I realized that many of my friends had divorced and remarried. Most of them seemed genuinely happy in their new marriages. One man I had grown up with admitted privately, "If I had been more mature, I'd probably be married to my first wife. I realize now a lot of our troubles were partly my fault." I assured him that such an awareness on his part is a good sign his present marriage will probably succeed.

SUMMARY

1. Much of the couple's adjustment in the early stages of marriage has to do with their respective roles as husband and wife. Other important areas of marital adjustment include the sharing of power in decisions and handling conflict. Although marriages tend to become devitalized over the years, there are many exceptions to the rule.

2. Sexual satisfaction and marital happiness go hand-in-hand, each enhancing the other. Probably the most common problem in sex is the discrepancy between the partners' desires for intercourse. Seasoned couples, especially those who are happily married, tend to emphasize the quality and mutuality of their sex life. More couples than in the past are choosing not to have children, are waiting until later to have their first child, and are having fewer children.

3. About two out of every three marriages now end in divorce, though the divorce rate is leveling off somewhat. The divorce experience is a complex process, including emotional and economical adjustments. Most divorced people remain committed to marriage, with more than three out of four divorced people remarrying, many of them successfully.

SELF-TEST

1. Today, more couples:
   a. share decisions about family life
   b. prefer conventional husband-wife roles

   c. expect the wife to pay the bills
   d. all of the above

2. Among couples, both men and women are more satisfied:
   a. in male-dominated relationships
   b. when men and women have equal say
   c. in female-dominated relationships
   d. when men have more say in sexual matters

3. The most common source of marital conflict is:
   a. sexual incompatibility   c. breakdown in communication
   b. money   d. problems with inlaws

4. The longer a couple is married, the less:
   a. their marital satisfaction
   b. the partners talk to each other
   c. their emotional involvement
   d. all of the above

5. The longer couples remain married, the more they:
   a. have sex with greater frequency
   b. stress the quality of marital sex
   c. engage in extramarital affairs
   d. talk about sexual matters

6. Marital infidelity is more likely to occur among women who:
   a. are working class
   b. never engaged in premarital sex
   c. work outside the home
   d. are happily married but adventuresome

7. _____ has become more acceptable to young married
   couples.
   a. a larger family   c. sacrificing for children
   b. voluntary childlessness   d. having the first child

8. The current divorce rate is about two out of every _____
   marriages.
   a. three   c. seven
   b. five   d. ten

9. The divorce process usually begins with the _____ divorce.
   a. legal   c. economic
   b. community   d. emotional

10. Most divorced persons:
    a. eventually remarry   c. never remarry
    b. remarry after 10 years   d. seldom marry a divorced
                                         person

EXERCISES

1. *What is your view of marital roles?* Do you hold to the traditional notion that certain responsibilities in marriage belong to the husband and others to the wife? If so, which do you associate with each spouse? To what extent do you agree with the trend toward more functional marriage roles, such that either the husband or the wife can assume a given responsibility like paying the bills?

2. *Do you and your partner have equal say in your relationship?* If you're married or going steady with someone, how is the power distributed in your relationship? Are you in a male-dominated or female-dominated relationship? Or do you have "equal say" about things pertaining to your relationship? In which aspects of your relationship do you enjoy the greatest and the least equality?

3. *Changes in marriage over time.* If you're married or have been going with someone for a year or so, how has your relationship changed over time? Write a paragraph or so describing how your relationship has changed. Compare the changes in your relationship with those in the typical marriage described in this chapter. To what extent are the changes in your relationship like or unlike those of the typical marriage?

4. *How important is sexual satisfaction in marriage?* If you're married, living together, or sexually active with someone, would you agree that sexual satisfaction and marital happiness go together? How realistic is it to expect a highly satisfying relationship with a mediocre sex life? Can you have a satisfying sex life in a lukewarm relationship? In the long run, would you agree that a satisfying sex life depends largely on the quality and mutuality of sex?

5. *Has your life been affected by divorce?* If you have experienced a separation or divorce, write a brief paragraph about it. Relate your experience to the six overlapping aspects of divorce described in this chapter. What was the worst part of the divorce for you?

    If you have children, how were they affected by the divorce? If you've grown up in a home broken by divorce, how have you been affected by your parents' divorce?

6. *For single parents.* Write a paragraph or so on your life as a single parent, including your thoughts on the following questions.

    What are some of the special opportunities and problems you face as a single parent? Has divorce or being unmarried encouraged you to develop your own interests and career? Has life as a single parent brought problems not fully anticipated? Is lack of money one of your biggest problems? How well have your children adjusted to the single-parent home?

Effective Communication

7

THE PROCESS OF COMMUNICATION
  Types of communication
  Nonverbal messages
  Common barriers
  Improving communication

EXPRESS YOURSELF EFFECTIVELY
  Be assertive
  Use "I" messages

BE A GOOD LISTENER
  The failure to listen
  Nonreflective listening
  Reflective listening

SUMMARY

SELF-TEST

EXERCISES

Robin, an attractive seventeen-year-old, lives with her mother, who is divorced. Sometime ago Robin reluctantly agreed to be home by 1 A.M. on Friday nights. But this Friday evening, Robin arrives home closer to 2 A.M. She unlocks the front door as quietly as possible, slips inside, takes off her shoes, and tiptoes toward her room. Suddenly her mother appears in the hall. Obviously upset, she asks, "Where were you?"

"At Michael's party just as I said. Why are you so suspicious?"

"I thought something had happened to you."

Making a sour face, Robin says, "Nothing bad happened, mother. We were having such a good time I forgot to check my watch until after one o'clock. Besides, why are you always imagining bad things?"

"So many kids are drinking and having accidents these days," replies her mother.

"I know," acknowledges Robin. "But you exaggerate so much. Don't you trust me?"

"I trust you," says her mother. "But I can't help worrying about you when you're out so late, especially at two o'clock in the morning. At least you could have given me a call."

"I'm sorry," Robin says remorsefully. "I thought about calling you. But it was so late I was afraid it would wake you up or frighten you."

"No, I'd much rather have you call than not know when you're coming home. I usually stay awake until you come in anyway."

"Aw, mother, that's ridiculous," protests Robin.

"It's *not* ridiculous."

"Well, *next* time, I'll call you, okay?"

"Promise?" asks her mother.

"Promise," reassures Robin.

"Now let's get some sleep," says Robin's mother.

"Goodnight," says Robin. "I'll be up by noon."

THE PROCESS OF COMMUNICATION

Like so many parents in a similar situation, Robin's mother vents her momentary feelings of anger more readily than the underlying anxiety over her daughter's safety. Reacting to her mother's anger, Robin becomes defensive and begins arguing with her mother. The result is miscommunication—people simply talking "at" each other with no real exchange of understanding. Fortunately, Robin senses her mother's concern for her safety. Similarly, her mother realizes Robin had a reason for not calling home. Gradually they begin communicating with each other more effectively. Yet you can imagine how such an argument might have easily gone the other way. It's no wonder that when it comes to getting along with others, parents and teenagers, husbands and wives, and practically everyone else admits that their major problem is "poor communication."

Types of communication

Communication ("making known") has to do with the exchange of information, signals, and messages. Communication is something which occurs, or fails to occur, *between* people. As such, communication is affected by a variety of influences, including attitudes, personalities, and relationships. For example, it's well known that individuals who are happily married are better able to pick up each other's nonverbal messages, like the readiness for sex, than unhappily married couples. Also, people communicate for different purposes, which is not always apparent in their words. This is why it helps to know *why* someone is taking the time and trouble to communicate with us and *what* they're trying to say, in order to "get the message."

Most of our communication can be understood in terms of five common types, described below.[1]

1. *Cognitive communication.* Here, the primary purpose of communication is to transmit content or information. *What* is being said or written is more important, though it is often difficult to separate the content from the speaker's personality and delivery. Common examples would be the instructor lecturing to a class or the TV newscaster giving the news.

2. *Expressive communication.* We also communicate to express our attitudes and feelings. It isn't always easy to find the right word to express our deeper subjective states of feeling, our needs, or our judgments about various things. An example is the communication between relatives grieving over the death of a loved one.

3. *Persuasive communication.* Here we're attempting to influence others. This could be an appeal to change an attitude, or a more action-oriented request such as the request that one buy something. Common examples are the politician persuading us to vote for him or her, or the salesperson explaining the merits of a given product.

4. *Social communication.* Much of our communication has to do with getting to know people or acknowledging their presence, i.e., with the maintenance of human relations. Social communication involves many "ritual" responses, such as "How are you?" and the "small talk" of social gatherings. Social communication tends to be guarded, with people telling mostly what they want us to know and withholding other information.

5. *Nonverbal communication.* We communicate through our facial features, especially our eyes and mouths, and also through our postures and gestures. Perhaps this is why we prefer face-to-face communication. In this way we get all those valuable nonverbal cues which help us to decipher someone's overall message.

Of course, in everyday life our communication is usually mixed. The lecturer communicating information may occasionally add his or her evaluations or feelings about what is being said. Similarly, the mother warning her child not to run into the street may scowl and point her finger to make the point. Also, in casual conversation, people may shift quickly from one type of communication to another. An example would be two friends who, after greeting each other socially, begin exchanging information about a class assignment.

[1]*Listen.* A recording. Sperry Corporation, 1980.

Figure 7-1

Nonverbal messages

One reason we have such a hard time figuring out what people are saying is that much of what is being expressed is nonverbal. It has been estimated that up to two-thirds of our face-to-face communication is nonverbal. The most likely explanation is that words alone fail to convey the full meaning of strong emotions. Our emotions also leak through our facial expressions and bodily gestures. We speak of people "bursting with pride," "trembling with rage," and "frozen with fear." Nonverbal communication is especially valuable in that much of it is unintentional and unconscious, thereby revealing a person's deeper feelings. Consequently, when we're getting "mixed signals" from someone, we tend to favor the nonverbal message.

Facial expressions tell much about what someone is feeling. The mouth and lips are especially expressive of emotions. Biting the lip indicates tension, pursing the lips reflects deep thought, and smirking lips usually accompany doubt or sarcasm. Because facial expressions are so important to communication, people often "mask" their unpleasant emotions. For example, when someone accidentally bumps into you, she may feel as annoyed as you do, but she will probably smile instinctively as if to express a polite apology. Such smiles appear forced, betraying a mixture of annoyance and apology.

The act of looking helps to regulate conversation in several ways. Eye contact is needed initially to establish interest. Avoidance of eye contact may

---

How's That Again?

I
know that
you think you
understand what I said.
But do you also realize that what
you heard is not what I meant to say?

---

indicate disinterest, guilt, or sometimes shyness. Yet too much eye contact or staring makes people feel uncomfortable. Throughout a conversation people tend to alternate looking and looking away. But, too much eye contact or staring makes people feel uncomfortable. When finished, a speaker tends to look directly at the listener as if to say, "I'm through, now it's your turn."

A good listener "reads between the lines," listening for more than the speaker's words. A good listener also notices the tone of voice, how loud or soft the voice is, and the rate of speech. People talk faster when they're excited or anxious. On the other hand, they usually talk more slowly when they're despondent, disgusted, grief-stricken, or just plain tired.

People also reveal their attitudes by the way they stand or sit or move various parts of their bodies. People who lean forward in their seat to speak or listen indicate more interest in communicating with us than those who remain slouched in a chair. Even something as simple as a nodding of the head helps the flow of conversation. Head nodding tends to reinforce the speaker, with the result that in a group the speaker may more directly address those who consistently nod their heads.

Facial expressions and gestures tell a lot about what someone is feeling.

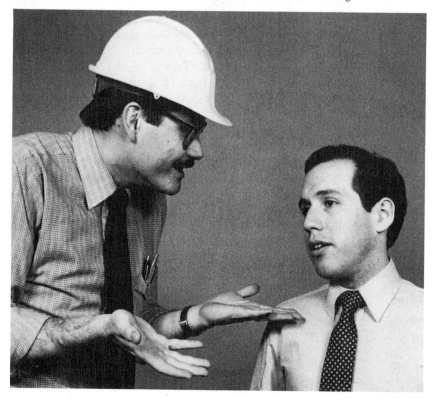

The importance of physical closeness for communication is reflected in popular figures of speech, such as "getting close" to people you like and "keeping your distance" from those you dislike. Mostly because of our upbringing, we feel more comfortable when we keep a certain distance between ourselves and others. This distance is known as *personal space*. The personal space we favor depends on the type of communication engaged in as well as on cultural influences. Generally, people from Latin American and Mediterranean countries tend to get closer than those from northern European countries. Americans fall somewhere in between. We like to keep at least 18 inches of personal space between ourselves and others, except for intimate communication as between lovers. Accidental invasions of this personal zone, as in a crowded elevator, are usually accompanied by avoidance of conversation and eye gaze to keep from giving the wrong signals. Most social communication between friends and acquaintances takes place between about one-and-a-half and four feet; most public communication further than four feet. When people sit or stand closer or further away than the appropriate distances, we tend to feel uncomfortable and form an unfavorable impression of them.

For example, speaking of a casual acquaintance in one of her classes, Carol says, "Michael makes me feel uncomfortable. He stands so close and talks right into my face. I can smell his breath. I don't know why he does that." Whether Michael realizes it or not, he has invaded Carol's personal space, and is paying for it with her negative impression of him.

Common barriers

There are many things which may hinder our communication with others besides conflicting nonverbal messages or inappropriate distances. We might call these *barriers* to effective communication. Some of the more common barriers to communication are described below.

1. *Passing judgment.* The biggest barrier to communication is our natural tendency to judge, to approve or disapprove of what is said. If someone tells you of a movie she has just seen, notice how your first response is something like, "Was it good?" "Did you enjoy it?" or, "Do you think I'd like it?" In other words, our first impulse is to judge and evaluate. Other types of judgmental responses are ordering, warning, advising, and moralizing. All such remarks tend to distort communication.

2. *Stereotypes.* These are widespread generalizations that have little or no basis in fact and which distort our communication with others. For example, two people who are equally competent apply for a position. One is physically attractive and well groomed; the other is homely and carelessly dressed. Which person is more likely to be accepted? Probably the first one because of all the positive qualities associated with attractiveness and physical appearance.

3. *Anxiety and self-centeredness.* When we're anxious, aroused, or wrapped up in ourselves, we don't communicate well. Listeners become rattled if we digress a lot. Preoccupied listeners become so wrapped up in themselves they don't really listen. Perhaps you've had this experience. Someone may say to you, "Did you hear what I just said?" and you reply, "I'm sorry, I was thinking of something else. What did you say?"

4. *Overreacting to emotional words.* People who are emotionally aroused or highly prejudiced often distort communication by using emotionally loaded words. They may call others a *bigot* or *liar.* If you get caught up in their emotional labels, you'll overreact to their emotions without hearing what the main message is. Calling someone a *bigot* and *liar* may be a defensive response to the experience of feeling hurt and offended, which is most likely the underlying message being communicated.

5. *Interrupting needlessly.* This is habitually done by people in positions of power, like executives, supervisors, teachers, and parents. Also, men tend to interrupt more than women, especially in man-woman communication. Needless interruptions confuse the communication by distracting the speaker and turning the conversation into a tug-of-war. The result is that both people may end up feeling frustrated.

6. *Hidden agenda.* When people enter a conversation or meeting with special interests or needs not evident on the surface, the resulting communication is distorted by "hidden agendas." An example would be the leader who comes to a meeting intending to make an unpleasant demand, but who begins by discussing matters of little interest or praising everyone. Others may begin wondering, "What's she getting at?" or "What's the purpose of this meeting?"

Improving communication

Anytime you can remove one of the barriers to communication, well and good. Withholding judgment and avoiding needless interruptions are especially helpful. Here are some further guidelines for effective communication. The better you observe them, the more you'll do your part to foster good communication.

Figure 7-2 Avoid interrupting

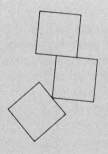

One-Way vs. Two-Way Communication

First, select one or more persons to do this exercise with. Then study the figure above. Tell the participants how to draw the figure without showing it or allowing any questions. When they have finished their drawings hold them until the completion of the exercise.

Now tell the participants how to draw the figure, but his time answer all questions, repeating your instructions if necessary. When the participants have completed their drawings, compare all of the drawings with the master copy. How accurately did the participants follow your directions with "one-way" communication? Did their drawings more closely resemble the master copy with "two-way" communication?

David Johnson, REACHING OUT: Interpersonal Effectiveness and Self-Actualization, © 1972, pp. 239–241. Reprinted by permission of Prentice-Hall, Inc., Englewood Cliffs, N.J.

1. *Adopt an accepting attitude.* Acceptance refers to a basic attitude of trust and positive regard toward others, regardless of whether or not you agree with what they are saying. When people feel accepted, they can let down their guard and express themselves more honestly, and in turn, listen more attentively. In contrast, negative attitudes such as distrust and suspicion put others on the defensive, making for guarded communication. Acceptance is critical for creating a favorable climate for communication.

2. *Be physically attentive.* Face your partner. Maintain appropriate eye contact. Make certain your posture and gestures reinforce your words. Sit or stand at an appropriate distance to put your partner at his or her ease. Remember, whether you're speaking or listening, you must concentrate to communicate.

3. *Listen for the total meaning.* Remember that people communicate for a variety of purposes, such as to express their attitudes and emotions. Listen for the feelings as well as the factual information. The person who says, "Damn, it's good to have that job done!" is expressing more than someone who says flatly, "The job is finished." In the former case, the person is expressing intense feelings of relief, which should also be acknowledged.

4. *Share responsibility for the communication.* Whether you're listening or speaking, be an active participant. Whenever you're unclear about something that has been said, let the speaker know by providing active feedback. For example, suppose your doctor says, "You can go home from the hospital soon." Rather than assume that "soon" means tomorrow, you might clarify this statement by asking, "How soon do you mean?" If the doctor says, "Let's say in two or three days," you'll probably be glad you asked. In this way, feedback allows both speaker and listener to adjust meanings in a way that avoids misunderstandings.

5. *Observe nonverbal communication.* Pay attention to the other person's body language as well as their words. Watch facial expressions. How much does that person look at you? Listen to his or her tone of voice, inflection, and rate of speech. How close or far apart does the person sit or stand? Does the person's body language confirm or contradict his or her words?

6. *Express yourself clearly.* Think about what you want to say. Choose your words carefully. Also, learn to speak in a way that makes people want to listen to you. Use nonjudgmental, expressive communication, such as the "I" message explained in the next section.

In the remainder of the chapter, we'll focus on the two main components of effective communication: expressing yourself effectively and being a good listener. Together they make for good communication.

EXPRESS YOURSELF EFFECTIVELY

People frequently fail to communicate because they don't express themselves clearly or forcefully enough. Or they may go to the other extreme, expressing themselves in such a belligerent way that they alienate others. Some people are simply shy and hesitate to express their feelings. Others, excessively needy of approval, may become so tactful that they don't get their message across. For example, Mary Ann is annoyed by the smoke from Wendy's cigarette. So she tactfully says, "I think I'll change places with Linda so I can be on the end of the row." Of course, Linda and Wendy may well ask why Mary Ann wants to change seats and inadvertently discover her annoyance. But Mary Ann could accomplish her goal more effectively by turning to Wendy and saying, "Would you please blow your smoke in the other direction," or "Perhaps you could move to the end of the row so your smoke wouldn't bother the rest of us."

Effective communication consists not only of saying what you mean but saying it in such a way that others listen and "get the message." An example would be the customer why says in a direct but pleasant manner, "I'd like to have this suit back from the cleaners by Friday noon." The clerk may say, "Okay, you can have it back by Friday noon," or "I'm sorry, we can't have it back until Saturday." But at least the clerk gets the message.

In this section, we'll focus on two crucial elements in effective communication; being assertive and expressing yourself in a nonjudgmental way.

Be assertive

In its simplest terms, assertiveness has to do with expressing your own thoughts, feelings, and rights in a way that respects those of others. People often confuse assertiveness with aggressive behavior, though the two are quite different. Aggression involves the violation of others' needs or rights. Aggressive people "put down," "blame," or "attack" others, consciously or not. Occasionally, unassertive people accumulate sufficient resentment after being taken advantage of by others that they go to the opposite extreme and behave aggressively. One of the goals of assertiveness training is to help people express themselves more effectively before they become angry and act in a self-defeating way.

People remain unassertive out of fear of losing other people's approval. Yet other people tend to feel sorry for and eventually become annoyed at such behavior. In contrast, by acting assertively you not only increase your self-respect and self-confidence, you're also more likely to satisfy your needs and preferences.

There are different types of assertive expressions. Basic assertion involves the expression of your feelings or the standing up for your rights, such as saying, "Excuse me, I'd like to finish what I was saying." Another type of assertiveness is the expression of positive feelings, such as, "I really liked the way you did that." There is also a type of assertiveness that requires confrontational skills, such as when someone's words contradict their actions. An example would be, "I said it was okay to include me provided you checked with me first. But you didn't." An escalating type of assertion is appropriate when people fail to respond to your earlier request. An example here would be, "This is the third time I'm going to tell you. I don't want to take advantage of your company's offer." Finally, there is the "I" message that is especially helpful in expressing your negative feelings, and we'll explore this in the next part of the chapter.[2]

An example of the way in which assertiveness can improve your life situation can be seen in one of my client's experiences. Karen, an unmarried woman in her late twenties, worked as a secretary in a large insurance company. Karen complained that her boss and co-workers were always taking advantage of her good nature, so that she worked harder than the other secretaries without extra pay. As a result, she felt resentful, depressed, and complained constantly about her job.

I pointed out that much of Karen's problem stemmed from her submissiveness. She had grown up a "good girl," complying with what was asked of

[2]P. Jakubowski, and A.J. Lange, *The Assertive Option* (Champaign, Ill.: Research Press Company, 1978), 157–166.

her, mostly to win the approval of her somewhat rigid parents. Gradually Karen learned to express herself more assertively. When the secretaries asked her to do extra jobs for them, she began saying *no* more frequently. She explained that she had plenty of her own work to do. She also spoke to her boss in private, expressing her resentment over being asked to cover for his colleague's secretaries without first being consulted. Her boss said, "I'm glad you spoke up. I didn't know you felt this way." They also agreed that in the future she would be asked ahead of time about any extra work, and paid for it.

By expressing herself assertively, Karen began to feel better about herself and her job. The more control she felt over her life, the less she complained. She also discovered that once people learn you are an assertive person, they're less likely to impose on you.

Practice Being Assertive

Think of situations in which you're usually not very assertive. Then practice expressing yourself more assertively. Consider the following suggestions:

The next time you're interrupted, say, "Excuse me, I'd like to finish what I was saying."

When invited to do something you don't want to do, say, "No thanks. But I appreciate being asked."

If a purchase is not satisfactory, return it to the store with a simple statement such as, "This product is defective."

Remember that assertiveness also involves expressing affection and appreciation for others. Consider the following:

If you enjoy someone's company, say, "I like being with you."

When you're grateful for a person's support, say, "I appreciate what you've done for me."

Tell a loved one, "I love you."

The expression of positive feelings not only enhances communication but also strengthens bonds of affections with others.

Use "I" messages

People hesitate to express themselves assertively because of the mistaken notion that if you're honest you'll alienate others. But this isn't necessarily true. A lot depends on *how* you express yourself. If you talk to people in the usual judgmental way, you may well alienate them. Our typical judgmental remarks tend to be "you" messages: "*You* shouldn't do this. *You're* acting like a baby. Why don't *you* shape up?" Such messages tend to put people on the defensive and tempt them to argue with us rather than make the desired changes in their behavior.

Figure 7-3

"I" messages are a more effective way of expressing yourself. Such messages enable you to say what you honestly feel, but in a way that people will want to listen to you. "I" messages are especially helpful in expressing negative feelings about behavior that bothers you. According to Thomas Gordon, an "I" message has four components: (1) an objective, nonjudgmental description of the person's behavior; (2) the concrete effects on me; (3) how I feel about this; and (4) what I'd prefer the person do instead.[3]

First, it is important to describe the person's behavior in nonjudgmental terms. This isn't as easy as it sounds, but you can learn to do it. Describe the person's behavior in specific terms. Avoid using fuzzy and accusatory responses, and try not to guess the person's motives. Otherwise, the person will become defensive and resist changing his or her behavior.

Second, point out the concrete effects of that person's behavior on you. In most instances, people are not deliberately trying to annoy or frustrate us. Instead, they are so preoccupied they are not fully aware how their behavior affects us. Once people become aware of how their behavior affects us, they're usually more considerate. Pointing out the tangible effects on us is a very important part of getting them to change their behavior.

Third, identify your own feelings. Remember, because of our judgmental tendency we tend to project our feelings onto others. We say things like, "You hurt me" rather than, "I feel hurt." In order to get our message across, we must identify our feelings and express them as such. A common difficulty here is recognizing our emotions accurately. For example, if another driver barely misses your car in a parking lot, you might feel momentary anger, though later you realize you were more frightened than angry. If you talked

[3]Thomas Gordon, *Parent Effectiveness Training* (New York: Peter H. Wyden, 1970), 115ff.

with the driver, it would be important to express your fear as well as your anger. Otherwise, a needless argument might follow.

Finally, an "I" message should tell people what you want them to do. For example, let's say you object to your boss criticizing you in public. In responding to your boss's objectionable behavior, be sure to specify what you'd prefer instead. You might conclude your "I" message with a phrase like, "When you criticize me, I'd prefer you do this in private."

Essentially, "I" messages are a way of expressing your reactions and requests in a way that encourages people to listen and cooperate. At first, "I" messages may seem a bit formal or stiff to you. But as you become comfortable using them, you may mix the four components in a way that matches your own style of communication. See the examples in Table 7-1.

BE A GOOD LISTENER

No matter how effectively people express themselves, communication isn't complete until someone listens. As Thoreau put it, "It takes two to speak the truth—one to speak, and another to hear." However, studies of the listening ability of thousands of people have shown that most of us fail to listen well. After hearing a ten-minute oral presentation, the average person understands and remembers only about half of what was said. Within the next forty-eight hours, up to one-half more is forgotten. In short, you can expect to retain only

Table 7–1 Examples of "I" Messages

Nonjudgmental description of person's behavior	Concrete effects on me	My feelings about it	What I'd prefer the person to do
1. When you're late picking me up after work	I waste a lot of time waiting for you	and I feel annoyed	I'd like to be picked up on time.
2. When you don't take down my telephone messages accurately	I don't have the information I need	and I feel frustrated	I'd appreciate your taking down my tele-phone messages more accurately.
3. Each time you cancel our plans at the last minute	It's too late to make other plans	and I feel irritated	Give me more advance notice when you think our plans are not going to work out.
4. When you criticize my work without tell-ing me what I'm doing wrong	I don't know how to improve it	and I feel frustrated and resentful	Tell me exactly what I'm doing wrong so I can correct it.

one-fourth of what you heard someone say just a couple of days earlier. When people have been asked to rate themselves as listeners, more than 85 percent rate themselves as *average* or *worse*. Fewer than 5 percent rate themselves as *superior* or *excellent*.[4]

How Well Do You Listen?

How would you rate yourself as a listener? Do you usually understand what people say to you the first time? Or do you frequently have to ask them to repeat what they've said? The next time someone initiates a conversation with you, ask youself, "Am I really listening?" or "Am I just waiting for my turn to talk?" Are you:

faking attention, or acting polite?
reacting to emotional words?
interrupting frequently?
tuning out uninteresting topics?
jumping to conclusions?
finding fault with the message?
thinking of what you want to say?

The more of these you find yourself doing, the less well you're listening.[5]

The failure to listen

To listen, according to Webster's *New World Dictionary,* is "to make a conscious effort to hear" or "to attend closely." Right away you'll notice that listening is more than hearing. Essentially hearing pertains to the physical reception of sound; listening refers to the perception of *meaningful* sound. Hearing is an involuntary act of the senses and nervous system. Listening is a voluntary act involving our higher mental processes as well. Listening requires effort and concentration. You have to want to listen.

There are many reasons why we fail to listen. One of the most common is that we're preoccupied. Patients anxious about their health may misinterpret their physician's warnings or reassurances. Workers enthusiastic about their performance or their program may shut out valuable criticism and suggestions lest these interfere with their plans. Couples preoccupied with their wedding plans characteristically ignore observations and suggestions about the future of their relationship. In short, as long as we're wrapped up in ourselves, we spend too much time talking and not enough time listening.

Sometimes we fail to listen because we don't want to hear. We're less likely to give someone a fair hearing on matters we feel emotional or opinionated about.

[4]*Listen,* op. cit.
[5]Eastwood Atwater, *I Hear You* (Englewood Cliffs, N.J.: Prentice-Hall, Inc. 1981), 2

Or we may be afraid to listen to something about which we feel anxious and insecure. Also, all of us tend to bristle in the face of personal criticism, though this is the one time we could most benefit from listening.

Another reason we don't listen is that we don't know how to listen. Actually, listening is one of the communication skills learned first and used most. Yet of all the communication skills it is the least taught and least mastered. Nor should this be surprising, considering that we learn to listen through personal example and imitation during the formative years. People who grow up in families plagued by poor communication tend to repeat faulty listening habits, such as competitive talking, mistaking silence for listening, and judging prematurely.

The most common reason we fail to listen is our tendency to judge. After many years practicing and teaching psychotherapy, Carl Rogers concluded that we do not hear very well because of "our very natural tendency to judge, to evaluate, to approve or disapprove the statements of the other person."[6] We say, "That was a stupid thing to do," or "that was great." We also label others, with such statements as "You're acting like a fool." Such judgmental habits tend to have a disruptive effect on communication, putting others on the defensive. Unfortunately, we tend to judge more out of habit than intent. But the effect is the same—we fail to hear what someone is saying to us.

> "We have been given two ears and but a single mouth, in order that we may listen more and talk less."
>
> Zeno of Citium

Nonreflective listening

This is the simplest form of listening. It makes good use of attentive silence and minimal vocal responses like "mm-hmm." At the least, this kind of listening avoids the habit of constantly interrupting. Furthermore, saying "mm-hmm" or nodding one's head usually has the effect of encouraging the speaker to talk for a longer period of time. Whenever possible, you should use responses which come to you naturally, as long as they are nonjudgmental. Some commonly used responses are:

Oh?
Go on.
Yeah?
I'd like to hear.
Really?

[6]Carl R. Rogers, *On Becoming a Person* (Boston: Houghton Mifflin Company, 1961), 330.

Often you can take your cue from the speaker's nonverbal expression. That is, people's facial expression, tone of voice, or gestures may suggest they have something to say. In such instances you can facilitate conversation by saying things like:

"You look happy."
"Worried about something?"
"You seem preoccupied."
"Is something bothering you?"

For example, Donna approaches her supervisor to complain about her new work assignment. The supervisor, recognizing Donna's need to ventilate her feelings, engages in nonreflective listening. The conversation might go something like this:

Donna: This is the last straw. It's too much.
Supervisor: How's that?
Donna: I'm already up to here with all the unfinished business from my last assignment.
Supervisor: Such as?
Donna: You know, we've got to replace the main unit at the downtown job. And I still haven't written up my report yet.
Supervisor: I see.

The supervisor's willingness to listen nonreflectively, especially in the early part of the conversation, helps to uncover some of the reasons for Donna's complaint. Whether the supervisor will agree or disagree with Donna's complaint, both parties will come away from this exchange with more understanding and respect for each other than they would with the usual judgmental listening. Nonreflective listening is more appropriate in some situations than in others. It is especially useful when people need to ventilate intense feelings, such as when spouses express frustration or pent-up anger. It is also helpful when people have difficulty expressing themselves to those in authority, such as workers talking to their bosses. It is also important to recognize that there are times when nonreflective listening is not enough. When the speaker mistakenly equates your listening with agreement, you may need to clarify your own view. Also, there are times when the speaker may need a more active form of support or reassurance than that afforded by nonreflective listening. At such times, reflective listening may be needed.

Reflective listening

Reflective ("giving back") listening is the process of giving the speaker nonjudgmental feedback as a way of checking on the accuracy of what has been heard. Professionals like psychologists and marriage counselors have long practiced

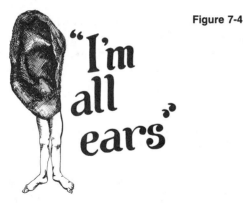

Figure 7-4

this type of listening as a way of understanding and helping troubled people. Now there is greater awareness that all of us need to know how to listen reflectively in order to communicate more effectively with each other.

Reflective listening is often necessary because of the *encoding* and *decoding* process inherent in communication. People encode what they want to say in socially acceptable ways. They must express their nonverbal feelings, needs, and preferences in verbal language. They try to choose the right words, but every word has more than one meaning. So there are many pitfalls in the encoding process. Sometimes speakers are too subtle; at other times they may become overly dramatic. In the process, they frequently fail to communicate exactly what they mean. Many times they aren't even sure what they're trying to say, much less how to say it. In order to avoid misunderstanding, we must decode the speaker's message. To do so, we have to provide the speaker with some nonjudgmental feedback as a way of letting the speaker know what *we* heard. Then the speaker may clarify the original message so that it more nearly matches the intended message. Reflective listening consists of this kind of give-and-take between speaker and listener.

Reflective listening requires the use of several related techniques, such as clarifying, paraphrasing, summarizing, and reflecting feelings. We'll describe each type of response separately for the purpose of explanation. Ordinarily, though, we use them in combination.[7]

The aim of *clarifying* responses is to get additional facts or meanings from the speaker. Frequently, such a response is all that is needed to alert speakers they are not making themselves clear. Such responses encourage speakers to say or do something more to clarify their communication. Although there is no one right way to phrase clarifying responses, the following may be useful:

"Would you clarify that?"
"What do you mean?"

[7]Eastwood Atwater, *I Hear You* (Englewood Cliffs, N.J.: Prentice-Hall, Inc., 1981), 46-53.

"I don't get it."
"Would you say that again?"
"I don't understand what you mean."
"Would you translate that?"

Paraphrasing responses go a step beyond clarifying in restating what we've heard. That is, we give back the essence of the speaker's message to see if we've heard correctly. It's important to paraphrase in your own words, otherwise, you'd be falling into the error of "parroting." Paraphrasing involves responding selectively rather than becoming mired down in exhaustive repetition, capturing the main points of the speaker's message.

Paraphrasing responses usually begin with phrases such as:
"You mean . . ."
"As I understand you . . ."
"From your point of view . . ."
"What I hear you saying is . . ."
"You think . . ."
"Correct me if I'm wrong . . ."
"In other words, your point is . . ."

Summarizing responses help to tie together the various parts of a conversation into a meaningful whole. In this way, you let the speaker know you've heard the overall message. Otherwise you may walk away from the conversation having only heard part of the speaker's message, probably the part you wanted to hear. The speaker, in turn, may be uncertain whether the message was fully communicated. Summarizing responses are especially appropriate in the discussion of differences and in problem solving. It's also helpful in groups in which the prolonged discussion of a subject may become unduly complicated, if not confusing. Also, summarizing may be helpful at the close of a telephone conversation when something is expected of you as the listener.

Some typical opening lines for summarizing responses are:
"Summing up what you've said . . ."
"What you've said so far . . ."
"Your key ideas, as I get it . . ."
"Recapping what you have been saying . . ."
"Everything you've said so far . . ."

Reflecting feelings makes use of many of the above responses, but the focus is on the feeling tone of the speaker's message. That is, we're trying to reflect or mirror back the speaker's feelings, attitudes, and personal meanings. This is important because people are often communicating what is personally meaningful, as well as factual information.

Avoid saying, "I know what you're feeling," a sure way to frustrate people. Instead, demonstrate that you understand by reflecting the actual feelings being expressed.

Some typical reflective responses are:

"You feel . . ."
"It appears that you feel . . ."
"I sense you feel . . ."
"You are feeling a bit . . ."
"Do you feel . . .?"
"You feel (sad, angry, etc.)"

An example of how the reflection of feelings may clarify communication occurred at the beginning of our family vacation. We had planned to drive all day and have dinner with old friends. But after a few hours, and considerable frustration, we had to return home to get the car repaired. Reluctantly I called our host to explain in detail why we wouldn't be there for dinner. Our friend, a psychiatrist, replied, "You've had a frustrating day!" At first, I was surprised by his response. I felt he was treating me like a client. But soon I breathed a sigh of relief. He understood. He realized what we'd been through. My friend also helped me to get in touch with my own feelings. I was so busy making all the necessary readjustments I was not fully aware of my feelings. By reflecting my feelings my friend helped me become more aware of my own inner state, which in turn helped me face my situation more realistically.

When people begin to listen reflectively, they often feel their responses are artificial. "It's not me," they say. They fail to realize that the acquisition of any new skill usually feels awkward in the initial stages. The same is true with reflective listening. It takes practice and patience to integrate these skills into your overall listening style. But the rewards of good listening will make all your efforts worthwhile. There's nothing so gratifying as being told, "Thanks ever so much for listening to me."

SUMMARY

1. Communication has to do with the exchange of information, signals, or messages between people. The five most common types of communication are cognitive, expressive, persuasive, social, and nonverbal communication. Our tendency to be judgmental is a major barrier to communication. Good communication not only requires a more accepting

attitude toward others, but also the ability to express yourself clearly and to listen accurately.

2. Effective communication requires that you express yourself in a clear and assertive way so that others will understand. "I" messages are especially helpful in expressing negative feelings. An "I" message consists of expressing yourself in a nonjudgmental way such that others are encouraged to listen and cooperate.

3. Communication is consummated in listening. Sometimes all that is needed is nonreflective listening, or the avoidance of interruptions and use of minimal responses. But often we need to listen reflectively, mostly because of the difficulties inherent in the encoding and decoding process of communication. Reflective listening consists of giving nonjudgmental feedback as a way of checking on the accuracy of the message. Reflective listening makes use of clarifying, paraphrasing, and summarizing responses as well as reflecting feelings.

SELF-TEST

1. The process of maintaining relationships with others takes precedence over the content of what is said in _____ communication.
   a. social
   b. cognitive
   c. expressive
   d. persuasive

2. The primary purpose of persuasive communication is to:
   a. express our feelings
   b. transmit information
   c. influence others
   d. maintain relationships

3. When we're getting "mixed" signals from someone, we tend to favor the _____ message.
   a. loudest
   b. nonverbal
   c. verbal
   d. "official"

4. The single biggest barrier to personal communication is:
   a. interrupting
   b. stereotyping
   c. passing judgment
   d. anxiety

5. We may improve communication with others through:
   a. being physically attentive
   b. expressing ourselves clearly
   c. adopting an accepting attitude
   d. all of the above

6. _____ people express their inmost thoughts and feelings in a way that respects the rights of others.
   a. aggressive
   b. nice
   c. assertive
   d. compliant

7. Which of the following is an "I" message?
   a. I think you're an aggressive person.
   b. When you're late I resent wasting the time.
   c. I feel you should have known better.
   d. I resent your sarcastic remarks.

8. When asked to rate themselves as listeners, more than three-quarters of the public rate themselves as:
   a. superior
   b. good
   c. average or worse
   d. very poor

9. We can encourage a speaker to talk for a longer period of time by:
   a. saying "mm-hmm"
   b. avoiding eye contact
   c. saying nothing
   d. interrupting frequently

10. _____ listening is often needed as a way of understanding the speaker's intended message.
    a. persuasive
    b. nonreflective
    c. analytic
    d. reflective

EXERCISES

1. *One-way vs. two-way communication.* If you didn't do this exercise earlier in the chapter, you may want to do it at this point. The instructions are described on page 133. The exercise can be done with just one other person or better still with a small group. It's also fun as a class exercise.

2. *Observing nonverbal communication.* Turn on the TV, without sound, to a program in which two people are carrying on a conversation. Then by simply observing their nonverbal communication, try to figure out what is being discussed. Which type of communication is involved? After you've made a guess at what they're talking about, turn up the sound and check on your hunches. How close were you? What were the most valuable clues?

3. *Practice expressing yourself assertively.* If you didn't do the exercise on assertiveness described earlier in the chapter, you may want to do it now. The exercise is described in the boxed item *Practice being assertive* on page 136.

4. *Sending "I" messages.* Think of a situation in which another person's behavior has become a problem for you. Then write out an appropriate "I" message. It may help to compose your "I" message under the four respective headings described earlier: (1) nonjudgmental description of the other person's behavior, (2) concrete effects on me, (3) my feelings, and (4) what I'd prefer the other person do about it.

5. *Listening with minimal responses.* The next time an appropriate opportunity presents itself, practice your nonreflective listening skills. You may

recall this type of listening is especially helpful when people are explaining a problem, ventilating their feelings, or having difficulty expressing themselves. Avoid interrupting the speaker throughout. Also, encourage the speaker to continue talking by occasionally nodding your head and saying "mm-hmm" or making some other neutral response. Did you listen more effectively than usual?

6. *The listening rule.* The next time you're involved in a disagreement with someone who understands reflective listening, simply adopt this rule. One person is to speak for no more than five minutes. The other person listens reflectively, i.e., restating the speaker's ideas and feelings as accurately as possible to that person's satisfaction. Then the roles are reversed, with the second person speaking an equal amount of time and the first person listening reflectively.

   You'll find this isn't as easy as you thought. You'll also discover a new level of understanding with the other person.

Handling Conflict

8

CONFLICT
>   Conflict is unavoidable
>   Types of conflict

STYLES OF CONFLICT MANAGEMENT
>   Defensive styles
>   Cooperative styles
>   Your personal style

COOPERATIVE PROBLEM SOLVING
>   Basic steps
>   Helpful hints

SUMMARY

SELF-TEST

EXERCISES

Bill and Ginny, a couple in their mid-thirties, live in the suburbs with their two small children. They've talked about adding a screen porch to their house, but they keep postponing definite plans because they can't agree on where to build it. One evening after dinner, while they are sitting on the back patio, the topic comes up again.

"We could really use that screen porch tonight," Ginny says as she swats a fly on her arm.

"All we have to do is to agree," Bill says, "and we can get started."

"Agree with *you*. You're the one who's being pigheaded."

"Look who's talking."

"Well," sighs Ginny, "I still say the back patio is the natural place for the porch."

"Sure," chimes in Bill, "because it's the *easiest* place to build it. You've already got the concrete floor."

"Isn't that a good reason for putting it here?" asks Ginny.

"Not necessarily," replies Bill. "Just because it's easier to build the porch here doesn't mean it belongs here."

"What do you means it doesn't *belong* here? The porch belongs wherever we decide to build it."

"What I meant," says Bill, "is we need to ask ourselves 'Why are we building this porch? What's it for?'"

"Okay, okay," protests Ginny. "We're back to that."

Pointing his forefinger into the air to make a point, Bill says, "We need a cool place to sit during the summer. And the best place is at the end of the house next to the living room."

"I know, I've heard this before," adds Ginny. "But I think we'd have more privacy if we put the porch back here. That way I can see the children playing."

"In other words, you're more concerned about keeping an eye on the children than staying cool?"

"Partly. But I don't think the location of the porch makes that much difference about the breeze anyway."

"I don't agree," argues Bill. "Just listen to the weather reports for this area. The wind usually comes from the west."

"I'm tired of arguing about it" sighs Ginny. "I just want to relax for a while."

Shaking his head, Bill gets up and heads for the house.

CONFLICT

Like most couples, Bill and Ginny occasionally find themselves at odds over something like a proposed screen porch. Some of their differences may be "pseudo" conflicts resulting from miscommunication. Bill and Ginny are so wrapped up in their own ideas about what they want they tend to talk past each other. Each needs to explain his or her views more clearly and listen more carefully to the other. Yet no matter how well they communicate with each other, at some point they must also deal with their conflicting views about the proposed porch.

Conflict is unavoidable

Conflict ("to strike together") has to do with the experience of antagonistic or incompatible forces. Some conflicts arise from opposing inner needs, such as the urge to eat a fattening dessert and the desire to keep your weight down. But many conflicts occur between people because of their different viewpoints, needs, lifestyles, values, or priorities. For example, suppose you're asked to cancel an important dinner date at the last minute because your boss insists you work late that evening. Do you disappoint your dinner date? Or do you say *no* to the boss and risk losing your job?

A certain amount of conflict is unavoidable in everyday life. You only have to look around you, read the newspapers, or watch the TV news. Rival political parties and candidates are constantly fighting over their respective interests and programs. Nations dispute their conflicting interests with the result that military confrontations and threats of war are always with us. The emphasis on individual rights and personal fulfilment in recent years has brought about even more conflict. One student may express her "rights" by playing the stereo loudly late at night, while another student in the dorm will insist she has an equal right to sleep in peace. People unable to settle their disputes may take them into the courts of law. Just take your local newspaper and count the number of articles about people or companies taking each other to court. Nobody wants to give in. We live in a contentious, quarrelsome age.

Conflicts are especially likely to occur when people live or work closely together. The greater the emotional involvement and day-to-day sharing, the greater the potential for conflict. Yet conflict is not all bad. Each conflict may become an opportunity for mutual problem solving and a strengthening of bonds between the partners. You may recall that partners in a devitalized or empty marriage tend to have few problems but also little satisfaction in their relationship. On the other hand, those in a vital marriage experience greater happiness despite occasional conflicts. The difference is that happily married couples use their differences and conflicts as the raw material from which to forge an even more satisfying relationship.

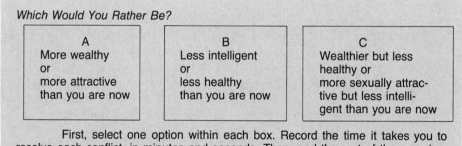

Which Would You Rather Be?

A	B	C
More wealthy or more attractive than you are now	Less intelligent or less healthy than you are now	Wealthier but less healthy or more sexually attractive but less intelligent than you are now

First, select one option within each box. Record the time it takes you to resolve each conflict, in minutes and seconds. Then read the rest of the exercise.

Which was the easiest conflict to resolve? Which was the most difficult or time-consuming conflict?

Studies have shown that conflicts between two attractive alternatives (A) are much easier to resolve than those between two unattractive alternatives (B), with conflicts between two mixed alternatives (C) falling somewhere in between. Was this true for you?

Types of conflict

Most conflicts can be classified into one of three types, depending on whether they involve desirable or undesirable alternatives.

> *Approach-approach* conflicts involve two desirable alternatives or goals. An example would be friends who have agreed they'd like to see either of two movies but can't decide which one. As you might suspect, such a conflict is rather easily resolved because both alternatives involve pleasant activities.
>
> *Avoidance-avoidance* conflicts involve two undesirable alternatives. An example would be an unhappily married couple trying to decide between a trial separation or remaining together while taking marriage counseling. Such conflicts are more difficult and time-consuming because both alternatives are unpleasant.
>
> *Approach-avoidance* conflicts involve both a desirable and an undesirable alternative. A common example is being attracted and repelled by the same person, a kind of "I love him—I hate him" response. Probably the most common type of conflict of all is the *double* approach-avoidance conflict. This type of conflict involves two alternatives, both of which present desirable and undesirable consequences. An older student once explained to me that he had originally returned to school because he had lost his job at a steel plant. But then after a

Figure 8–1. Approach-Avoidance Conflict.
Both the approach and avoidance tendencies increase as one gets closer to the goal or decision time. But the tendency to avoid increases more rapidly than the tendency to approach.

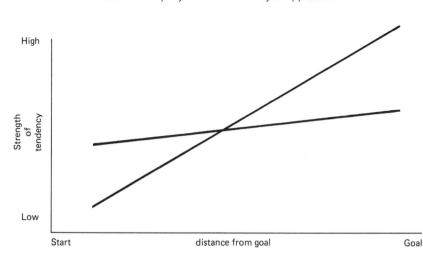

few months, he experienced a conflict because he was offered his old job back. He reasoned this way: "If I go back to my old job, I won't have to worry about supporting my family. But I'll always wonder when the next layoff is coming. On the other hand, if I keep my present part-time job and stay in school, I'll have to struggle to make ends meet. But eventually, I'll get an even better job." You may be interested to know that he decided to remain in school.

Conflicts usually become more intense and agonizing as the time for a decision draws near. Psychologists explain this in terms of goal gradients. That is, each alternative or goal exerts both an attracting and a repelling force, much the same as a magnet does with metal. The closer you approach each goal the greater the attracting and repelling forces, though the repelling force is usually the stronger of the two. At some point, when both approach and avoidance goals are involved, the person may waver indecisively. A man who has threatened to quit his job suddenly changes his mind as the time for a final decision draws near. Or the bride who has looked forward to getting married gets "cold feet" on the morning of the wedding, but proceeds with the marriage anyway, fortunately so in retrospect. The more neurotic people are, the more difficulty they have resolving such conflicts. Fortunately, most of us realize that even the best decisions are accompanied by some risks, and we proceed with positive action in spite of certain reservations.

Figure 8-2

STYLES OF CONFLICT MANAGEMENT

When faced with a conflict, how do you handle it? "Well, a lot depends on the conflict and the people involved," you might say. And that's true. At the same time, most of us have developed a distinctive style of managing conflicts, depending partly on our personalities and partly on the way we've grown up. Early on we learn a lot about managing conflict by observing and imitating our parents. If your father cursed and intimidated others with his anger, you may be tempted to do likewise. If your mother sulked, nagged, or broke into tears when fighting with your father, you may have picked up some of her ways. As a result, we go through life reacting to conflicts in a way that feels natural to us, without too much awareness of our particular style of conflict management.

This is why in dealing with couples I often ask each partner, "How did your father handle conflicts? How did your mother deal with them? How is your style of conflict management like and unlike those of your parents? How does it differ from your spouse's way of handling conflicts?" In this way I hope to make each partner more aware of the way he or she handles conflict.

In this section, we'll describe the all-too-common defensive reactions to conflict along with the more cooperative styles of conflict management. Then we'll turn to your own personal way of managing conflicts.

Defensive styles

These are the most common ways of reacting to conflict partly because they're the easiest. That is, they occur mostly at the unconscious level. As the word *defensive* implies, such responses serve to reduce anxiety and protect self-esteem, but in ways that may alienate others. Most defensive reactions to conflict fall into one of three types: avoidance and denial, domination, or capitulation.[1]

Avoidance and denial.   Many people go out of their way to avoid a conflict. In some instances, they are driven by a strong need for love and approval. Their hidden assumption is that conflicts aren't worth the price that must be paid. In other instances, people have developed a rigid mechanism of denial which prevents them from acknowledging conflicts that are obvious to everyone else. Whenever conflicts break out between themselves and others, such people quickly patch things up or refer to the incident as "just a little problem, nothing more." As a result, feelings are denied, needs go unmet, and goals are surrendered.

[1]Robert Bolton. *People Skills* (Englewood Cliffs, N.J.: Prentice-Hall, Inc., 1979), 233–236.

Sometimes avoiding conflict seems to be the only way out.

Marge works as a secretary in the history department of a large urban university. Marge refused to join the majority of her colleagues in organizing a bargaining unit to improve their working conditions. Even though she complained as loudly as everyone else about the low pay and miserable working conditions at the college, she refused to face up to the conflicts between the clerical workers and the college administration. Her official view was, "Things aren't really that bad." Privately, she admitted, "It's just too upsetting to fight with your superiors."

Domination. People who handle conflict by dominating others are apt to be driven by a need for power. In some instances, domination is mistaken for leadership and is regarded as necessary for "taking charge" or "winning." In other instances, people may enjoy the challenge of a fight. Getting the best of others becomes a way of asserting their authority or displaying their prowess. Also, some people simply enjoy controlling others. Unfortunately, when you dominate people you impose your own solution to a conflict and remain insensitive to their needs, often at the price of limited cooperation. Such an approach almost always generates deep feelings of resentment on the part of those who are dominated. The high price of domination can be seen among unduly rebellious adolescents with domineering parents, and among "unmotivated" workers whose bosses insist on running the company autocratically.

The Ultimate Solution

One way to resolve a conflict is to do away with the person who opposes you. Recently, *Psychology Today* magazine asked its readers, "If you could secretly push a button and thereby eliminate any person with no repercussions to yourself, would you push that button?"

Of the more than 650 people who responded to that question, 60 percent said *yes*. Men are somewhat more likely than women to push the button. Over two-thirds of the men said *yes,* compared to just over half of the women. Men tended to direct their anger at public figures, with Ronald Reagan and the Ayatollah Khomeini being the two favorite targets. Women were more apt to select their victims from their bosses, ex-husbands, former boyfriends, or men who had victimized them sexually.

Many people wanted to wipe out entire groups, such as murderers, rapists, and violent criminals.

How would you answer this question? If you could push such a button, would you? Who would you most want to put away? Why?

"The Ultimate Solution" Nick Jordan, "The Ultimate On-Off Switch," *Psychology Today,* October 1983, 14. Reprinted from *Psychology Today Magazine.* Copyright © 1983 American Psychological Association.

Capitulation.   People may also deal with conflicts in this way. For example, "If you can't lick 'em, join 'em." Those who habitually give in to others may be motivated by the fear of authority or the fear of rejection. They tend to be unassertive people who are more concerned about maintaining their relationships than getting their own way. Sometimes people give in because of their self-image as "victim." Believing they are powerless, they reason, "Why try anyway?" Chronic capitulation breeds resentment toward those who dominate you. This is especially true in close relationships. If you're constantly sacrificing yourself for someone you love, you'll probably end up hating that person. For example, the hen-pecked husband may constantly give in to his wife to "keep peace in the family," but despise her for bossing him around. Another example is that of the worker who meekly complies with her boss's every request, but is usually the first one to criticizes the boss behind his back.

Cooperative styles

A conflict doesn't have to be a tug-of-war between opposing sides. Conflicts can also be an opportunity for change and mutual gain. At least, that's what the proponents of negotiation and problem-solving approaches contend. The two most familiar cooperative styles of conflict management are compromise and cooperative problem solving.

Compromise, though superior to domination and capitulation, is often a measure of last resort. People rarely begin negotiating with the goal of compromising. Yet when two opposing sides reach a stalemate, compromise may be appropriate. Agreement is reached through each party giving up something or making concessions. Even though the gains may be largely offset by the losses, the relationship between the two parties is maintained. An example of this would be a threatened strike that is avoided only by the workers agreeing to accept a minimum salary raise and management getting only minimum concessions from the workers on productivity. A strike is avoided, but neither side is very happy about the results.

Cooperative problem solving, more popularly known as negotiation, is the preferred method of conflict resolution whenever possible. This approach is so important, the last part of the chapter will be devoted to explaining it in greater detail. Conflict here is viewed as an opportunity for mutual problem solving. As in compromise, both parties desire to preserve their relationship. But unlike compromise, the emphasis is on maximizing each party's gains, rather than on making concessions. Obviously, this approach is superior on ethical grounds because it is based on cooperation. It also makes good sense on practical grounds. Because each party has a stake in maintaining their relationship, both tend to achieve long-range objectives, not just short-term advantages.

A large state university, plagued by costly faculty strikes in two consecutive years, turned to a more cooperative approach to their problems out of desperation. The change in climate began when college administrators and the faculty union received a timely invitation to a workshop on mutual-gains bargaining. Both administrative officials and faculty were wary at first. But eventually three representatives from the faculty union and three key administrators, including the college president, agreed to attend the workshop. There they joined similar teams from other colleges in exploring ways to deal with their problems in a more cooperative manner. After this, a monthly "meet-and-discuss" meeting was set up in which faculty leaders talked over current issues with a key administrator. So far, one of the most tangible proofs of the mutual-gains approach has been a one-year extension of the current contract. Nobody believes this approach is a cure-all. But it has helped to create a more receptive climate in which both sides can discuss the issues and, hopefully, avoid an all-out confrontation.

Your personal style

At this point, you may be wondering, "How do I manage conflict? Do I tend to avoid conflicts? Am I inclined to dominate people or give in to them? Or do I tend to negotiate and use problem-solving skills?" Many of us adopt a characteristic style of managing conflicts, depending on our personalities and the way we've grown up. Then we continue to rely on this approach whether it is appropriate or not.

Ideally, it's best to use the style of conflict management most appropriate to the conflict at hand. Naturally, this changes from time to time and from one situation to another. When neither the goal nor the relationship is very important, it may be wiser to *avoid* a conflict. An example would be avoiding unnecessary involvement with a stranger on the highway who wants to engage in competitive passing. When your goal is important, though the relationship is considerably less important, *domination* may be more appropriate. For example, when you're buying a house, you want the best possible bargain, regardless of whether the seller or real estate agent feels you are a nice person or not. On the other hand, when the relationship is paramount, *capitulation* might be the better strategy. An example would be giving in to a neighbor's request on a matter he or she feels strongly about but which means little to you.

When both the goal and the relationships are important to you, then the most appropriate approach would be some type of *cooperative problem solving*. An example would be a happily married couple, like Bill and Ginny who disagreed over the proposed screen porch. They're not only concerned about the type of porch they plan to build, they also want to keep up a good relationship. They want a solution they can live with. Hence both of them have much to gain through some type of cooperative problem solving.

COOPERATIVE PROBLEM SOLVING

People call cooperative problem solving by a variety of names, including *negotiation, mutual gains bargaining*, and *mediation*. But the process is essentially the same: Once you've discovered you have a conflict, you come together to find a solution acceptable to all parties. The attitude is positive, with an emphasis on cooperation. This is also a mutual-gains approach because all parties stand to gain more through cooperation than through defensive self-seeking.

Figure 8-3

Basic steps

Books on conflict management cover a wide variety of procedures, suggesting that there is probably more "art" than "science" in resolving conflicts. Much depends on the parties involved, their experience, their orientation, and their preferred style of handling conflict. Despite the variety of labels and approaches, however, there are some basic steps involved in conflict resolution. The following procedure should be seen as a suggested sequence of steps which in actual practice often overlap, rather than a scheme to be followed to the letter of the law.[2]

1. *Acknowledge the conflict.* As simple as this sounds, it's probably the most neglected part of the process. Conflict arouses so much anxiety that many people habitually avoid it, deny it, or attempt to resolve it prematurely by dominating or giving in. Instead, it's better to admit openly that conflict exists. This may clear the air and set the stage for a constructive solution. Remember that some conflict is unavoidable in life, especially among those who live or work together. What matters most is *how* we handle it.

2. *Agree on a procedure.* When it's obvious that a conflict is not going to be resolved in the meeting at hand, it's best to agree on the process to be used rather than to continue haggling. That way you're beginning with some sort of agreement. You might say something like, "Suppose we meet Monday afternoon just to explore possible solutions, okay?" or, "Let's meet on Tuesday morning to review the whole situation and identify some of the issues that need to be worked out." It's best to agree on who will participate when there are more than two parties involved. Because people feel more comfortable in their home turf, it's usually wise to alternate meeting places between the two parties, or to select a neutral meeting place.

3. *Define the conflict.* The main idea here is to define the conflict in terms of a mutual problem to be solved. Right away, the "we" approach taps the motivation of both parties to cooperate in reaching a mutually satisfactory solution. Both parties should say how they see the conflict, how they feel about it, and especially how each contributes to it. Equally important is what the respective parties are *not* saying or doing. Whenever possible, try to smoke out the "hidden agendas" and personal grievances that may aggravate the basic conflict. As much as possible, focus on specific actions, needs, and issues rather than personalities. Avoid interpreting other people's motivation, or attributing their behavior to personality factors.

[2]Robert Bolton. op. cit., 329ff.

4. *Explore possible solutions.* One of the most helpful ways of accomplishing this is *brainstorming*—the uninhibited offering of ideas and suggested solutions by all members of a group. Everyone should be encouraged to participate. All suggestions should be listed without being judged or associated with any person's name. Avoid criticizing or praising these suggestions. Simply list all the ideas, no matter how crazy they may initially appear. Your goal is to explore as many possible solutions as you can.

   I recall how brainstorming helped a church building committee break through a stalemate. After a number of conventional suggestions had been expressed, one member asked, "Why not sell the church, buy some land, and start over?" Although this suggestion wasn't adopted, mostly because of the strong sentiment attach to the existing building, it served to stimulate the members' imaginations in reaching a more creative solution than might have otherwise occurred.

5. *Reach an agreement.* Eventually, the participants must evaluate all the suggestions and select a solution. To be mutually satisfying, agreement should be reached through some sort of consensus. When there are only two people involved and the issue is not very important, a "sense of the meeting" may be sufficient. When there are more than two or three participants, especially when the issues are more important, it's best to take a vote. Ordinarily, a hand vote is acceptable, though on crucial issues a written vote may minimize the influence of group conformity.

   Herbert Cohen suggests you write down a *memorandum of agreement.*[3] This is sometimes called a *letter of intent* or a *memo of understanding.* But the purpose is the same: to define the commitments of all the parties involved. Such a written agreement then serves as a reminder of the verbal agreement for future occasions. The agreement

Figure 8-4

[3]Herb Cohen. *You Can Negotiate Anything* (New York: Bantam Books, 1980), 219.

should preferably be written in simple, common-sense language, though in more formal negotiations, such as collective bargaining in schools and businesses, it's customary to use conventional legal terms as well.

6. *Put the plan into action.* In order to facilitate this, both parties should be clear about what is to be done, when, where, and by whom. Sometimes this is included in the written agreement. It's desirable to initiate the action as soon as possible after an agreement has been reached. Otherwise, delays may arouse doubts and suspicions.

   I recall a group that was having difficulty getting things done until one of the members, a successful executive in a large corporation, made an innovative suggestion. He requested that at the end of each meeting the secretary summarize what the group had decided to do together with the names of those responsible for initiating the action. Such a reminder just before the meeting adjourned helped to define what was expected. Consequently, the group got more accomplished.

7. *Evaluate the solution.* Most people evaluate the solution to their conflicts, whether asked to or not. Such judgments are apt to be expressed in their private "mutterings" or small, informal gatherings after the official meeting has adjourned. Why not provide them with an opportunity to make a more objective evaluation? In this way, participants may learn more about the negotiating process itself. Each participant should be asked questions like: How satisfied are you with the solution? Do you feel "railroaded"? Or do you feel there have been mutual gains? What do you like best about the solution? What do you like the least? What do you wish had been included that was not? What can we do better next time?

Helpful hints

Skilled negotiators are well aware that the problem-solving process is influenced by a variety of factors. Many of these are intangibles like the attitudes, motivations, and needs of the participants. People's assumptions and stereotypes can also make or break a series of negotiations. With this in mind, here are some suggestions for enhancing your efforts at cooperative problem solving.

1. *Create a climate of cooperation.* Participants can help to create a cooperative atmosphere the moment they meet. This is why it's so important to spend a few minutes at the beginning of each session with some "icebreaker" conversation. Also, when you're meeting over several days, it helps to share a meal or some social time. During the sessions, it's important that people from both sides talk for an equal amount of time. Otherwise, those who talk the most may dominate the negotiation.

Furthermore, from time to time you should emphasize what you have agreed upon and your progress to that point. All this helps to build the sense of trust and cooperation so essential to successful negotiations.

A mediator I know makes it a habit to arrive quite early and spend a fair amount of time in small talk with people from the respective parties he is dealing with. He readily admits this is a way of establishing trust between himself and others before they get down to business.

2. *Communicate clearly.* Most of the things which make for good communication have been discussed in the previous chapter. The two most pertinent points here concern presenting your points effectively and listening.

In order to present your points clearly, you must do your homework. Skilled negotiators stress the value of preparing for negotiations. The use of prepared statements, charts, and tables of appropriate figures, and the developing of specific points, all help to make your case effectively. Also, the way you organize your information helps to communicate your priorities.

Listening is crucial to understanding other people's views. Use clarifying and summarizing responses as a way of inviting others to correct and elaborate on your understanding of their position. Questions are often helpful, though excessive questioning is to be avoided. When you ask too many questions, you begin to assume more control over the conversation, thereby putting the speaker on the defensive. Finally, listening to others helps to model the kind of response you want from them. People are much more likely to listen to you if you've sincerely tried to listen to them.

3. *Manage your feelings.* Contrary to popular understanding, emotions are important in problem solving. First of all, it's usually when you feel strongly about a matter that you're motivated to do something about it. Once you've begun the problem-solving, however, it's important to control your emotions. Otherwise you'll become irrational.

The best way to manage your feelings is to express them in an appropriate way—as in the "I" message. That is, rather than rant and rave, explain why you feel the way you do and what needs to be done about it. A good example of this occurred in our college. The maintenance workers would always wait until the first hot spell to turn on the air conditioning in one of the classroom buildings. Shortly afterwards, at the worst possible time, it would always break down. One day I joined several other faculty members to see what could be done about the situation. The college official, accustomed to handling such problems, was quite businesslike, but one of the maintenance workers was very emotional and defensive. "Don't blame us," he said, "it's the college's fault." Fortunately, the other maintenance worker, though equally annoyed, was more in control of his feelings. He said, "The reason the air conditioning keeps breaking down is that we never really fix it. We keep patching it up to stay within our budget. As soon as the college gives us enough money to fix it properly, it'll work. It's as simple as that." It took three weeks to fix the air conditioning properly. But it hasn't broken down since.

Managing Anger

There's a widespread belief that when you're angry, it's better to express the emotion than to hold it in. "Blowing off steam" not only makes you feel better but makes known your grievance in no uncertain terms. But does it always work?

Not necessarily, especially when it's your boss or someone in authority you're telling off. There's also the danger that ventilating anger may actually *increase* anger to the point that you lose control. As a result, you not only may say or do things you'll later regret, but you're also more likely to alienate others.

The reflective approach to anger is usually more effective than the exclusive suppression or ventilation of anger. That is, you're encouraged to keep in touch with your feelings but not to take them at face value. Suppose you feel angry about something your boss told you. Rather than rushing in to tell him, or suffering in silence, think over the situation. Was there a good reason for what your boss said? Are you being defensive? Only after you've calmed down and thought things through does it help to express your anger. At this point, you're more likely to express it in a way that makes your grievance more effective, as in an "I" message. The reflective use of anger is especially helpful to people exposed to constant provocation and conflict, such as police officers, complaint managers, supervisors, mediators, and those in various positions of responsibility.

---

4. *Stay open to new information.* Skilled negotiators realize that additional information becomes available during negotiations, and they incorporate this. For example, suppose your opponent says, "My initial offer is so-and-so." Right away, use of the word *initial* implies that subsequent offers will be made. Such knowledge then helps you to remain more patient in bargaining for the price you want.

   The simplest way to increase your information is to ask questions. Another way to get information is to give it. People are reluctant to communicate beyond the chit-chat level until the risk in giving information becomes reciprocal. By providing some carefully worded information, you'll get additional information in return. Still another source of information is nonverbal communication, as discussed in the previous chapter. A change in voice intonation or facial expression is often a telltale sign of a person's real feelings about the matter at hand.

5. *Use of positive power.* The term *power* carries a negative connotation, suggesting the use of force. Yet power simply means the ability to get things done. As such, power is in itself neither good nor bad; it depends on how it is used.

The most important point here is that each of us has a great deal more positive power at our disposal than we realize. Power is first and foremost based on perception. Too often, people surrender their power by believing there's nothing they can do about it. Instead, when you're convinced you *can* do something about a problem or conflict, you're well on the way to a solution. There are many ways you can increase your positive power, including expertise, fresh options, persistence, and risk taking, to name a few.

Persistence is often the key to success. For many years, an advertising man in a large soft-drink firm was in constant conflict with his superiors over the company's unimaginative ads. Gradually he rose to a policy-making position and at last persuaded those in charge to try more innovative ads. When they did, sales increased dramatically, and the company's stock soared to unprecedented heights. The adman became the company hero and also became a millionaire because of his stock holdings in the firm.

6. *Set a deadline.* It's essential to set a deadline for any type of conflict resolution, or negotiations tend to expand to fill the time available. When you set a deadline, all parties adjust their negotiations accordingly.

Two crucial points should be noted here. First, it is important that everyone involved agree on the deadline. Otherwise, if your opponents know your deadline and you don't know theirs, they have the advantage. For example, suppose your partners in a business deal meet you at the airport and ask when your return flight leaves. If you say "Tomorrow evening at 8:30 P.M.," you're immediately giving them an unnecessary advantage in the bargaining process. Second, many significant transactions occur just before the deadline expires, or sometimes during an extension that is mutually agreed upon. Realizing this, you may negotiate with more patience. For example, in a lunch meeting during a tense series of negotiations at a large metropolitan newspaper, the chief negotiator for the company humorously quipped, "Nothing much happens until the deadline anyway." That disclosure, which eventually proved to be true, provided the workers with much needed encouragement during the early stages of a seemingly fruitless series of talks.

In closing, remember that conflict is a natural part of human existence. Yet this does not mean that life must be a constant battle of winning and losing. The cooperative approach suggests that we view each conflict as a problem to be solved, as an opportunity to find a creative solution to the issues at hand. It's not a matter of how to "cut up the pie" to see who gets the bigger piece. Both parties need to work together to create a bigger pie so that there will be more for everyone. Our goal is mutual satisfaction.

SUMMARY

1. Conflict, or the experience of incompatible forces, is inevitable in everyday life. Most conflicts fall into one of three types: approach-approach, avoidance-avoidance, or approach-avoidance. The most common type is the double approach-avoidance conflict, in which both alternatives have desirable and undesirable consequences.

2. People may handle conflict in a variety of ways, including defensive avoidance, domination, and capitulation. Alternatively, they may use one of the more cooperative approaches, like compromise or cooperative problem solving. Although we each tend to adopt a characteristic style of conflict management, it's best to vary the approach depending on what is appropriate for the situation.

3. Cooperative problem solving is the preferred approach to conflict resolution because all participants gain more than they lose, and all have a stake in maintaining good relationships. All parties work to: (1) acknowledge the conflict; (2) agree on a procedure; (3) define the basic conflict; (4) explore possible solutions; (5) reach an agreement; (6) put the plan into action; and (7) later evaluate the solution. This approach works best when everyone observes certain guidelines, such as creating a cooperative climate, communicating clearly, and setting a deadline.

SELF-TEST

1. _____ has to do with our experience of antagonistic or incompatible forces.
   a. negotiation
   b. conflict
   c. compromise
   d. power

2. Most of our conflicts can be classified in terms of _____ conflicts.
   a. approach-approach
   b. avoidance-avoidance
   c. approach-avoidance
   d. all of the above.

3. Having to decide between two courses of action both of which offer advantagess and disadvantage is known as a(n) _____ conflict.
   a. approach-approach
   b. approach-avoidance
   c. avoidance-avoidance
   d. double approach-avoidance

4. Defensive styles of handling conflict include:
   a. compromise
   b. domination
   c. negotiation
   d. all of the above

5. Whenever possible, it is preferable to resolve conflicts through:
   a. domination
   b. avoidance
   c. negotiation
   d. capitulation
6. When neither the goal to be achieved nor the relationship involved is very important, it may be wiser to handle the conflict through:
   a. avoidance
   b. domination
   c. negotiation
   d. capitulation
7. Cooperative problem solving may be labeled by a variety of terms like:
   a. bargaining
   b. negotiation
   c. mediation
   d. all of the above
8. The first step suggested in cooperative problem solving is to:
   a. define the conflict
   b. explore solutions
   c. acknowledge the conflict
   d. agree on the procedure
9. Which of the following is true in regard to the use of power in cooperative problem solving?
   a. the use of power usually has harmful effects
   b. in itself, power is neither good nor bad
   c. the use of power is always good
   d. financial power is especially ineffective
10. For successful problem solving, skilled negotiators suggest that we:
    a. communicate clearly
    b. manage our feelings
    c. set a deadline
    d. all of the above

EXERCISES

1. *Easy/hard conflicts.* Draw a line down the middle of an 8½-by-11 sheet of paper. Label one column *conflicts easily resolved,* and the other *conflicts resolved with difficulty.*

   Now think of five to ten conflicts or problems you've resolved one way or the other in the past year. Include an equal number of easy and hard conflicts. Then go back and code each conflict in terms of the three basic types explained in this chapter: Ap-Ap (approach-approach), Av-Av (avoidance-avoidance), and Ap-Av (approach-avoidance).

   Do you find that most of the easy conflicts were of the approach-approach type? Were most of the hard conflicts either an avoidance-avoidance or approach-avoidance type? What other factors makes a conflict easy or hard?

2. *How do your parents handle conflict?* Think back to the way your parents handled problem situations in the home. How did your father deal with confict? How did your mother handle conflict? How is your own characteristic style of handling conflict like and unlike your parents' approach?

3. *Your personal style of conflict management.* Write a brief paragraph describing your characteristic style of handling conflict. Include your strong points as well as your weak ones. To what extent do you use some type of cooperative problem solving? Are you satisfied with the way you handle conflict? In what way would you like to improve your style of conflict management?

4. *Defining the conflict.* Take a problem or conflict you're currently having with someone and define it as carefully as you can. How does each of you view the problem? What does each of you say or do, or not do, that contributes to it? If possible, get the other person's ideas and feelings about all this. To what extent do all parties involved agree on the basic conflict?

5. *Cooperative problem solving.* Apply the suggested procedure for cooperative problem solving to some conflict you're experiencing with another person. Adapt the procedure to your own situation, making allowances for the nature of the problem. Alternatively, select a recent experience in which you have successfully resolved an interpersonal problem or conflict. Then compare your experience with the suggested steps for cooperative problem solving explained in the chapter. How similar was your approach to the suggested procedure?

6. *Conflict and intimacy.* Select a close relationship you have, either with your spouse, someone of the opposite sex, or a friend. Then describe how each of you handles conflicts within this relationship. Does either of you become defensive or take a long time getting over a disagreement? Or have you both learned how to "fight fair" and make up afterwards? Would you agree that a good fight sometimes clears the air and improves your relationship?

Managing Stress

9

UNDERSTANDING STRESS
    What is stress?
    Stressful events
    Individual, situational factors

REACTIONS TO STRESS
    Physiological effects
    Defensive coping
    Other coping devices

EFFECTIVE STRESS MANAGEMENT
    Modifying your environment
    Altering your lifestyle

SUMMARY

SELF-TEST

EXERCISES

Marci, a twenty-five-year-old, attends college in the mornings and works as a waitress at a Holiday Inn several evenings a week. Recently divorced, she lives with her three-year-old son John in an apartment.

One evening, while preparing to close up at work, Marci talks with a waitress friend, Sandy.

"I dread going home," Marci says.

"Something the matter?" asks Sandy.

"For one thing, I'm having trouble keeping babysitters."

"That's too bad."

"Most of my sitters are high-school students. And they don't want to stay up this late."

"I can understand," says Sandy. "Why don't you let John stay at your parents' house?"

"That's okay once in a while. But if I do it too often my mother will say, 'Why don't you move back home, Marci?' No way am I going to do that."

"I can't say I blame you," says Sandy sympathetically.

"Anyway, that's not my only problem these days," Marci continues. "John's just getting over the measles. He's been so demanding lately."

"Honestly, I don't know how you manage to do everything you do."

"That's just it. I'm not doing very well right now," admits Marci. "I'm also having trouble keeping up in school. I have a paper that's overdue in my English class. To make matters worse, my car has broken down twice. I was late for a test the other day. It's been so frustrating!"

"Maybe you need a little social life to take your mind off things," suggests Sandy.

"Not right now, thank you," protests Marci. "That's all it would take to push me over the edge."

"Well, hang in there," Sandy says cheerfully. "Better days are ahead."

"Let's hope so," sighs Marci, as she prepares to go home.

UNDERSTANDING STRESS

As so often is the case, much of Marci's stress comes from the combination of things happening in her life. The recent divorce is still fresh in her mind. Living on her own has brought added responsibilities. Working while attending school has proven to be more demanding than she anticipated; in addition, she is a single parent. Also, she has not made sufficient allowance for the unexpected, such as John getting the measles. How well Marci copes with the changes in her life remains to be seen. Hopefully she'll gain a better understanding of stress as well as an ability to manage stress successfully. This is what this chapter is about.

Too often, people believe stress is something bad we must get rid of. But we can't. More and more, we're coming to understand that stress is an unavoidable aspect of life. What really counts is learning to understand stress and to manage it successfully.

What is stress?

One reason stress is so hard to define is that it means different things to different people. Some people see stress mostly as stressful events, like job pressures or the death of a loved one. Others think of stress more in terms of reactions to such events—our worrying about job pressures or our feelings of bereavement.

The truth of the matter is that stress includes both. It consists not simply of stressful events or our reaction to them, but of the *interaction* between the two. Stress refers to any adjustive demand that requires a response from us in order to meet our needs. As such, it is an inevitable part of life. Even when we're asleep we're under stress, as expressed in the rapid moving of our eyes and the pounding of our heart while we dream. The crucial question is not whether we'll escape stress, for we can't. What counts is what kind of stress we experience, how much, and how well we're managing it.

Stress is so multifaceted we need different words to describe it. Hans Selye, the noted physician who studied the bodily effects of stress, has described and labeled four basic types of stress. Things that have a harmful effect on us may properly be called *distress*. Much that we call stress is really distress. But stress may also have a beneficial effect on us. Examples are the stresses associated with beginning a new and exciting project at work, or learning a challenging sport like skydiving. Selye suggests we call this *eustress*, or *good stress*. He has also written of two more types of stress: *overstress* and *understress*. Overstress (or *hyperstress*) usually occurs when stressful events pile up and stretch the limits of our adaptability. Understress (or *hypostress*) is more apt to occur when we're bored, lacking stimulation, or unchallenged. The need for stress may be associated with the familiar sensation-seeking behaviors, such as experimenting with drugs, engaging in risky sports, and seeking greater variety in sexual behavior.[1]

Stressful events

Almost any event can be stressful depending on our reaction to it. Yet some events tend to be more stressful than others. The stress potential of various events has been measured by instruments like the College Life-Stress Scale shown below. Studies using this instrument have shown that despite differences in age, sex, and individual experience, some events are generally more stressful than others. Nor are these simply negative events like the loss of one's job. Positive events such as entering college and getting married can be stressful too. It is the total impact or combined effect of various changes in one's life that produces stress. Furthermore, studies have shown that the impact of stressful events can stay with us for up to a year or longer.

Stress doesn't cause sickness as much as it lowers the body's resistance, thereby predisposing us to illness. As a result, people with the highest amount of stress tend to have more health problems or illnesses than those with medium and lower levels of stress. Naturally, the particular illness depends on a person's makeup as well as the bacterial and viral agents present. Negative events like the death of a spouse are especially likely to predispose us to physical illnesses.

[1]Hans Selye, "The Stress Concept Today," in *Handbook on Stress and Anxiety: Contemporary Knowledge, Theory, and Treatment*, eds. I. L. Kutash et al. (San Francisco: Jossey-Bass, 1980), 142.

The College Life-Stress Scale

Designed specifically for college students by Marx, Garrity, and Bowers, the College Life-Stress Scale helps to predict illness in college students.

Simply indicate in the blank to the right of each item how often you have experienced this event in the past twelve months. Put *0* if you haven't experienced this event; *1* if the event happened once; *2* for twice; *3* for three times; and *4* for four or more times. After you have completed all items, multiply the number of occurrences of each item by the value assigned to that item. For example, item 29, *major change in responsibilities at work,* has a value of 47. If you've experienced this three times in the past year, you would multiply 47 by 3.

Add your scores, then compare the total with the table below to find your chances of getting ill or having health problems.

1. Entered college	50	_____
2. Married	77	_____
3. Trouble with your boss	38	_____
4. Held a job while attending school	43	_____
5. Experienced the death of a spouse	87	_____
6. Major change in sleeping habits	34	_____
7. Experienced the death of a close family member	77	_____
8. Major change in eating habits	30	_____
9. Change in or choice of major field of study	41	_____
10. Revision of personal habits	45	_____
11. Experienced the death of a close friend	68	_____
12. Found guilty of minor violations of the law	22	_____
13. Had an outstanding personal achievement	40	_____
14. Experienced pregnancy or fathered a pregnancy	68	_____
15. Major change in health or behavior of family member	56	_____
16. Had sexual difficulties	58	_____
17. Had trouble with in-laws	42	_____
18. Major change in number of family get-togethers	26	_____
19. Major change in financial state	53	_____
20. Gained a new family member	50	_____
21. Change in residence or living conditions	42	_____
22. Major conflict or change in values	51	_____
23. Major change in church activities	36	_____
24. Marital reconciliation with your mate	58	_____
25. Fired from work	62	_____
26. Were divorced	76	_____
27. Changed to a different line of work	50	_____
28. Major change in number of arguments with spouse	50	_____
29. Major change in responsibilities at work	47	_____
30. Had your spouse begin or cease work outside the home	41	_____
31. Major change in working hours or conditions	42	_____
32. Marital separation from mate	74	_____
33. Major change in type and/or amount of recreation	37	_____
34. Major change in use of drugs	52	_____
35. Took on a mortgage or loan of less than $10,000	52	_____
36. Major personal injury or illness	65	_____
37. Major change in use of alcohol	46	_____

38. Major change in social activities	43	_____
39. Major change in amount of participation in school activities	38	_____
40. Major change in amount of independence and responsibility	49	_____
41. Took a trip or a vacation	33	_____
42. Engaged to be married	54	_____
43. Changed to a new school	50	_____
44. Changed dating habits	41	_____
45. Trouble with school administration	44	_____
46. Broke or had broken marital engagement or a steady relationship	60	_____
47. Major change in self-concept or self-awareness	57	_____

Association between amount of life change and number of health problems

Amount of Life Change	*Number of Health Problems*
High (total score greater than 1434)	3.6
Medium (total score between 348 and 1434)	2.9
Low (total score less than 348)	2.2

Reprinted with permission from *Journal of Psychosomatic Research,* 19, M. B. Marx, T. F. Garrity, and F.R. Bowers, "The Influence of Recent Life Experience on the Health of College Freshmen." 1975, pp 87–98 Pergamon Press, Ltd.

Do you sometimes feel that it's the little things get you down? If so, you may be correct. Richard Lazarus and his colleagues found evidence of this in their investigation of the effect of minor but frequent daily events on illness. They identified two types of minor daily events: *hassles* and *uplifts.* Hassles are the irritating, frustrating, or distressing events like misplacing the car keys or having too many things to do. Uplifts include such pleasures as getting along well with your spouse or lover, completing a task, or eating out.

People vary widely in what bothers them. Among college students, the most commonly reported hassles are anxiety over wasting time, anxiety about meeting high standards, and loneliness. Middle-aged people are bothered more by health matters and economic concerns. Professional people often feel they have too much to do and not enough time to do it in, and they have trouble relaxing as well. Several hassles were common to all groups: misplacing or losing things, anxiety over physical appearance, and excessive obligations.

Two of Lazarus's findings are of special interest. First, uplifts do not significantly offset the negative impact of hassles. In fact, for some strange reason, for women uplifts may have a negative effect on their emotions and mental health. Second, hassles are generally better predictors of psychological and physical health than major life events. Those who suffer frequent and intense hassles tend to have the poorest health, with the link between major life events and health being weak. It seems that what happens to us on a daily basis, whether provoked by a major life crisis or not, has a major impact on our health health and sense of well-being. Would you agree?[2]

[2]R.S. Lazarus, "Little Hassles Can Be Hazardous to Health," *Psychology Today* (July 1981): 58–62.

Automobile accidents are almost always stressful.

Individual, situational factors

Our overall experience of stress is affected by a variety of influences, some social and situational, others highly individual.

Among the situational factors, we've already mentioned the importance of the combined effect of stressful events. An airline pilot with a sick child at home, a troubled marriage, and a health problem will probably experience more stress in a professional emergency than a pilot with a happier personal life. The severity of stress also varies with the situation, the death of a spouse being more stressful than the difficulty of paying the bills. The threat of harm generally intensifies stress. People engaged in military combat are under greater stress than those taking part in competitive sports. One young woman taken hostage and held at gunpoint reported developing an ulcer in a matter of days. Unpredictability is a very important factor in stress. People in emergency rooms and bomb squads often complain of having to be alert all the time. Lack of control makes stress all the worse, which is why, in stress management courses, people are taught what they *can* do even in the most difficult of times, such as cooling down and approaching their situation in a rational, problem-solving manner.

Many personal factors affect our experience of stress. How you perceive stressful events is vital. An athlete who panics after making a mistake in a game puts himself under greater stress than one who begins looking for a way to redeem himself before the game is over. As one professional football player put it, "Everyone makes mistakes. It's knowing how to recover from your mistakes that counts." Certain personality traits also aggravate stress. People who are ambitious, competitive, and have an intense drive to get things done generally suffer more from stress than those without these qualities. Such people have been labeled as Type A personalities and are more prone to heart attacks and other stress-related illnesses. On the positive side, individuals who are reasonably intelligent, flexible, and resourceful are better able to take stress in stride through the intelligent use of problem-solving methods.

An individual's characteristic level of self-esteem also affects his or her tolerance for stress. People with low self-esteem are apt to take criticism of their work as a personal affront, while those with high self-esteem might accept the same criticism and use it as a means of improving their work. Last but not least, the amount of experience you have in a particular activity or task affects in a positive way your tolerance for the stress associated with it. The more you've spoken in public, for example, the less worry and wasted effort will be associated with that activity for you.

REACTIONS TO STRESS

We experience stress totally, with both our minds and our bodies affected. Coping with a viral infection, especially if it's severe and persistent might depress us. Similarly, frustration and anger at work may weaken our bodily resistance so that we are more apt to get a cold. Some people claim to be so aware of their bodies that they can feel a cold coming on in its earliest stages, take the proper preventive measures, and avoid the full-blown infection. Others seem to be oblivious to their bodies. One executive, for example, kept up an extraordinarily busy schedule until he collapsed with a bleeding ulcer. He was as surprised as his doctors to discover he had an ulcer. But his doctors were even more amazed at how someone could experience so much stress with so little awareness of its devastating effects.

We'll begin by looking at some of the physiological effects of stress. Then we'll examine some typical psychological reactions, such as defensive behavior and other coping devices. Keep in mind throughout that we experience stress with our whole being, so that there is often a mixture of physical and emotional symptoms.

Physiological effects

Hans Selye spent much of his life investigating the effects of stress. He uncovered a complex chain of reactions to stress and labeled it the *general adaptation syndrome* (GAS). Selye proposed that even though each *stressor* (i.e., stress-producing agent) produces specific effects on the body, such as heat causing us to sweat; the general effects of the syndrome are common to all forms of stress.

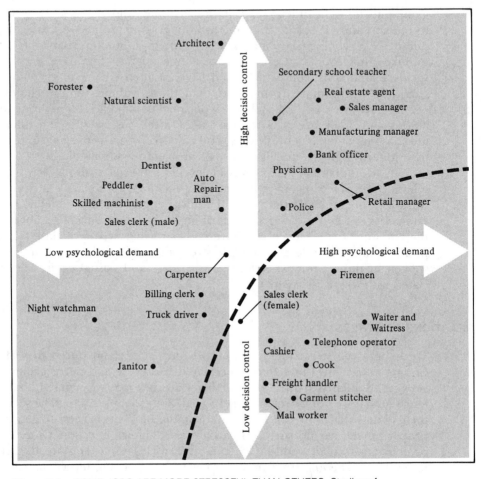

Figure 9-1 SOME JOBS ARE MORE STRESSFUL THAN OTHERS. Studies of male workers suggest that those whose jobs involve high psychological demand but little decision making or control over their work, like cooks, waiters, and assembly-line personnel, are five times more likely to develop coronary heart disease than workers who exercise greater control over their work.
Source:*Columbia University Department of Industrial Engineering and Operations Research.*[3]

The general adaptation syndrome consists of three overlapping stages: the *alarm reaction,* the *resistance stage,* and the *exhaustion stage.*[4]

In the alarm reaction, the body mobilizes its defenses for an all-out response to the stressor. The arousal of the autonomic system and the adrenal glands makes our hearts beat faster, gives us quick energy, and arouses the

[3]*Columbia University Department of Industrial Engineering and Operations Research,* 1983.
[4]Hans Selye, *Stress Without Distress* (Philadelphia: Lippincott, 1974),

appropriate emotions. Common bodily symptoms of this reaction are headaches, aching muscles and joints, and an overall feeling of fatigue. We become more anxious, unable to concentrate or sleep well, and generally upset and defensive.

If the stressor continues and we can tolerate it, we enter the resistance stage. Although the level of bodily arousal is not as high as it was in the alarm stage, it remains higher than usual, thereby giving us greater protection against the initial stressor. As a result, our bodies adapt to the continued stress to the point where we're no longer aware of the earlier symptoms. But our bodies pay a price all the same, and one of the "diseases of adaptation" may result. Among the common stress-related illnesses are high blood pressure, strokes, heart attacks, ulcers, and ulcerative colitis. Stress also plays a major role in a host of other medical complaints such as allergies, arthritis, and premenstrual syndrome. As we mentioned earlier, it is not clear why some people suffer from high blood pressure and others get ulcers. But it is probably related to an interaction of hereditary weaknesses, lifestyle, and environmental stress. For example, blood pressure is generally higher among blacks than whites. Yet high blood pressure is more common in both groups in those who tend to repress their anger. What kind of stress-related illnesses run in your family? How about yourself?

When the stressful events are intense or persistent we reach the exhaustion stage. Because our bodies cannot handle excessive stress indefinitely, they quickly wear out, manifesting many of the signs of aging. Such symptoms, when stress related, are more or less reversible with rest and treatment, however. Sometimes severe stress leads to mental and emotional breakdown. In these cases, individuals may exhibit bizarre thinking and behavior, or extreme withdrawal. Chronic or intense stress may even lead to death.

Defensive coping

Often our experience of stress is mental rather than physical. This is especially true with the various types of psychological stress like anxiety, frustration, and conflict. For instance, when we become frustrated at not being able to meet an important deadline at work, we become anxious and defensive. We may make lame excuses, lash out at innocent people, or curse and say things we later regret. These spontaneous reactions are called *defense mechanisms*—automatic, unconscious mechanisms that protect our self-esteem against anxiety. They do not get rid of the stress. They simply reduce our awareness of it temporarily, thereby giving us time to mobilize ourselves against it. Yet defensive coping involves gross self-deception and makes us act in socially inappropriate ways. It is actually an emergency response to be superseded by more

Figure 9-2

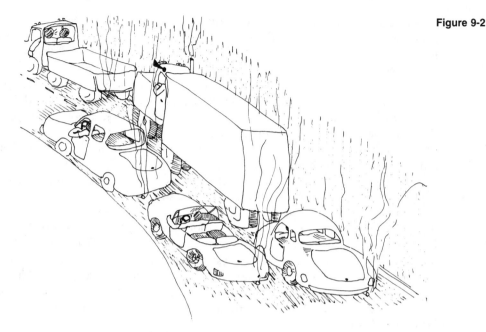

rational, appropriate behavior as quickly as possible. Some of the more common defense mechanisms are described below.

> *Denial* is the refusal to see or hear unpleasant or threatening things. Many smokers continue their habit oblivious to its dangers and heedless of the surgeon general's warning on the package. Similarly, people who engage in hazardous activities like racing or sky-diving commonly adopt the attitude that it "won't happen to me." Even terminally ill patients characteristically react to the news of their impending death with denial. Only gradually does denial give way to reality.

> *Repression* is the unconscious blocking from consciousness of a threatening impulse or idea. But those impulses continue to be expressed indirectly. The man who says he isn't angry about having been passed over for promotion may nevertheless show up late for work and have a sullen attitude toward his superiors. Repression should not be confused with *suppression*—the conscious, deliberate control of an unpleasant thought or impulse. Ordinarily, suppression is a healthier response because it involves less self-deception and permits the individual greater control over his or her behavior. For example, the above-mentioned man might say, "I'm disappointed about not getting promoted, but I'm not going to let it get to me."

Displacement involves discharging your negative emotions onto safer objects. Thus, the boss chastizes the manager, who in turn takes out her anger on those working under her. The workers go home in a bad mood and proceed to take out their frustration on members of their family. Similarly, when a team loses, there's usually a search for a suitable scapegoat to explain the failure—often ending with the coach's head.

Projection is the mechanism whereby we see in others those unpleasant things we can't accept in ourselves. The person who starts an argument may say, "You're the one who is angry. I'm not," despite having a flushed face and clenched fists. Sexually inhibited people may have fantasies about being tempted by someone else's seductive behavior, or being coerced to engage in sex, thereby protecting themselves from an acknowledgment of their own sexual desires.

Regression is falling back to patterns of behavior more appropriate to an earlier age. People who resort to temper tantrums when they don't get their way, or those who cry in the face of every little frustration, are exhibiting forms of regression. Other familiar examples are nail-biting, name-calling, overeating, and excessive use of drugs or alcohol.

Sublimation is the redirection of basic desires toward more socially valued activities. Sublimation is evident in a group like *MADD:* mothers against drunk driving. Mothers who've lost a son or daughter because of someone else's drunk driving have good reason to be angry. But they may accomplish more by directing their anger toward changing the laws and helping to save other people's lives.

Rationalization is an attempt to explain unacceptable behavior in a way that makes us look good. People who hurt our feelings or fail to keep their promises often resort to rationalization to justify their behavior. Similarly, students who miss a test or fail to submit their papers on time may think they have a "good reason" for their behavior, though it's seldom convincing to experienced teachers.

Reaction-formation is the attempt to deny unacceptable desires or feelings by adopting exaggerated feelings of the opposite type. Someone who habitually avoids getting angry may be regarded as an exceptionally "nice" person. But such an individual might well lose control when he, or she, does get angry. Other examples of reaction-formation can be seen in overly tough, macho men, and the compulsively cheerful people who can't afford to admit they're ever depressed.

Stress Carriers

At the turn of the century, an itinerant cook became known as *Typhoid Mary* because she was a carrier of the highly infectious typhoid fever. Invariably, wherever she worked the people became infected with typhoid fever, with an untold number of deaths resulting. Eventually, Typhoid Mary was caught and incarcerated to prevent further spread of the dreaded disease.

Today we have *stress carriers* who, like Typhoid Mary, unwittingly spread stress to those around them. Although stress carriers may not suffer greatly from stress themselves, they make other people's lives miserable. There are the dictatorial types who never make mistakes; only their subordinates do. There are also the insecure, anxiety-ridden bosses who shirk responsibility, thereby intensifying fear and uncertainty in others. Then there are the "doomsday foresayers," who always expect the worst, thus evoking fear and pessimism in others around them. There are also the "detail drones," who manage to make mountains out of molehills, thereby creating stress where there wasn't any before.

Perhaps you can think of other types of stress carriers. Do you live or work with a stress carrier? Would anyone consider you a stress carrier?

Other coping devices

There are also other stress-reducing reactions that operate automatically. Typical examples are cursing when we accidentally hit our thumb with a hammer, overeating or overdrinking when under nervous tension, or sleeping late when we're feeling depressed. These reactions occur spontaneously, though they are influenced by learning. For example, Kathy grew up in a family which condoned the regular use of hard liquor by all adult members of the family. Later, it was no surprise to learn that when Kathy was going through a severe marital problem she turned to the bottle.

Let's take a look at some of the common coping devices for stress.

The comforts of *food, drink,* and *drugs* are so familiar as to be taken for granted. The psychological value of oral pleasures probably derives from their association with the primal food, mothers milk. When under stress, some people constantly nibble, while others gorge themselves at mealtime. People may smoke or drink to excess to ease nervous tension. In recent years, many people have turned to drugs. Although drugs may be taken for a variety of reasons, habitual or compulsive drug use often reflects an attempt to escape stress.

Touching, hugging, and *physical intimacy* may also help to alleviate stress. Handshakes and hugs serve to reassure us of the trust and affection of partners and friends. Even sexual intimacy involves more than just erotic arousal and orgasm. It also affords an opportunity to touch each other's bodies in ways that make us feel emotionally as well as physically close. Even when the explicit sexual activity is not fully satisfying, partners often derive pleasure

Alcohol and drugs are familiar, but potentially dangerous, ways to relieve stress.

from the time spent together. In times of sorrow, when words easily fail us, it's natural to reach over and put your hand on someone's shoulder, or to put your arms around her in a silent hug.

Laughing, crying, and *cursing* are all familiar ways to alleviate stress. Perhaps you've noticed all the joking and nervous laughter that goes on among students just before a test. Cursing and crying are also common reactions to frustration, disappointment, and loss. Though both sexes today feel less constrained by old stereotypes, many men still have great difficulty shedding tears, largely because they've grown up with the notion that "real men" don't cry.

Reflection and *talking it out* are common reactions to stress. After a disappointment or hurt, we may want some time to be alone. Reflection is especially valuable for sorting things out when we're confused or overwhelmed. At other times, we may feel a need to express our troubles. Simply putting them down on paper or talking to a computer has been found to be helpful. Even more valuable is talking to a friend. What is usually needed is not so much advice as the opportunity to express our feelings, which usually helps us to clarify our thoughts.

Vigorous physical activity is an excellent way to alleviate stress, especially when we're feeling frustrated or angry. Biking, jogging, and walking all help us to maintain our psychological health as well as our physical fitness. Some people prefer to "work it off." One man I know likes to cut firewood on weekends; a woman friend prefers to work in her graden. *Sleep, dreams,* and *fantasy* are time-honored ways of achieving temporary relief from stress. In addition to screening out unpleasant things, fantasy helps us to picture things as we'd like them to be. We may fantasize about being a celebrity, hero, or finally being recognized after years of mistreatment.

Like defense mechanisms, any of these reactions may alleviate tension in the short run. But there is a danger of habitually relying on such coping devices instead of seeking more effecient methods of stress reduction. For example, the troubled person who turns to drink may find temporary relief only to compound his or her problems in the long run.

EFFECTIVE STRESS MANAGEMENT

To manage stress successfully, you must do more than alleviate the symptoms of stress, helpful as this may be. You must also modify the source of the stress. Ordinarily, this is done through problem-solving strategies, most of which fall into two categories: those aimed at modifying our environment, and those aimed at modifying ourselves. Effective stress management employs a combination of these approaches, along with the various symptom-reducing reactions discussed earlier.

Modifying your environment

Suppose you're sharing an apartment with two friends. One of them plays the stereo late into the night. The other often types late. As a result, you're having trouble getting to sleep. Yet you must get up early in the morning for work. What can you do? You could ask your friends to stop playing music and typing so late at night. Or, if they're not receptive to your request, you could find another place to live. The most likely solution would be to work out some sort of compromise arrangement in which you and your friends make mutual adjustments.

These three responses to the problem illustrate the basic ways of modifying your environment: the assertive approach; withdrawal; and compromise. Let's examine each one of them.

The *assertive* approach is generally preferred whenever there is a reasonable chance of success. This involves saying or doing things that will modify your surroundings in a direct, positive way. Much of this has already been explained in regard to assertiveness in the earlier chapter on communication. You may recall that "I" messages are especially effective in expressing your desires in such a way that people are likely to listen and cooperate. Examples of the assertive approach for stress reduction would be: asking your boss for a more interesting assignment; requesting a friend not to smoke while riding in your car; and renegotiating a loan.

Tom was having trouble with the number of assignments he was given at work. While still busy with one job, his boss would pop in and say, "I'd like this done by tomorrow." Tom usually agreed, but he felt deeply resentful about being so overwhelmed with work. He would go home, drink a lot, argue with his wife, and yell at his kids. Occasionally he would blow up at his boss. Once he was in counseling, however, Tom began acting more assertively to modify his work situation. Whenever the boss handed him an additional assignment, Tom would say, "When I have so many jobs to do at once, I get very frustrated. I'd like to know which job you want completed first. That way, we can avoid misunderstanding and I can pace my work better." In this way, Tom got rid of much of the stress arising from trying to do the impossible. And as is so often the case, his boss was surprised to learn how much of a problem all this had been for Tom, saying, "I wish you had spoken to me about this earlier."

Sometimes *withdrawal* from stress may be the most appropriate strategy. In itself, withdrawal is neither good nor bad. Much depends on the situation, and whether or not you're withdrawing to escape from something that must be dealt with. Withdrawal is usually more constructive when it is used as a temporary strategy rather than a habitual lifestyle. This was the case with Mike. After graduating from law school, he failed the state bar exam. He retook the exam twice in the next couple of years, but each time he flunked. Worse still, each time he received word of his failure, he became violently ill, with severe headaches and vomiting. Upon a therapist's suggestion, Mike turned his energies elsewhere for a while. He took a job in the university library and spent more time with his wife and young son. Eventually he took the bar exam again and passed. "I was just spinning my wheels," he said later. "I had to back off to find out what I was doing wrong and make a fresh approach."

Frequently, some type of *compromise* is the most realistic approach to stress. Compromise allows you to remain in a difficult situation through the making of certain concessions, in order to achieve desirable gains. The three most common types of compromise are conformity, negotiation, and substitution.

Conformity may be especially useful when dealing with people in positions of authority, situations in which the penalities for being assertive or withdrawing can be prohibitive. An example is the middle-aged worker who reluctantly changes his way of doing things under a new boss, mostly because he feels he would lose too much by changing jobs. Of course, the price of conformity may be too high. When going along with others results in undue hardship or excessive concessions, conformity may not be worth it.

Negotiation, which involves *mutual* concessions and gains, is an even more promising way of achieving a compromise in difficult situations. Long valued in the arenas of labor-management and political conflict, negotiation is now being applied to practically all areas of life. As a result, marriage partners informally negotiate everything from sex to household chores. And parents and teen-agers may negotiate curfew hours and use of the family car.

Substitution is still another type of compromise. Sometimes, when one means of achieving your goal seems impossible, you may choose a substitute means. An example would be the student who discovers that he cannot attend school full time if he wants to keep his job, and decides to continue his schooling on a part-time basis instead. Sometimes a substitute goal may solve the problem. A single mother who felt that becoming a dentist was out of the question for her decided instead to become a dental hygienist.

Altering your lifestyle

A good deal of the stress we face is self-generated. We panic in the face of an upcoming deadline at work, we overreact to a friend's well-meant criticism, or we get too anxious about receiving a traffic ticket. In these situations, stress reduction calls for changing some facet of ourselves or our lifestyle. Such a change might involve acquiring more tolerance for stress, controlling distressful thoughts, or changing one's pace of life.

Greater *tolerance for stress* always helps. This involves both the amount of stress you can handle, and the length of time for which you can handle it without acting in an irrational and disorganized fashion. An airline clerk says, "I can take a lot of pressure at the ticket counter until someone starts making nasty remarks at me. Then I hit the ceiling." Learning to take such emotional encounters in stride rather than overreacting to them would increase her tolerance to stress. Let's look at some of the other ways to increase your stress tolerance.

Tolerance for the stress that is associated with pressure usually comes with greater experience and skill in the tasks at hand. For example, police

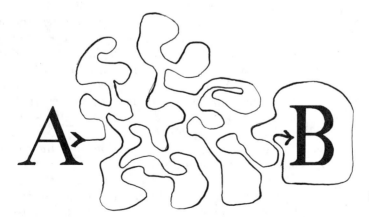

Figure 9-3 How much stress is too much?

recruits sometimes react to the pressures of their job by becoming cocky and authoritarian—once known as the *John Wayne syndrome*. In due time, most of them discover that a macho manner actually aggravates stress on the job, not to mention in their home lives. With greater experience, most police officers not only take the stress of their jobs in stride, but learn how to defuse potentially dangerous situations.

Tolerance of frustration can be increased by such means as keeping in good physical shape, selecting tasks suited to your abilities, and adjusting your expectations to match more closely the realities of everyday life. This last point is especially important. Expecting too much of a job or relationship often sets the stage for misunderstanding and disappointment.

Greater tolerance for conflict comes not only through experience in dealing with it but also with the realization that conflict and decision making are unavoidable aspects of life. Rather than fret and fuss in the face of all the situations that require a choice to be made, look at them as normal parts of daily life. Learning to evaluate such situations and arrive at a decision in a matter-of-fact, problem-solving manner will enable you to avoid overreacting to stressful events.

Relaxation Exercises

A time-tested technique for relaxation consists in alternately tensing and relaxing a given set of muscles.

First, sit or lie down in a comfortable position, and let yourself relax. To begin, clench your right fist tighter and tighter. Observe the tension in your wrist and forearm. Now relax your fist. Repeat the same sequence with your left fist. Then proceed to practice the alternate tensing and relaxing procedure with the desired group of muscles. To relax your entire body, you'll want to include the muscle groups associated with your head, face, throat, and shoulders; chest, stomach, and lower back; and finally your hips, thighs, calves, and feet.

You may enhance muscle relaxation by combining it with deep breathing. That is, breathe with your diaphragm, keeping your chest wall as immobile as possible. As you relax, breathe in deeply, filling your lungs as full as you can. Hold your breath for a moment. Then breathe out slowly, observing your relaxation. Breathe normally for a few seconds while you think about being relaxed. Now repeat the sequence of deep breathing and normal breathing several times, concentrating on the pleasant feeling of relaxation.

The next time you take a test, practice deep breathing a few moments before you begin the test. See how it helps you to relax.

Controlling distressful thoughts is also a valuable means of reducing stress. Often we aggravate matters by overreacting or panicking in the face of a stressful situation. Glancing at the first test question, an anxious student starts imagining that she is bound to fail. Such negative self-monitoring then interferes with her performance. Or at the first signs of chest pain, a middle-aged man feels panic. He imagines he is having a heart attack. His anxiety makes his heart pump even faster, thereby lessening his chances of successfully surviving such an attack.

You can control thoughts of failure and disaster by use of the following procedure. First, get in touch with your distressful thoughts through careful observation. Notice how you often assume the worse? Then formulate thoughts that are incompatible with your distressful thoughts, such as, "I know I'm going to make it," or, "I'll just take one thing at a time until I finish," or, "I'll keep doing the best I can." Finally, reward yourself when you've successfully changed your thought patterns. You might give yourself a mental pat on the back or treat yourself in some way. Karen regularly excused her poor performance in school by saying she had test anxiety. But with the help of a counselor, Karen learned how to think in positive ways. When faced with a hard question on a test, she would say to herself, "I'll come back to this one after I've done the ones I know," "The more relaxed I remain, the better I'll do." Also, rather than view anxiety as a signal to become upset, she learned how to visualize herself as coping with the anxiety by means of slow, deep breathing and positive instructions for improving her performance. Each time she improved her test grade, she rewarded her newly acquired self-mastery by buying some article of clothing she especially wanted.

Changing your pace of life is especially effective in reducing stress. Too often, we jump out of bed in the morning, gulp down our morning coffee, and rush off to class or work. By noon we're already tired. After the evening meal, we may be wondering where all the energy went. Often, much of it was wasted rushing around. Sometimes all that's needed to improve the situation is better time management. In other cases, you can benefit from less needless overstimulation. The specific adjustments will vary with each of us. But consider adopting as many of the following suggestions as apply to you:

Awaken to music. Buy a radio-alarm clock. Tune it to your favorite station.

If you do special exercises, do them while listening to music rather than the news. It's more relaxing.

Get up early enough to enjoy your breakfast without rushing.

Avoid scheduling too much in a day. Don't arrange all your classes back-to-back.

Make a list of things to do. Put the "must do" things at the top of your list.

Space out your errands. Don't get your car fixed the same day you do laundry and pay bills.

Leave some time for relaxation on the weekends. It breaks the vicious cycle of stress.

Allow ample time for your drive to school or work.

Save some time for coffee breaks and daily pleasures. A walk or a hot bath refreshes.

Take time to enjoy your meals even if eating alone. Try to share at least one meal a day with others.

Avoid excessive use of caffeine, alcohol, or drugs.

Talk more slowly. You'll be more thoughtful and people will listen more carefully.

Walk deliberately, without rushing. An unhurried pace helps keep you relaxed.

Drive more slowly. You'll get there just as soon without the needless frustration of competitive driving.

How you choose to alter your lifestyle is up to you. The important thing to remember is this: You *can* do something about stress. You need not simply react to stress. You can also put it to work for you. Properly managed, stress makes life challenging and satisfying. It becomes a means of personal growth. Effective stress management is a lot like adjusting the pressure on the strings of a musical instrument. Too little pressure and the strings squeak. Too much and they snap. But apply just the right pressure and you get beautiful music. So it is with managing stress in your everyday life.

SUMMARY

1. We began the chapter by explaining that stress is something we experience in relation to our environment. As such, stress includes our reactions to events as well as the events themselves. Although some events are ordinarily more stressful than others, it is the combined effect of stressful events, both big and small, that makes life stressful. Our subjective experience of stress depends on a variety of individual and social factors, like the severity of the stress and the amount of control we have over our lives.

2. We experience stress totally, with our minds and bodies affecting each other. According to Selye's General Adaptation Syndrome, the price of adapting to stress is often manifested in illnesses like high blood pressure. Defense mechanisms serve to temporarily reduce the symptoms of stress; but often they can involve socially inappropriate behavior, such as blaming others for our mistakes. We also rely on a variety of other coping devices to alleviate the symptoms of stress, like the comforts of food and drink as well as laughing, crying, and cursing.

3. Effective stress management also requires certain problem-solving strategies that reduce the stress itself. Most of these fall into two categories: those aimed at modifying our environment and those aimed at

altering ourselves. Although the assertive approach is generally preferable in modifying our surroundings, there are times when withdrawal or compromise may be more appropriate. Among the many ways of altering ourselves, we discussed increasing one's stress tolerance, controlling catastrophic thoughts, and changing one's pace of life.

SELF-TEST

1. Which of the following is a true statement?
   a. stress always makes us more productive
   b. stress is an inevitable part of life
   c. all stress is distressful
   d. we can never have too little stress

2. The impact of stress depends largely on:
   a. the combined effect of various life changes
   b. socially undesirable events
   c. major life events only
   d. all of the above

3. An everyday hassle common to all age groups is:
   a. insufficient time for meals
   b. misplacing or losing things
   c. loneliness
   d. too little time for sleep

4. According to Selye's General Adaptation Syndrome, headaches and anxiety are apt to occur in the _____ stage.
   a. resistance   c. exhaustion
   b. maladaptive   d. alarm

5. _____ is the unconscious blocking of a threatening idea or impulse from consciousness.
   a. suppression   c. repression
   b. denial   d. displacement

6. A person who reacts to a low mark on a test by saying, "I can't believe I did that poorly," is relying on the defense mechanism called:
   a. denial   c. suppression
   b. displacement   d. acting out

7. _____ is an excellent way to alleviate stress associated with frustration and anger.
   a. crying   c. eating
   b. physical exercise   d. hugging others

8. In returning a defective shirt to the store, an assertive response would be:
   a. threatening to sue the store
   b. complaining about the cheap clothes sold there

c. asking for another shirt without the defect

d. apologizing for returning the shirt

9. A student who cannot afford to attend school full time but continues on a part-time basis while working is modifying stress through:

    a. assertiveness

    b. withdrawal

    c. compromise

    d. denial

10. _____ is a valuable means of alleviating stress through altering your lifestyle.

    a. controlling distressful thoughts

    b. progressive relaxation

    c. changing your pace of life

    d. all of the above

EXERCISES

1. *Taking inventory of your stress.* Use the College Life-Stress Scale to assess the degree of stress in your life. Remember to include the changes that have happened to you over the past twelve months. If you've experienced some major change not listed in the scale, you might assign this a numerical value by comparing it to a similar event in the rating scale. Then multiply it by the number of times it occurred in the past year, as with the other life changes.

    Add up your total score. How much stress does your score indicate—high, medium, or low? When you think back over the past year, does your physical health reflect this level of stress? If you've functioned better than your score would suggest, how do you account for this?

2. *Daily hassles that bother you.* Make a list of the little things that annoy you the most in daily life. Compare your list with the survey of daily hassles described in this chapter. Are there some items common to both lists? Which ones? Select two or three hassles in your list and suggest better ways to cope with them.

3. *Your use of defense mechanisms.* Recall one or two recent stressful situations in which you probably reacted defensively. Were you more aware of your defensive coping after the fact than at the time? Which defense mechanisms did you rely on? How well did you cope with these situations? If you were to face a similar situation in the future, would you handle it differently?

4. *How do you cope with stress?* Read over the list of *Other Coping Devices* for stress. Which ones do you use most frequently? Has this been a problem for you? Do you use a variety of these coping reactions? Or are you inclined to employ just one or two of them?

5. *Managing stress assertively.* Select some stressful situation that you handled assertively. An example would be successfully returning a defective product to the store. Describe the situation, tell how you handled it, and how it turned out. As an alternate exercise, think of a similar situation that you wished you had handled in a more assertive manner. How did you handle the situation? Why were you not more assertive?

6. *Changing your pace of life.* Look over the list of suggestions for changing your pace of daily life. Which of these suggestions most clearly apply to you? Are there any changes you would like to add? Select two or three of the suggested changes and apply them to your daily life for a week. How helpful was this?

Exploring the Workplace

10

THE PLACE OF WORK IN OUR LIVES
    Why do people work?
    How work affects us

ATTITUDES TOWARD WORK
    Changing attitudes toward work
    Motivating the worker
    What do people look for in a job?

THE PROCESS OF CAREER CHOICE
    Stages of career choice
    Influences on career choice
    Work experience

SUMMARY

SELF-TEST

EXERCISES

Jim works as a salesman for an expanding pharmaceutical company. Since he feels strongly about his family responsibilities, he does his best to get home for the family dinner each evening. Lately, however, he has been having difficulty leaving the office on time. The main reason is Marvin, Jim's new sales manager. Marvin is very ambitious and is pushing everyone to work harder, largely, Jim feels, to make a name for himself. One evening Jim reaches for his coat to go home just as Marvin appears in the doorway.

"Is that new demonstration ready for the Chicago show?" asks Marvin.

"Not quite," replies Jim. "It still needs a little work."

"You'd better get on it. The time is getting short."

"We'll have it ready for you," says Jim.

"Not at this rate," says Marvin emphatically, shaking his head.

Heaving a short sigh, Jim says, "Well, I've got to get home on time this evening. My son has a little league game."

"Jim, I told you to forget the clock. Just get the work done."

"Trust me," Jim says. "The job will be done on time."

"You like that nice suburban lifestyle, don't you?" asks Marvin.

"You bet."

"Just remember how you pay those bills."

"Believe me, I'm glad to be working here," says Jim. "But I think a lot of these hasty deadlines are unrealistic. We need more advance notice to do the right kind of job."

"I don't always have that much advance notice myself. Why should you?"

"Well, frankly, I think there are other things in life besides work," complains Jim.

"Not as far as I'm concerned," Marvin says. "Work comes first."

THE PLACE OF WORK IN OUR LIVES

What claim does work have upon our lives? Should work always come first, as Marvin insists? Or is it more realistic to balance the demands of work and family, as Jim suggests? Obviously, there is no easy answer to such questions. Much depends on the individual, the situation, and the person's reasons for working.

Why do people work?

The obvious reason is money. Most people have to work because they need money to pay for the essentials of life, like food and housing. Money is also important as a means for satisfying other needs. People who value achievement may regard their incomes as a tangible measure of how well they are doing. Those who value security may see money as a means of satisfying that end. In short, money provides people with financial freedom to fulfil a variety of needs.

However, when people of various ages were asked if they would continue to work if they had enough money to live comfortably for the rest of their lives, the majority said *yes*.[1] Clearly, people work for reasons other than just money. Some of the major motives for work are as follows:

1. *Personal fulfilment.* When people of various ages are asked why they work, the single most common response is, "I enjoy what I do." Increasingly people are looking for jobs that will develop their abilities and make them feel good about themselves.[2]

---

[1] P.A. Renwick and E.E. Lawler, and the *Psychology Today* staff, "What Do You Really Want from Your Job?" *Psychology Today* (May 1978): 58.

Figure 10-1

2. *Identity.* We derive much of our personal and social identity from the work we do. At social gatherings, notice how people identify themselves by their jobs. People whose work is challenging and fulfilling may identify more closely with their jobs than those in boring, dead-end jobs.

3. *Structure and security.* Work fills our time and helps to prevent boredom. Our jobs determine what time we get up in the morning, where we spend most of the day, and what people we associate with. Work also provides us with a sense of security. And the greater our emotional and financial security on the job, the more satisfied we feel in our jobs.

4. *Serving others.* People who work in service-oriented fields, like teaching, counseling, and social work, are apt to cite this motive. For others also the social value of their work is an important factor.

5. *Status and approval.* Jobs continue to be a major source of status in our society. An occupation like a white-collar or supervisory job will often be chosen for its status. Conversely, people may hesitate to take a lower-status job if it involves getting their hands dirty. Yet, if you like

[2]Ibid., 57.

the job and are good at it, you'll eventually achieve recognition and respect whatever the work.

People generally work out of mixed motives, many of which may be unclear to them. Furthermore, motivation changes with age, experience, and personal growth. This is especially true of the financial incentives of work. Once people are making enough money to take care of their material well-being, they tend to be motivated more by a desire for fulfilment, recognition, or service. A physician spent years building up a thriving practice in eye care, then one day volunteered his skills for a two-week stint in a Third World country. After doing this for several years, he spent a month visiting Third World countries in an airplane refurbished as an eye clinic. He was especially interested in teaching other doctors how to do specialized eye surgery in their own countries. He found this work so satisfying he eventually took a full-time position as coordinator of such volunteer activites. Although he receives a much lower income, he finds the work immensely satisfying, especially now that he is in his late fifties.

How work affects us

Studs Terkel traveled throughout the country talking to people in all sorts of jobs, like truck drivers, waitresses, and sales managers. He concluded from his research that ordinary people are aware of a sense of personal worth, or more often of a lack of it, in the work they do. Good or bad, work helps to determine how we feel about ourselves.[3]

How your job affects you depends on many things, such as how much you enjoy the work activity itself, your working conditions, the level of stress involved, and your attitude and motivation. People who are engaged in work that is routine and lacking in challenge, like assembly-line jobs, frequently find such jobs boring. To escape the drudgery they may take drugs on the job or vary the routine in a way that jeopardizes their work or safety. Unfortunately, the growing use of technology promises to increase the number of such jobs. At the other extreme are people who are engaged in work that is highly meaningful and enjoyable, like entertainers, musicians, and self-employed workers of all types. They generally find their work very rewarding, often to the point of ignoring the need for vacations. Such people are especially apt to suffer from worker "burnout." Motivated more by inner drives than by money, and lacking a clear, measurable output as a way of evaluating their performance, they risk becoming over-involved in their work. Such people may find it helpful to structure their jobs better, deliberately setting aside time for leisure pursuits.

Working conditions are also an important facter here. Workers generally feel satisfied when they have sufficient freedom on the job, are recognized

---

[3]S. Terkel, *Working* (New York: Pantheon, 1972), xxiv.

for their achievements, have friendly co-workers, and possess job security. Good working conditions may compensate somewhat for unchallenging, repetitive work. One large pharmaceutical company keeps a long list of applicants for its lower-level jobs, mostly because of the good pay and favorable treatment of its employees. Elsewhere, though, dissatisfied workers tend to complain about excessive rules and regulations, lack of recognition, low pay, and lack of opportunities for advancement.

Job stress is another factor. Some workers, like air-traffic controllers, experience a good deal of stress because of constant pressure and the responsibilities associated with this job. But did you know that people like sales clerks, waiters, waitresses, telephone operators, cashiers, and secretaries also work under heavy stress? The major reason is that their work involves much responsibility with little control over the job. Of course, the amount of stress you experience on the job depends on many other factors, such as your attitude toward the job, your motivation, and your overall life situation. A secretary who is unhappily married and works mostly to help pay the bills will experience more stress on the job than someone with a happier home situation and more interest in the job.

Perhaps you've heard people complain that their jobs are "killing" them. They may be right. People who remain in a job despite intense dissatisfaction with it are more likely to suffer from stress-related illnesses like ulcers and high blood pressure than those who are happy in their jobs. They will also be hospitalized more frequently and live shorter lives. One of my clients, a middle-aged man, so despised his job reading water meters that it made him

Figure 10-2

physically ill. As soon as he arrived home after work he took to his bed. I suggested that he find a job that agreed with him better. But he was convinced that this was the only type of job a person of his age and lack of education could get, and he remained in it despite my warnings that he was shortening his life. Consider now what Bob Newhart the comedian did. He began his career as an accountant. Yet he became so bored with the job that he sought comic relief in make-believe conversations on the office phone. He enjoyed these telephone monologues so much he began performing them on stage. Eventually, he switched to professional acting. And the rest, as they say in Hollywood, is history.

ATTITUDES TOWARD WORK

The early settlers of our country believed that work was a virtue and idleness was a sin. They worked hard to survive in a difficult environment. They took pride in their work, and honored industriousness and success. As a result, the *work ethic* has become deeply embedded in our society, and many of its assumptions are taken for granted. One is the widespread notion that the most important characteristic of a man is being a "good provider." Another is the idea that hard work leads to success, with the payoff of owning your own home, raising a family, and enjoying the good things of life. As a result, to a large extent people's self-respect is tied up with their achievement in the world of work.

Changing attitudes toward work

Attitudes toward work are changing, however. This was initially seen in the sharp drop in the number of college students who believed that hard work always paid off. In the mid-1960s, about three-quarters of all students agreed with this view. But by the mid-1970s, the number had fallen by about half. Other surveys of public opinion have shown that the majority of Americans feel people take less pride in their work, have less motivation to work, and do not work as hard today as they did ten years ago.[4]

> "Friends say, 'I admire you for what you're doing.' But my job isn't all that different. Sure, some days when I've been especially helpful with a patient, I feel real good. Other days, I feel more like quitting. Everyone has days like that. Basically, though, I love what I'm doing."
>
> Barbara Seeman, nurse

[4]D. Yankelovich, *The New Morality* (New York: McGraw-Hill, 1974), p. 68.

Yet it would be a mistake to conclude that the traditional work ethic is dead. The findings of a *Psychology Today* survey of work attitudes are significant in that most of the respondents were young, college-educated, and half were women. Over half of them felt that hard work makes you a better person. More than three-quarters felt that people who are capable of working but choose not to are a drain on society.[5]

Daniel Yankelovich believes the work ethic is very much alive but is not sufficiently used by employers. He has found that very few people work primarily for money. Instead, four out of five American workers feel "an inner need to do the very best job I can regardless of pay." Also, a clear majority of workers feel they exercise some control over their jobs. Yet only one out of five admits to using that control to fulfil an inner need to do his or her best. Why so few? The answer may be seen in the responses of the workers themselves. When asked whom they thought benefited from their productivity, only 10 percent felt that they themselves did. Most assumed that the major benefits went to the consumers, managers, and stockholders. Yankelovich holds that Americans are generally willing to work harder and turn out a high-quality product, and in fact, their self-esteem demands they do so; but they must have sufficient incentives.[6]

Motivating the worker

A well-known theory of worker motivation distinguishes between Theory X, with the emphasis on extrinsic satisfactions like money, and Theory Y, with the emphasis on intrinsic satisfaction like the work activity itself.

According to Theory X, the average worker is lazy and disinterested in work, prefers to be told what to do, and must be closely supervised in order to become productive. Theory Y, by contrast, holds that the desire to work is as natural as play, and that when people are sufficiently rewarded they will assume the necessary responsibility to become productive workers. It has traditionally been assumed that all blue-collar and many white-collar workers are attracted by extrinisic rewards, while professional and executive people are more attracted by the intrinsic satisfaction of their work.

"Some of my colleagues dread answering the phone. But I find it exciting. You never know who's going to call next. When someone calls about a house, I can't wait to meet that person. Oh, occasionally, I run into someone who is a real 'pill.' But I really enjoy getting to know most of the people. The way their faces light up when they like the place I've found. Ah, there's nothing to compare with it."
Brad Smith, realty broker

---

[5]Renwick and Lawler, op. cit.: 56.
[6]D. Yankelovich, "The Work Ethic Is Underemployed," *Psychology Today* (May 1982): 5–8.

Figure 10-3

EMPLOYEE
APPRECIATION
NIGHT

William Ouchi has developed an alternative approach to Theory Y known as Theory Z. Inspired by the success of Japanese business, Ouchi stresses the importance of involving the worker in the "corporate culture." Instead of having a nine-to-five job, workers become part of the company's family. Each person is made to feel that he or she is very important to the company and contributes something essential to the success of the overall organization. Activities such as morning fitness exercises and monthly "beer busts" help to foster the "we" feeling among workers.

Admittedly, Theory Z characteristics may not be easily transplanted to American society for a number of reasons. Most Japanese workers spend their entire lives in one company, are slow to get promotions, and subordinate their initiative to group consensus and long-term results—all of which are at odds with the American emphasis on individuality and short-term results. Despite this, several American companies, including General Motors and the giant electronics firm of Hewlett-Packard, have adopted aspects of the Theory Z approach. Such an approach shows how the involvement of the individual worker can improve both job satisfaction and company productivity.[7]

[7]W.G. Ouchi, *Theory Z: How American Business Can Meet the Japanese Challenge* (New York: Avon Books, 1981), 57–136.

What do people look for in a job?

Workers make a sharp distinction between what they *like* about their work and what they think is most *important* in their jobs. At least, this was one of the findings in the *Psychology Today* survey of work attitudes. As indicated in Table 10-1 the most satisfying aspects of work have to do with the personal atmosphere at work, such as the friendliness of co-workers, the degree of freedom you have on the job, and the respect you receive from people you work with. On the other hand, the most important aspects of work have to do with the fulfilment of psychological needs, such as the chance to do something that makes you feel good about yourself, to accomplish something worthwhile, and to learn. Many of these psychological needs are integral to the concept of self-actualization.

Is self-actualization more important than money? Apparently so for many people, especially when they've already achieved a satisfactory level of pay and job security. When respondents were asked whether they would accept a higher-paying job that was less interesting, almost two-thirds said *no*. However, almost half indicated they would not want a more interesting job if it paid less than their present job. Those less willing to take a pay cut were divorced women, married men, widows, and single women living with someone, in that order. Admittedly, though, much depends on the individual. Circumstances also change our priorities. In hard times when jobs are difficult to get, workers may become less choosy and put a greater value on pay and job security. Furthermore, in the near future many people in our society may not find much fulfilment in their jobs because of the greater number of openings in low-paying service and data-handling jobs. If personal fulfilment is important to them, individuals may have to seek it in their families, in volunteer work, and in leisure activities.[8]

THE PROCESS OF CAREER CHOICE

You don't choose the kind of work you want to do suddenly. You've probably been thinking about it for a long time, mostly unconsciously. From the time you reach adolescence, people ask what it is you want to do. You may not have the slightest idea, but all that pressure starts you thinking about it. Each time you select your courses in school you become more aware of the need for a career goal. Not surprisingly, college students who lack a career goal drop out of school in greater numbers than those who do have one. But even when you have a career goal, it's natural to modify it as you gain more understanding and experience.

[8]Renwick and Lawler, op. cit.: 57.

Table 10–1 What People Look for in a Job[9]

	Importance	Satisfaction
Chances to do something that makes you feel good about yourself	1	8
Chances to accomplish something worthwhile	2	6
Chances to learn new things	3	10
Opportunity to develop your skills and abilities	4	12
Amount of freedom you have on the job	5	2
Chances to do things you do best	6	11
The resources to do your job	7	9
The respect you receive from people you work with	8	3
Amount of information you get on job performance	9	17
Chances to take part in making decisions	10	14
Amount of job security you have	11	5
The amount of pay you get	12	16
Way you are treated by people you work with	13	4
Friendliness of people you work with	14	1
Amount of praise you get for job well done	15	15
The amount of fringe benefits you get	16	7
Chances for getting a promotion	17	18
Physical surroundings of your job	18	13

Adapted from Patricia Renwick, Edward Lawler, and the *Psychology Today* staff, "What You Really Want from Your Job," *Psychology Today* (May 1978): 56.
Respondents were asked, "How satisfied are you with each of the following aspects of your job? And how important to you is each one?" Based on the averages of their responses, items were ranked from 1 (most important or most satisfying) to 18 (least important or least satisfying). Reprinted from *Psychology Today Magazine.* Copyright © 1978 American Psychological Association.

Stages of career choice

According to Eli Ginzberg, while growing up we go through three broad stages of choosing our life work: the fantasy, the tentative, and the realistic stages of career choice.[10]

1. *The fantasy stage.* Throughout childhood, career preferences are mostly the products of imagination and fantasy. Children assume they can become whatever they want to be, whether it's an astronaut or a police officer. They're constantly trying out these roles in their play. I recall coming back from the circus and wanting to be a lion tamer. All afternoon I kept snapping my whip at make-believe lions. Can you recall any of your childhood aspirations? Parents normally express little concern over such choices, and for good reason. Most childhood aspirations have little influence on our adult choices.

[9]Ibid., 56.

[10]E. Ginzberg, "Toward a Theory of Occupational Choice: A Restatement," *Vocational Guidance Quarterly* 20 (1972): 169–176.

2. *The tentative stage.* During adolescence, young people begin thinking in a more mature way. As a result, they start viewing career choices differently. They initially identify career preferences in terms of their interests. Later they think about career choices more in terms of their abilities. Gradually, they begin relating their career choices to the opportunities available. Their ideas about their career change greatly during this period. Perhaps you can recall some of your career aspirations during this stage.

3. *The realistic stage.* From the late teens on, most young people start thinking about career choices in a more realistic manner. The extent to which they do so, however, depends greatly on the individual's motivation and resourcefulness. At this stage it is desirable for young people to investigate various careers, preferably with the guidance of parents, school counselors, and others. Yet this does not always occur. A survey of 32,000 high-school students in thirty-three states reveals that although nine out of ten had talked with their parents about their career plans, less than half of them had discussed their plans with a school counselor, teacher, or a worker in their chosen field. More than two-thirds of them had never taken a course in career guidance or participated in a career day. So it is that many people fail to familiarize themselves with the full range of possibilities before making a commitment to a specific career.[11]

College students of all ages tend to worry when they haven't settled on a firm career choice. Perhaps you've felt this way at one time or another. If so, you should realize that a sense of direction and active progress toward a career choice are far more important than quickly arriving at a decision. Even if you've already decided on your career, you should remember that career choice involves a continual refining of that decision in the light of experience. Making up your mind too quickly can be disastrous, especially if you later find yourself trapped in a job you dislike. On the other hand, if you're floundering over the choice of a career, it may be helpful to talk with an interested teacher or school counselor.

I remember a woman in her mid-thirties named Marie who was returning to the classroom now that her children had reached school age. She had majored in art before dropping out of college to get married, but now she was more interested in working with people. She had enrolled in the human services program in our college, but she was uncertain of her career goal. I suggested that she might benefit from a two-credit course in career guidance offered by the counseling center. She decided to take it. During the course,

[11]R.J. Noeth, J.D. Roth, and D.J. Prediger, "Student Career Development: Where Do We Stand?" *Vocational Guidance Quarterly* 23 (1975): 210–218.

Marie got a good deal of feedback from various career guidance inventories as well as from class exercises. In one exercise, a person sits in the "cool" seat. Then everyone else shares his or her impressions of the kinds of positions most appropriate for this person. To her surprise, most people saw her as someone who takes charge and supervises others. She discovered she was a "natural" at organizing and directing people. Soon after getting her degree in human services, she obtained an administrative position in a mental health clinic. When I saw her at a meeting several years later, the first thing she mentioned was how helpful that course in career guidance had been.

Influences on career choice

When Suzanne told her school counselor she was interested in a nursing career, the woman counselor said, "I'll bet you have sisters at home, don't you?" "Yes, I do," replied Suzanne. "But how did you know?" "I didn't," said the counselor, "I was simply guessing." Then the counselor went on to explain how our career choices are influenced by our families, whether we're aware of it or not. As a matter of fact, the family is the single most important influence on

Figure 10-4

career choice throughout the adolescent years, though this diminishes some-what as we enter early adulthood. Through our families we are exposed to adult models in the workaday world, to career opportunities, to encourage-ment, work values, and the influence of brothers and sisters. The counselor pointed this out in Suzanne's case. Her parents were college educated and supported their daughter's career aspirations. Both parents worked in service-oriented careers: her father was a dentist, and her mother an elementary-school teacher. Furthermore, Suzanne had two younger sisters, which probably accentuated the influence of the feminine sex role on her choice of career. How about you? In what ways has your choice of a career been influenced by your family?

Our career choice is also influenced by people like teachers, counselors, and coaches. Such people are called *mentors*—people of greater experience and seniority who take an interest in us and act as sponsor or advisor in our career development. Mentors are especially helpful in the early stages of a career when the right opportunity or support is so crucial. O. J. Simpson, the well-known football player and commentator, acknowledges that his own career was inspired by Willie Mays, the famous baseball player. Simpson came from a

Mentors are especially helpful in the early stages of a career.

broken home with little parental supervision. He ran around with delinquents, and had already been in jail several times before meeting Mays, to whom he was introduced through his school counselor. Mays quickly observed that Simpson's great talent was going to waste. He talked to Simpson about his talent, his future, and the importance of getting on the right track. Simpson says it was largely Mays's influence that helped him to decide to attend college and become a professional football player.[12]

Sex role has become a diminishing influence on career choice. Traditionally, the career choices of both men and women have been highly sex typed, with men considering a wider range of careers than women, and more apt than they to choose the high-status careers. Today the situation is changing. More women are attending college, working outside the home before marriage, delaying marriage longer, and combining a career with family responsibilities. Also, both men and women are being encouraged to choose their life work from a wider range of careers. Yet the lingering influence of sex-role stereotypes can be seen in the uneven distribution of the sexes in some careers, especially those shown in Table 10–2 below.

Work experience

Work experience is also a valuable part of choosing a career, though it is not always apreciated as such. Too often, work is seen as something you *have* to do, either during the summer months while you attend school, or after you graduate from school. Students work mostly to gain independence by having money of their own. Also, the types of jobs available to students are generally in clerical work, sales, fast food, or manual labor. As a result, students often don't

Table 10–2   Uneven Distribution of the Sexes

Selected male-dominated careers	*percent men*
Plumbers	99.2
Auto mechanics	99.0
Dentists	96.7
Police	93.3
Carpenters	93.0
Selected female-dominated careers	*percent women*
Secretaries	99.2
House servants	95.9
Registered nurses	95.6
Bookkeepers	92.0
Telephone operators	91.9

Source: U.S. Bureau of the Census, *Statistical Abstract of the United States 1984*, 104 ed. (Washington D.C.: Government Printing Office, 1984).

[12]J.W. Santrock, *Adolescence,* 2nd ed. (Dubuque, Iowa: Wm. C. Brown Publishers, 1984), 579.

find their work interesting. Nor do they pick up much technical knowledge in their jobs. But they do acquire practical knowledge from their work experience, one of the most important skills being how to find and hold a job. Students also learn how to budget their time and take pride in a job well done. Probably the most valuable lesson of all is how to get along with people at work.[13]

People learn even more from work experience when they can choose a job in which they're interested and be supervised in it. This was demonstrated in a study of almost two thousand students, of whom two-thirds were in various work-study programs and the other third simply held part-time jobs. Students in the supervised work-study programs were significantly more satisfied with their work than those who only held part-time jobs. The major reasons given involved: doing meaningful work; having adult role models available; opportunities for team work; and receiving valuable feedback regarding their performance. In addition, graduates with relevant work experience generally found it easier to find employment in their chosen fields.[14]

Work experience continues to be a valuable means of clarifying one's career goal throughout life. I often see people in their late twenties and older who are at last pursuing satisfying careers partly because of what they've learned from their varied work experience. Some people have to try out different things until they find what they like to do.

After graduation from high school John spent the next several years in the Marine Corps. Upon his discharge from the Marines, he enrolled in a community college with a major in business administration. He also worked part time with a community ambulance team, though he disliked the irregular schedule as well as the pay. One day he answered an ad for management trainees in a fast-food chain. He not only liked the work, but was pleasantly surprised to discover the company would pay for his college expenses. John switched his major to hospitality management. Later he obtained his degree and worked for several years with the company. Eventually he opened his own restaurant, and was even happier with his career.

Other people have less trouble discovering what they want to do, but they too find work experience helpful in clarifying their career goal. Kathy knew from her experience as a volunteer in a hospital during high school that she wanted to be a nurse. Later she obtained a nursing degree and began working as an R.N. on the wards of a local hospital. At first, she was happy just to be working as a nurse. But she gradually became disenchanted with her generalized job description. After talking with more experienced nurses, Kathy decided she might be happier in a specialized role that made better use of her abilities. Eventually she took advanced training which prepared her to be an anesthetist, someone who administers anesthesia before surgery.

[13]S. Cole, "Send Our Children to Work?" *Psychology Today* (July 1980): 44–68.
[14]H.F. Silberman, "Job Satisfaction among Students in Work Educational Programs," *Journal of Vocational Behavior* 5 (1974): 261–268.

Work experience can be especially valuable in clarifying career goals because during our years in school we are isolated from the working world. But no amount of work experience will automatically confirm the choice of a career. At some point, you must sit down and take stock of yourself. You must explore realistically some of the many career options open to you, and eventually settle on the most promising one. All this can be hard work, which is why so many people never get around to it until relatively late. Yet the process of choosing a career may be richly rewarding for those who take the time and trouble to do it, as we'll explain in the next chapter.

SUMMARY

1. Although money is a major reason for working, it isn't the only one. Other motives for work include personal fulfilment, identity, security, service to others, and status. The way our jobs affect us depends on a variety of influences, such as how much we enjoy the work activity itself, the working conditions, and job stress.

2. We pointed out that attitudes toward work are changing, with fewer people believing that hard work always pays off. Yet most people want to take pride in what they do, as long as there are sufficient incentives in the work. People generally look for a job that is interesting and makes them feel good about themselves. But overall satisfaction on the job also depends on things like friendly co-workers.

3. Individuals begin thinking about their careers in a more realistic manner as they reach late adolescence and adulthood. Although the choice of a career is a personal matter, it is usually influenced by a variety of factors like the family, mentors, and sex-role. Work experience may also help to clarify one's career goals, while providing practical knowledge of the working world.

SELF-TEST

1. Other motives for work in addition to money are:
   a. personal fulfilment   c. serving others
   b. identity   d. all of the above
2. Once people _____ in their jobs, they tend to be more motivated to achieve fulfilment and recognition, and to help others.
   a. have achieved status
   b. are making enough money
   c. have become bored
   d. are secure

3. _____ tend to report high levels of stress in their work because it involves much responsibility with little control over the job.
   a. sales clerks   c. secretaries
   b. waitresses   d. all of the above

4. According to Daniel Yankelovich, the American work ethic is:
   a. dead for most workers
   b. not sufficiently used by employers
   c. strongest among the working class
   d. overused by employers

5. The most important thing people look for in a job is:
   a. satisfying work   c. pleasant surroundings
   b. good pay   d. chances for promotion

6. According to the *Psychology Today* survey on work, the major source of job satisfaction is:
   a. learning new things   c. friendliness of co-workers
   b. the pay you get   d. praise received on the job

7. From the late teens on, most young people enter the _____ stage of career choice.
   a. idealistic   c. realistic
   b. tentative   d. fantasy

8. _____ is the single most important influence on the individual's career choice.
   a. The family   c. Sex
   b. Social class   d. Education

9. Which of the following careers has the most uneven distribution of the sexes?
   a. high-school teachers   c. auto mechanics
   b. physicians   d. newspaper columnists

10. Work experience helps young people to learn how to:
    a. find and hold a job   c. get along with people
    b. budget their time   d. all of the above

EXERCISES

1. *Would you work if you didn't have to?* Suppose you had just won a large sum of money—say $100,000 or more per year for twenty years. Would you continue to work? Explain your answer. To what extent is your need to work influenced by the motives discussed in this chapter, i.e., personal fulfilment, identity, need for structure, service to others, and status?

2. *Job stress.* Write a brief paragraph about the stress in your present job or jobs you've held in the past. What has been the most stressful thing

for you? Would you agree that a great deal of responsibility combined with very little control over your job is a major source of stress at work?

3. *Do you think hard work always pays off?* Or are you more of the opinion that "it's who you know more than what you know" that counts? Write a short paragraph explaining your attitude toward work. To what extent are you motivated by the American work ethic?

4. *What do you look for in a job?* Take the eighteen criteria listed in Table 10–1 and rank them according to what you think is most important in a job. Then compare your rankings with those in the table. In what ways are your responses like and unlike those in the survey?

5. *How has your career choice been influenced by others?* Write a paragraph or so describing some of the ways your choice of a career has been influenced by your family, other people, and events. To what extent has your choice of work been influenced by other factors such as work experience, money, status, and the desire to help others?

6. *Your work experience.* What kinds of jobs have you had? Include full-time, part-time, and summer jobs. What would you say you've learned from these jobs? Would you agree that work experience can be helpful in making a good career choice?

Choosing a Career

11

CHOOSING A COMPATIBLE CAREER
    Self-assessment
    Exploring careers
    Identifying compatible careers
    Making a decision

PREPARING FOR A CAREER
    Apprenticeship programs
    On-the-job training programs
      in business and industry
    Colleges and universities
    Vocational and technical schools
    Military service and other
      government programs

CAREER OUTLOOK
    Trends and projected growth
    Your career outlook
    Changing your career goal

SUMMARY

SELF-TEST

EXERCISES

Upon graduation from high school, David decided to work instead of attending college. But after several years in "dead-end" jobs, he began taking evening courses at a nearby community college. David enjoyed his courses so much that he eventually enrolled on a full-time basis as a general studies major.

At a teacher's suggestion, David talked with someone in the college counseling center about his career goals. Dr. Smith, David's counselor, gave him the Strong-Campbell Interest Inventory, which is widely used for people who are undecided about their career goals. We find them going over the results.

Dr. Smith says, "If you'll look at the number IV category labeled *Occupational Scales,* you'll notice that your highest scores appear under the investigative careers. For example, there's geologist, physicist, computer programmer, and mathematician."

"That's interesting," muses David. "My father is a chemist, and my brother is an engineer. But I'm not interested in those fields."

"Have you taken courses in any of them?"

"Yes, I took algebra, trigonometry, and physics in high school."

"How did you do?"

"I made an *A* in algebra and a *B-plus* in trig and physics."

"Did you enjoy math?" asks Dr. Smith.

"Pretty much," replies David. "I liked the practical problems and applications better than the abstract part."

"Have you ever taken any training in computers?"

"Not really," says David. "I couldn't work it into my schedule in high school. I've played around with the computer in my brother's office. It's kind of fun."

"You might try one of the courses here in our computer science department," suggests Dr. Smith.

"I'd thought about taking that introductory course in data processing."

"That might be a good idea," says Dr. Smith. "Computers would combine your interests in math and practical problems."

They continue discussing David's scores on the other occupational scales, including the careers to which he was not suited. At the end of their session, Dr. Smith says, "Well, I hope you've found this discussion helpful."

"It's been quite useful," replies David. "I still don't know what I want to do. But I've got some good leads, especially the idea about computers. I think I've got a sense of direction now."

CHOOSING A COMPATIBLE CAREER

David is wise to seek help in the choice of a career. Choosing a career, like marrying, is one of those crucial decisions we must make before we have the knowledge, judgment, or self-understanding to choose wisely. Too often, people choose on the basis of their momentary interests. Or they simply select their life work from the limited number of careers they are familiar with, rather than seeking out the most compatible one. But the choice of a compatible career is like solving a puzzle, involving four closely related processes: taking stock of yourself, especially your interests, abilities, and personal traits; exploring the variety of careers available to someone with your educational aspirations; identifying the best careers for you; and finally making a decision. Let's examine each of these tasks.

Self-assessment

A good place to begin is to ask yourself what you like to do. Which school subjects do you most enjoy? Which sports? Which types of activities are you most involved in—artistic, community-oriented or recreational? In each case, try to determine what it is that most interests you, the activity itself or the people you're doing it with.

Also, ask yourself what you are good at. People often freeze up at this question. They'll say something like, "I've spent years in school, but I'm not really good at anything," or, "I've been busy raising a family; I don't have any marketable skills." But the picture changes dramatically when people are asked if they can type or manage a budget, or supervise people. At this point, students and homemakers alike realize they have more marketable skills than they give themselves credit for. Remember there are different types of skills—working with things or people, or handling information.

Keep in mind that your interests and abilities may not always match. It's not uncommon to be interested in something you're not especially talented in, or to be good at something you aren't too interested in. For example, a certain musician after some years managed to become only an average singer. Then, almost by accident, he began writing songs and discovered that he composed rather easily. As the satisfaction and the income from his publications increased, he made the transition to songwriting, and found that he was really happier than when he had been singing for a living.

Personality is another important consideration in selecting a career. Your personal make-up is a unique combination of personal traits, needs, and motives which make some occupational pursuits more compatible than others. For example, a woman who kept a meticulous house and managed a large family well was told by an experienced teacher in the computer field that she might be good in data processing, a field which requires the ability to manage details with precision.

Figure 11-1

Ultimately, your choice of a career hinges on your personal values—those things which you most care about. We often take our values for granted, becoming aware of them mostly when we're faced with an important decision. Common American values include immediate pleasure, prestige, security, helping others, love, companionship, self-fulfilment, family, honesty, creativity, money, independence, responsibility, and education. Perhaps you can add others to the list. Although values are more difficult to measure than interests and aptitudes, there are various inventories to determine your work-related values. These are usually available in your school counseling center or career guidance center.

Exploring careers

With more than twenty thousand different careers to choose from, it's difficult to know where to begin. Even career counselors must regularly consult directories and handbooks to keep abreast of the various careers. Fortunately, there are many such resources to help you explore the various possibilities. Yet, many people either do not know about these resources or do not take advantage of them. Instead, they select a career on the basis of the hundred or so fields most familiar to them. Even worse, they may choose a career on an emotional basis, and enter their father's profession or follow in the footsteps of an admired friend.

A major resource for exploring the various careers is the *Occupational Outlook Handbook* (OOH) published by the United States Department of Labor. The handbook contains more than 20 basic occupational or career groups, with many related careers in each group. For example, the group for *service occupations* includes such careers as barbering, hotel housekeeping, and police work. For each career, the handbook provides information on the type of work, places of employment, entrance requirements, working conditions, and employment outlook. The OOH is revised regularly and is available in most libraries. Other helpful resources are the *College Blue Book* series (five volumes), which includes information on the appropriate technical schools, and the *Occupational Encyclopedia*.

Identifying compatible careers

In selecting a compatible career, it may be advisable to talk over your plans with someone like an interested teacher or school counselor. Professionals in school counseling centers or career guidance centers spend a good part of their time assisting people with their career planning. Fortunately, they have access to a variety of tests and inventories that help individuals match themselves with a compatible career. Although such inventories do not in themselves provide some magical right choice, they usually furnish valuable leads, especially when the results are shared with a counselor. Some of the more well-known inventories are described below.

John Holland's *Self-directed Search* (SDS) may, as the name implies, be completed by yourself. But as we've just indicated, you'll find it even more useful to share your results with a counselor. Students indicate their responses to a number of choices regarding their career daydreams, activities, abilities, career preferences, and self-estimates. The results are tabulated to indicate which three personality-occupational types they most resemble and in what order. Then, using a separate occupation-finder booklet, they match their preferred personality-occupational types with compatible careers.

Another widely used inventory is the *Harrington-O'Shea Career Decision-Making System* (CDM), especially the self-scored edition, published by the American Guidance Service. Choosing among prescribed lists in the inventory booklet, students indicate their preferences in regard to their careers, school subjects, future plans, job values, abilities, and interests. Then they tabulate their results to arrive at several career clusters which are suggested for further exploration.

If you have access to a computer, there's also the *System of Interactive Guidance and Information* (SIGI), pronounced Siggy, published by the Educational Testing Service in Princeton, N.J. Students sit at a terminal and enter into dialogue with the computer, making career decisions in a multiple-choice format. Students proceed at their own pace through six subsystems. In the process, they examine their own values, explore career options systematically, and formulate tentative career choices that can be tested realistically and revised. In the face of the enormous uncertainty associated with career choice, SIGI helps the student learn strategies that will result in an informed and rational choice.

One of the most widely used inventories administered by a professional counselor is the *Strong-Campbell Interest Inventory* (SCII). Students indicate their preferences (*like, dislike,* or *indifferent*) for a number of careers, school subjects, activities, amusements, types of people, and their own personal characteristics. Computer-scored printouts present the student's results organized around Holland's six occupational-personality types in terms of general occupational themes, basic career interests (with norms for each sex), and specific careers. Discussion of the results with a counselor usually provides valuable guidelines as to which careers might be best for you.

Students often ask whether these tests really help. I usually reply that much depends on how they are used. If you rely on them as a substitute for making a decision, the answer is *no.* But if you use the results as a guide in reaching your own decision, the answer is more positive. Occasionally, I hear someone complain that he took one of those tests, and was told that he should choose a certain career. What probably happened was that the counselor indicated careers that would be compatible with someone with that individual's profile, and the person mistakenly took that to be what he *should* do. This is a common *misunderstanding* of such inventories.

Holland's Six Personality-occupational Types

The following are descriptions of Holland's six personality-occupational types. These descriptions are, most emphatically, only generalizations. None will fit any one person exactly. In fact, most people's interests combine all six themes or types to some degree. Even if you rank high on a given theme, you will find that some of the statements used to characterize this theme do not apply to you.

The archetypal models of Holland's six types can be described as follows:

REALISTIC: Persons of this type are robust, rugged, practical, physically strong, and often athletic; have good motor coordination and skills but lack verbal and interpersonal skills, and are therefore somewhat uncomfortable in social settings; usually perceive themselves as mechanically inclined; are direct, stable, natural, and persistent; prefer concrete to abstract problems; see themselves as aggressive; have conventional political and economic goals; and rarely perform creatively in the arts or sciences, but do like to build things with tools. Realistic types prefer such occupations as mechanic, engineer, electrician, fish and wildlife specialist, crane operator, and tool designer.

INVESTIGATIVE: This category includes those with a strong scientific orientation; they are usually task-oriented, introspective, and asocial; prefer to think through rather than act out problems; have a great need to understand the physical world; enjoy ambiguous tasks; prefer to work independently; have unconventional values and attitudes; usually perceive themselves as lacking in leadership or persuasive abilities, but are confident of their scholarly and intellectual abilities; describe themselves as analytical, curious, independent, and reserved; and especially dislike repetitive activites. Vocational preferences include astronomer, biologist, chemist, technical writer, zoologist, and psychologist.

ARTISTIC: Persons of the artistic type prefer free unstructured situations with maximum opportunity for self-expression; resemble investigative types in being introspective and asocial but differ in having less ego strength, greater need for individual expression, and greater tendency to impulsive behavior; they are creative, especially in artistic and musical media; avoid problems that are highly structured or require gross physical skills; prefer dealing with problems through self-expression in artistic media; perform well on standard measures of creativity, and value aesthetic qualities; see themselves as expressive, original, intuitive, creative, nonconforming, introspective, and independent. Vocational preferences include artist, author, composer, writer, musician, stage director, and symphony conductor.

SOCIAL: Persons of this type are sociable, responsible, humanistic, and often religious; like to work in groups, and enjoy being central in the group; have good verbal and interpersonal skills; avoid intellectual problem-solving, physical exertion, and highly ordered activites; prefer to solve problems through feelings and interpersonal manipulation of others; enjoy activities that involve informing, training, developing, curing, or enlightening others; perceive themselves as understanding, responsible, idealistic, and helpful. Vocational preferences include social worker, missionary, high school teacher, marriage counselor, and speech therapist.

ENTERPRISING: Persons of this type have verbal skills suited to selling, dominating, and leading; are strong leaders; have a strong drive to attain organizational goals or economic aims; tend to avoid work situations requiring long periods of intellectual effort; differ from conventional types in having a greater preference for *ambiguous social tasks and an even greater concern for power, status, and leadership; see themselves as aggressive, popular, self-confident, cheerful, and sociable; generally have a high energy level; and show an aversion to scientific activities. Vocational preferences include business executive, political campaign manager, real estate sales, stock and bond sales, television producer, and retail merchandising.*

CONVENTIONAL: Conventional people prefer well-ordered environments and like systematic verbal and numerical activities; are usually conforming and prefer subordinate roles; are effective at well-structured tasks, but avoid ambiguous situations and problems involving interpersonal relationships or physical skills; describe themselves as conscientious, efficient, obedient, calm, orderly, and practical; identify with power; and value material possessions and status. Vocational preferences include bank examiner, bookkeeper, clerical worker, financial analyst, quality control expert, statistician, and traffic manager.

Reprinted from David P. Campbell and Jo-Ida C. Hansen, *Manual for the Strong-Campbell Interest Inventory,* Form T325 of the *Strong Vocational Interest Blank,* 3rd ed., with the permission of the distributors, Consulting Psychologists Press Inc., for the publisher, Stanford University Press. © 1974, 1977, 1981, by the Board of Trustees of the Leland Stanford Junior University.

However, the results of inventories such as the SCII have proven quite helpful in predicting which individuals will remain in a given field. Those who choose a career very similar to one indicated by their career profile tend to stay in that field, whereas those who enter a career very dissimilar to what their profile suggests usually drop out. But these inventories cannot predict your actual success in a given field, as there are many subjective factors involved, especially personal motivation.

Making a decision

You may well end up with a choice among several compatible careers. Ultimately, you must make a decision. A helpful strategy in making such an important decision is use of the "balance sheet." High school seniors, college students, and adults of all ages have found that the balance sheet helps them to identify their goals, their gains and losses, and their obstacles and frustrations. It also points out areas in which more information is needed. Studies have shown that people who use the balance sheet are more likely than nonusers to stick to their decisions and express fewer regrets about the options not taken.[1]

Essentially, the balance sheet consists of listing the pluses and minuses of a given course of action. To use the balance sheet method, simply divide a sheet of paper into three columns. Label the first column *projected consequences,*

[1] Irving Janis and Dan Wheeler, "Thinking Clearly about Career Choices," *Psychology Today* (May 1978): 75.

the second column *positive anticipations,* and the third column *negative anticipations.* Then under the *projected consequences* column list the following areas to be considered: *tangible gains and losses for me; tangible gains and losses for others; self-approval or disapproval;* and *social approval or disapproval.*

Ellen is a twenty-four-year-old woman completing her second semester of college. Since high school she has wanted to be a math teacher. But several years as the bookkeeper in a construction company, plus the encouragement of her favorite teacher, has modified her career aspirations. She's seriously considering being an accountant. To reach a decision, she uses the balance sheet method as shown in Table 11-1. As you can see, Ellen lists as many negative anticipations as positive ones. As she looks over the balance sheet, however, she realizes many of the negative anticipations consist of social disapproval. Yet she has already seen how social disapproval can often be exaggerated in one's mind, and that one can easily overcome it, as she did in her earlier job. She also realizes that her desire to teach can be satisfied in other ways, either in business seminars or in volunteer activites. Also, she feels the positive gains of good job opportunities, solid income, and the possibility of self-employment far outweigh the negative fears such as failing the state exam. As a result, Ellen switches to an accounting major; it's a decision she can live with.

Table 11–1: Ellen's Balance Sheet

Projected Consequences	Positive Anticipations	Negative Anticipations
Tangible gains and losses for me	1. good job opportunities 2. solid income 3. possibility of self-employment	1. hard courses 2. fear of using math 3. fear of failing state exam
Tangible gains and losses for others	1. substantial help with family income 2. positive role-model for daughter	1. conflicts between career and family goals
Self-approval or disapproval	1. confidence in mastering challenge 2. pride in being an accountant	1. lingering doubts about teaching career
Social approval or disapproval	1. admiration for a woman accountant	1. mother may be disappointed in me 2. future husband may disapprove of wife as accountant 3. Some people frown on women in business

PREPARING FOR A CAREER

You may prepare for a career in a variety of ways. Some careers are normally entered through an apprenticeship, vocational school, or on-the-job training program. Others require either a two-year or four-year college degree. Professions like medicine require an advanced degree and some sort of professional training. Do you know the educational requirements for your chosen career? Where are the appropriate schools located? What are the entrance requirements? How long is the training? If you're not sure of the answers, such information can be found in the *Occupational Outlook Handbook* and other resources in your school library.

Since most of you are already enrolled in some sort of post-high school educational program you have probably begun the appropriate training for your career. But you should also be aware of the other pathways to careers, especially if you should ever change your career goal. Such knowledge will also help you appreciate other peoples' training in different types of careers.

Apprenticeship programs

An apprentice is someone who agrees to work for a specified length of time for a master craftsman in return for instruction in a skilled craft or trade. The practice of apprenticeship dates back to the Middle Ages, when young workers normally acquired their knowledge and skill through service to a master craftsman. Those who successfully completed an apprenticeship were accepted by the guild or union as an independent craftsman. In colonial times, Benjamin Franklin became a printer by serving as an apprentice under his older brother.

Today, apprenticeship programs provide entry into more than three hundred skilled trades, such as carpentry, plumbing, and upholstery. The route to an apprenticeship depends primarily on how unionized the trade is in a given area. Where the trade is controlled by a union in a "closed shop," applicants tend to be tested and ranked for admission. In other places where the trade is practiced in small, nonunion shops, the entry requirements are more informal. There are many ways to enter an apprenticeship program. The most common way is by formal testing. But other factors are often involved, such as connections, appropriate schooling, persistence about your career aspirations, and willingness to start at a lower level.[2] Because Jeff's uncle was a carpenter, Jeff began working in summer construction jobs during high school. Later he had no trouble being admitted to an apprenticeship in carpentry. When some workers were laid off during a slow spell in construction, Jeff was kept on. Well aware of the value of his connections, Jeff worked extra hard to justify his good luck and was well regarded by other carpentry apprentices.

[2]Charlotte Lobb, *Exploring Apprenticeship Careers* (New York: Richards Rosen Press, Inc., 1978), 17–27.

Under federal regulations, apprenticeship training must last at least two years, though most programs last longer. Also, the applicant usually works under a written agreement registered with a state apprenticeship program. Although women have long been trained to be cosmetologists, medical technicians, and optical laboratory technicians, they are now being encouraged to enter a wider variety of trades, as are minority groups.

The advantages and disadvantages of apprenticeship training depend on the particular trade and program. Some possible advantages are: (1) opportunity to develop highly valued skills; (2) recognition as a skilled craftsman; (3) assurance of wages with regular increases; and (4) opportunities for employment. Possible disadvantages include: (1) unrealistic entry requirements in some cases; (2) some programs are inflexible; (3) some programs require unduly long periods of training; and (4) the demand for apprentices fluctuates with the business cycle.

On-the-job training programs in business and industry

Many companies now conduct educational and training programs of their own. The main purpose is to train workers in the special skills required by the company. The training programs in the automobile industry provided by General Motors, Ford, and Chrysler are well known.

There are a variety of such training programs. In some instances,

Figure 11-2

companies offer such programs to potential employees. The training is usually free, though the individuals are seldom paid while taking it. In other instances, companies provide a series of training programs for their employees, including an initial training program for new employees. Trainees in these programs are usually paid while they learn, either at a special trainee rate or at their regular salary. There are also independent training programs conducted in cooperation with other agencies, like the public schools, state employment services, or human service agencies. In addition, some well established companies like IBM support educational programs leading to an advanced degree. In a typical arrangement, the company will give the worker an opportunity to study on company time with paid tuition, either on the company premises or at school.

On-the-job training programs have both advantages and disadvantages. On the plus side, individuals get: (1) free instruction; (2) training in a marketable skill; and (3) guaranteed employment, or a high probability of it. On the minus side, individuals face: (1) stiff entrance requirements; (2) limited application of their newly acquired skills; and (3) commitment to one company.

Colleges and universities

Until recently, the advantages of going to college were mostly taken for granted. College is supposed to make you better informed and provide access to the higher-status, better-paying careers. Yet today many young people are thinking twice before attending college. One reason is the increased cost of a college education, especially at private colleges and universities. Another factor is the high rate of unemployment in our society, including that of many college graduates.

The reevaluation of college education has led to several major changes. More students are now delaying their entry into college, out of the need for money or more experience, before deciding on a career. Almost half the college-bound youth wait a year or more before enrolling. There is also a marked increase in career-oriented programs like business and computer science. This is especially evident in the two-year community colleges, which now enroll about half of all students in the first two years of college. Furthermore, students carrying liberal arts majors tend to stay more flexible, with some of them carrying a dual major like education and psychology, or business and computer science. There is also less reluctance to change one's career goals or drop out of college to get a clearer sense of direction in one's career. Almost three-quarters of the students in two-year community colleges interrupt their education at one time or another, though many of them reenroll at a later date.[3]

Admittedly, college graduates continue to have the highest lifetime earnings. According to one projection, a twenty-five-year-old male who has a four-year college degree can expect lifetime earnings of about $1,165,000, as

[3]Eastwood Atwater, *Adolescence* (Englewood Cliffs, N.J.: Prentice-Hall, Inc., 1983), 232.

against $918,000 for someone the same age who has a two-year college degree, and $803,000 for a high-school graduate.[4] College graduates also have lower unemployment rates than high-school graduates. Yet a college degree does not guarantee a job, as we'll discuss later in this chapter. Nor do college graduates necessarily enter the same careers as their college majors. In one survey, two-thirds of the men and half of the women decided on their careers after leaving college. When asked whether their college education had given them the necessary skills for their current jobs, 38 percent replied that it had been "very useful," while another 50 percent said it had been "somewhat useful." Only 12 percent felt that college had been a waste of time. When asked which courses they felt had been most helpful in their careers, the favored courses dealt with how to communicate, how to get along with people, and how to handle figures and general business practice.[5]

The potential advantages of a college education include: (1) learning how to learn; (2) becoming better informed; (3) greater communication skills; (4) development of valued personal traits through extra-curricular activities; (5) entry into the higher-status jobs; and (6) higher lifetime earnings. Some potential disadvantages of college are: (1) the high cost; (2) lost earnings while in school; (3) danger of a premature career commitment; (4) having to follow a prescribed program of studies, including subjects you aren't interested in; and (5) no guarantee of a job upon graduation.

Vocational and technical schools

These institutions provide post-high-school training to prepare individuals for careers other than those that require a college degree. They provide training in such areas as business skills, secretarial skills, cosmetology, and arts design. They are also trade schools, as well as a variety of technical institutes.

Vocational and technical schools enroll students of a wide range of ages, ability levels, and educational backgrounds. As in the past, such schools continue to attract young people who have either graduated or left high school without a marketable skill. Many come from low-income and minority backgrounds, and may choose from a variety of federally aided vocational programs. But today, such schools attract many other types of people as well, including those who are unemployed or underemployed, those whose skills are no longer marketable, those who want to update their skills, and apprentices in various skilled trades and technical careers.

After Dawn dropped out of college and got married against her parents' wishes, she looked for training in some marketable skill. Aided by her husband and some borrowed funds, she attended a secretarial school for a year and then found work in a large bank. Dawn realized she would not want to

---

[4]U.S. Bureau of the Census, *Statistical Abstract of the United States, 1984,* 104th ed. (Washington, D.C.: U.S. Government Printing Office, 1984), 470.
[5]*New York Times,* November 7, 1976.

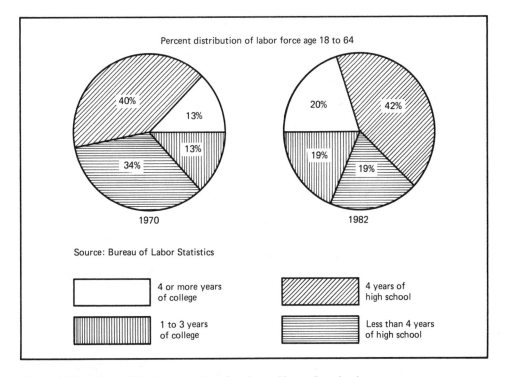

Percent distribution of labor force age 18 to 64

1970

1982

Source: Bureau of Labor Statistics

4 or more years
of college

4 years of
high school

1 to 3 years
of college

Less than 4 years
of high school

Figure 11-3. Since 1970, the proportion of workers with a college back-
ground has increased substantially. From *Occupational Outlook
Handbook,* 1984–85 Edition (Washington, D.C. Government
Printing Office, 1984), 16.

remain a secretary all of her life, but she felt this was the quickest way to get
the financial independence she needed right then.

Attitudes toward vocational and technical schools are decidedly more
positive today than they were in the past, when such schools were considered
inferior to college. Much of the change has to do with the increased value of
marketable skills in a society where job seekers face intense competition and a
high rate of unemployment. Also, there is a greater appreciation of the fact
that there are many people to whom college has little to offer. Such individuals
are in no way inferior to college students, but prefer a more practical education. It should be added that the goal of vocational and technical education is
not just to transmit technical skills needed on the job. The goal is also to help
students acquire the social and thinking skills needed to continue learning from
experience and growing as a person.

Vocational and technical schools have their advantages and disadvantages, and included among the former are: (1) an education relevant to one's
immediate interests; (2) the acquisition of marketable skills; and (3) a high
probability of employment. Disadvantages include: (1) the limited scope of the

education offered; (2) a high drop-out rate—mostly because promise outstrips performance in some of these schools—and (3) possible discrimination in the workplace as graduates of such schools may earn less than college graduates doing the same job.

Military service and other government programs

Some individuals may discover their best educational opportunities are in one of the armed forces—the Army, the Navy, the Marine Corps, the Air Force, or the Coast Guard. A select group will compete for places in one of the service academies that train officers, like Annapolis, West Point, or the Air Force Academy. Most will enter one of the services as enlisted personnel. In fact, many young people volunteer for the service in order to get the special training they want while earning pay. The emphasis is realistic, focusing on training people for the skills needed in the service. Yet many of these skills are useful in civilian life. Examples of workers trained in the military would include electronics technicians, auto mechanics, construction equipment operators, plumbers, and printers.

Don, the youngest of five children, joined the navy as a way of getting a

Marketable skills are especially valuable in today's competitive job market.

practical education while earning pay. When tested, he demonstrated a high aptitude and interest in mechanical skills, and was placed in a training program for aircraft mechanics. After serving a three-year hitch, he signed on as a mechanic with one of the major airlines, which required only a short period of reorientation.

There are also a wide variety of government-sponsored training programs. These range from the federally aided vocational programs for the unemployed, to work-study programs and internships in a variety of governmental agencies. In addition, there are training programs offered by state and municipal governments. You should also keep in mind that the federal government is the single largest employer of college graduates, employing about twenty thousand recent college graduates each year. Many of these graduates will enter the civil service. Jobs are classified under an eighteen-grade general schedule (GS) system. Individuals with a two-year college or associate's degree, or the equivalent appropriate experience, would start at the *GS 4* level; those with a four-year college or bachelor's degree, or equivalent appropriate experience, would start at the *GS 5* level. Employment and advancement in the civil service is based on the merit system, with all administrative decisions being subject to judicial review.

The educational opportunities of the military service and government offer certain advantages and disadvantages. Among the advantages are: (1) a reserved place while in high school (for qualified candidates); (2) pay while learning; (3) assurance of employment; and (4) pride in serving your country. Possible disadvantages include: (1) fixed terms of military service; (2) little control over job transfers; (3) coping with governmental bureaucracy; and (4) distaste for a military career.

CAREER OUTLOOK

Cliff retired from the army after twenty years of service as a machinist. Still in his mid-forties, Cliff took a job as a clerk in a hardware store. The job was not unlike his army job in that he enjoyed regular hours and nondemanding work with plenty of time for leisurely coffee breaks and some occasional fishing. Whenever customers inquired about getting their lawnmowers or chainsaws fixed, Cliff supplied them with the names of repairers recommended by the store. He began to notice that there were more machines to be repaired than there were places to take them. Soon he began repairing lawnmowers on his own time in the evenings. As his reputation for high-quality work spread, so did the number of lawnmowers brought to him. Eventually he opened his own full-time repair service and today he is busier than ever. He works harder but seems happier. When asked about this, Cliff readily admits, "I have a brighter future now."

Do you feel this way about your chosen career? Or do you sometimes wonder what you'll be doing twenty years from now? In this section, we'll take a look at some of the influences that affect your career outlook. We'll examine some of the major trends and projected growth in various careers. Then we'll ask you to apply this to your own personal future. Finally, we'll discuss the important matter of changing your career goal, if this becomes necessary.

Trends and projected growth

The predicted job openings in a given field generally depend on a number of factors, especially the rate of growth or decline in the field, the need to replace workers who retire, changes in technology, and social changes.[6]

The trend toward consolidation in business and farming, along with the increased use of technology, is producing significant shifts in employment patterns. As a result, farm workers and unskilled laborers will continue to have trouble finding jobs. On the other hand, professionals, technical workers, managers, sales people, and clerical workers will have much better job opportunities.

Another trend is the rapid growth in service industries as compared to goods-producing industries like steel factories. As a result, employment opportunities should be more favorable in such fields as finance, real estate, government, and data processing. An even greater proportion of job openings will be available in the lower-paying service jobs, like janitor, sales clerk, hospital aide, and fast-food worker. One of the most dramatic increases in job openings will be in clerical work. The reason is in part the growth of new jobs associated with electronic technology like word processors, and in part the need to replace workers who retire, return to school, or simply stop working, perhaps to care for a family.

There is also an increase in the number of jobs associated with the development of technology. This is especially true in the computer field, where a wide variety of jobs in software, like computer programmer, are opening up. There are also opportunities associated with the manufacture, sales, and maintenance of computer hardware. As we move into the electronic age there will in addition be many new adaptations of computer technology, such as computer mail and home offices linked by a computer to a central office. However, the rosy picture of high-tech jobs painted by the mass media has been exaggerated. In reality, the vast majority of new jobs in this area will be the low-paying service jobs, with many more openings for data clerks than for computer systems analysts.

Job openings will also be affected by certain demographic trends, based on a projection of population statistics. A major trend involves the maturing of the "baby-boom" generation—those born in the period between World War II and the mid-sixties. This huge group of eighteen- to thirty-six-year-olds, now representing about a third of our population, has become a formidable army of consumers. Their interest in self-gratification, self-improvement, and leisure-

---

[6]*Occupational Outlook Handbook,* 1984–85 edition (Washington, D.C.: U.S. Government Printing Office, 1984), 13–20.

Workers (millions)[1]

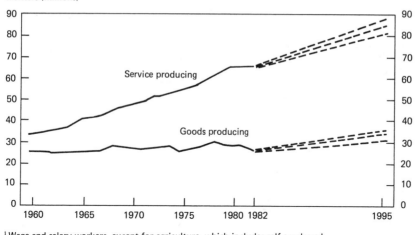

[1] Wage and salary workers, except for agriculture, which includes self-employed and unpaid family workers

NOTE: Dashed lines represent low, moderate, and high projections
SOURCE: Bureau of Labor Statistics

Figure 11-4. Growth of Service Producing Industries. From *Occupational Outlook Handbook,* 1984–85 Edition. (Washington, D.C. Government Printing Office, 1984), 17.

enhancing lifestyles will translate into more business for the housing market, travel agencies, child-care centers, restaurants, frozen-food makers, convenience stores, and high-tech equipment manufacturers. Another demographic trend is the growth of the retired population, with a corresponding increase in the need for medical care facilities, alternatives to hospital care, retirement homes, and limousine services.

Job prospects also depend on the level of education achieved. Now that the median[7] educational level of the work force is over twelve years, those without a high-school education are at a distinct disadvantage. Poorly educated young people with few marketable skills will continue to have the highest unemployment rates. Those who have pursued some post-high-school education and have acquired a marketable skill will be in a much better position, though this varies with the individual and with the field. College graduates will continue to have the lowest unemployment rates. Yet even they are not without their problems. Because the number of college graduates has been increasing faster than the number of positions appropriate for them, about one out of five college graduates may have to settle for a job previously held by someone with less than four years of college.[8] In some instances, college graduates will have to bide their time to find a position in their chosen field. Persistence and previous work experience will be helpful in finally landing the desired job.

[7] The midpoint in the distribution of scores: Half fall above and half fall below this number.
[8] *O.O.H.* op. cit., 14.

TABLE 11–2   Career outlook for the next decade.

Projected Employment Change, 1982–95	Numerical	%
ADMINISTRATIVE & MANAGERIAL OCCUPATIONS		
Accountants and auditors	344,000	40
Bank officers	193,000	45
Retail and wholesale buyers	76,000	30
Health-service administrators	175,000	58
Hotel managers and assistants	15,000	23
Personnel, labor specialists	47,000	23
Purchasing agents	52,000	27
School administrators	20,000	15
Underwriters	16,000	21
ARCHITECTS, SURVEYORS & ENGINEERS		
Architects	33,000	40
Surveyors	19,000	43
Engineers	584,000	49
Aerospace engineers	18,000	41
Chemical engineers	24,000	43
Civil engineers	73,000	47
Electrical engineers	209,000	65
Industrial engineers	67,000	42
Mechanical engineers	109,000	52
Metallurgical engineers	6,600	47
Mining engineers	1,300	22
Nuclear engineers	3,000	48
Petroleum engineers	5,700	22
NATURAL SCIENTISTS & MATHEMATICIANS		
Actuaries	2,700	33
Computer-systems analysts	217,000	85
Mathematicians	3,000	28
Statisticians	5,700	28
Chemists	20,000	22
Geologists and geophysicists	11,000	24
Meteorologists	500	14
Physicists	6,900	37

	Numerical	%
Agricultural scientists	4,000	19
Biological scientists	19,000	36
SOCIAL SCIENTISTS & RELATED WORKERS		
Lawyers	159,000	34
Economists	8,000	27
Psychologists	27,000	33
Sociologists	1,400	25
Urban and regional planners	3,100	15
Social workers	71,000	21
Recreation workers	28,000	23
EDUCATIONAL EMPLOYEES		
Elementary-school teachers	511,000	37
High school teachers	128,000	13
College teachers	−111,000	−15
Counselors	15,000	10
Librarians	19,000	13
HEALTH PRACTITIONERS & TECHNICIANS		
Chiropractors	6,900	27
Dentists	41,000	24
Optometrists	6,900	25
Physicians	163,000	34
Podiatrists	6,700	52
Veterinarians	11,000	30
Dietitions	18,000	40
Occupational therapists	15,000	60
Pharmacists	41,000	27
Physical therapists	25,000	58
Physician assistants	6,000	27
Registered nurses	642,000	49
Respiratory therapists	21,000	45
Speech pathologists and audiologists	12,000	29
Clinical lab technologists	83,000	40
Dental hygienists	30,000	43
EKG technicians	7,700	37
Health-record technicians	9,400	43

Licensed practical nurses	220,000	37
Radiologic technologists	47,000	43
Surgical technicians	14,000	40

WRITERS, ARTISTS & ENTERTAINERS

Public-relations specialists	26,000	29
Announcers and newcasters	15,000	28
Reporters and correspondents	15,000	29
Writers and editors	42,000	35
Commercial/graphic artists	34,000	26
Designers	73,000	41
Photographers	16,000	18
Actors and actresses	15,000	43
Dancers	3,300	43
Musicians	31,000	25
Singers	4,400	21

TECHNOLOGISTS & TECHNICIANS OTHER THAN HEALTH

Air-traffic controllers	900	4
Computer programmers	205,000	77
Drafters	15,000	5
Electrical/electronics techs	222,000	61
Legal assistants	43,000	94
Library technicians	3,000	10

MARKETING & SALES OCCUPATIONS

Cashiers	744,000	47
Insurance agents	90,000	25
Manufacturers' sales workers	64,000	15
Real estate agents/brokers	112,000	33
Retail-trade sales workers	898,000	27
Securities sales workers	28,000	36
Travel agents	26,000	43
Wholesale-trade sales workers	327,000	30

ADMINISTRATIVE-SUPPORT OCCUPATIONS

Bank tellers	154,000	29
Bookkeeping/acctg. clerks	272,000	16
Computer-operating personnel	157,000	27
Mail carriers	−11,000	−5
Postal clerks	−55,000	−18

Receptionists	267,000	45
Transportation ticket agents	2,100	2
Secretaries	719,000	29
Shipping and receiving clerks	66,000	18
Stenographers	−20,000	−7
Teacher aides	130,000	28
Telephone operators	25,000	8
Typists	155,000	16

SERVICE OCCUPATIONS

Correction officers	36,000	33
Firefighters	22,000	9
Guards	300,000	47
Police and detectives, public	43,000	8
Bartenders	121,000	32
Cooks and chefs	402,000	33
Waiters and waitresses	562,000	34
Dental assistants	64,000	42
Medical assistants	48,000	47
Nursing aides, orderlies	423,000	35
Building custodians	779,000	28
Barbers	12,000	10
Cosmetologists	103,000	20
Flight attendants	15,000	29

MECHANICS & REPAIRERS

Aircraft mechanics	20,000	19
Automotive mechanics	324,000	38
Diesel mechanics	48,000	28
Appliance installers/repairers	13,000	17
Computer technicians	53,000	97
Line installers/cable splicers	53,000	27
Radio and TV technicians	22,000	27
Phone and PBX repairers and installers	37,000	28
Air-cond./refrig. mechanics	56,000	33
Industrial-machinery repairers	95,000	29
Millwrights	30,000	33
Office-machine repairers	40,000	72

CONSTRUCTION OCCUPATIONS

Bricklayers and stonemasons	41,000	33
Carpenters	247,000	29

Table 11–2 (*cont.*)

Drywall applicators and tapers	31,000	41		Job and die setters	26,000	27
Electricians	173,000	32		Lithographers and photoengravers	20,000	29
Floor-covering installers	23,000	29		Machinists and layout markers	62,000	26
Glaziers	14,000	35		Photo-process workers	11,000	17
Insulation workers	20,000	44		Tool and diemakers	33,000	21
Ironworkers	36,000	39		Machine-tool operators	200,000	22
Painters	82,000	23		Printing-press operators	32,000	18
Paperhangers	4,700	24		Assemblers	332,000	25
Plumbers and pipefitters	131,000	34		Automotive painters	17,000	46
Roofers	27,000	27		Welders and flamecutters	105,000	21
Sheet-metal workers	40,000	46		**TRANSPORTATION & MATERIAL MOVING**		
PRODUCTION OCCUPATIONS				Airplane pilots	23,000	29
Blue-collar supervisors	320,000	27		Bus drivers	78,000	17
Bookbinders	6,100	20		Building-machinery operators	89,000	44
Butchers and meatcutters	−12,000	−6		Industrial truck operators	70,000	18
Compositors and typesetters	−7,600	−7		Truck drivers	578,000	24
Dental-laboratory technicians	13,000	26				
Jewelers	4,000	13				

These figures show the number of new jobs expected between 1982 and 1995, together with the percentage gain these numbers represent. The general trend is toward an increase in jobs. But where job opportunities are expected to decline, the change is shown with a minus sign, as with college teachers. A rate of growth in the 20 to 29 percent range is average; increases less than 19 percent are slower than average, and increases more than 29 percent are faster than average.

Source: Tom Nardone, "The Job Outlook in Brief, *Occupational Outlook Quarterly,* U. S. Department of Labor, Bureau of Labor Statistics. Spring 1984. (Washington, D.C.: U.S. Government Printing Office, 1984): 9–24.

Your career outlook

What is the outlook for your career? Have you investigated this? Are the job openings expected to grow faster than the average? Or are job prospects expected to grow more slowly than the average? You should keep in mind that your own career outlook involves a number of special factors like the unusual opportunities available to you, your special abilities and experience, and especially your personal drive. For example, if you want to work in a field like agriculture or farming, you will have to be particularly persistent and resourceful. Also, you may have to be more flexible. Instead of owning your own farm, which is increasingly expensive and risky, you may have to settle for a job managing someone else's farm. Or you could take another job and farm on a part-time basis.

Also keep in mind emerging work patterns. Each year about 2 million *new* jobs open up.[9] Are you aware of these newer types of jobs? For example, few people anticipated all the new jobs that opened up following the energy crisis of the '70s. Yet some alert individuals have made a profitable career selling smaller, more economical cars, or energy-saving devices for the home. Another possibility is the growth in self-employment. Individuals who work best on their own are increasingly apt to form small companies. For example, one man founded a small firm which handles toxic waste material. This is a service for which there will be growing need in the future. A woman who quit her secretarial job to have children later organized a secretarial service that enables homemakers to earn money on a part-time basis without sacrificing their responsibilities at home. Also, people are putting together more than one job to make a career. A man I know, for example, teaches drafting in a small college, serves as a consultant in industrial design, and manages several pieces of real estate with his wife. Some individuals hold down not two or three, but four or five part-time jobs, all of which add up to one full-time career, providing interest and variety.

Changing your career goal

If you're uncertain or unhappy about your career goal, you may want to change it. As you may recall, one of the main pitfalls in choosing a career is the refusal to modify your original goal. It has been estimated that about two-thirds of entering college freshmen start out taking courses leading in the wrong direction. Fortunately, many of them change their majors. Yet as many

[9]R.N. Bolles, *What Color Is Your Parachute?* (Berkeley, CA: Ten Speed Press, 1984), 175.

as 50 percent of those who graduate from four-year colleges and universities find they majored in the wrong subject.[10] As unsettling as this may be, what is more disturbing is that even when students realize they are on the wrong educational track, many of them refuse to change. They would rather complete the wrong program than pay the price of switching. But why?

Students may be reluctant to change their career goals for any number of reasons. Sometimes they would rather stick with their original goal than risk disappointing their parents and peers. Students forget they are choosing for themselves, not for their parents. Switching goals may also be seen as an admission of failure. Yet to continue in a direction you have misgivings about will only make matters worse. In addition, students may overestimate the price of changing career goals. Switching goals usually involves some backtracking, such as taking a few required courses. But after getting all the facts, the penalties may not be as great as expected.

Now that we've considered some of the reasons people refuse to change career goals, how about you? If you realized you were on the wrong educational track or were in an incompatible career, would you admit it? Have you weighed the short-term losses with the long-term gains? Do you realize that a small sacrifice now may greatly increase your career satisfaction for the rest of your life? Whatever your responses to these questions, keep in mind that roughly one worker in nine changes his or her career each year.[11] In most cases, the positive gains far outweigh the costs involved, for there's nothing to compare with really enjoying what you do in life, and being paid for it as well.

SUMMARY

1. We began the chapter by emphasizing the value of choosing a compatible career. Such a process usually requires an understanding of your own interests and abilities, an exploration of various career options and, most important of all, matching yourself with a compatible career. Use of the "balance sheet" method may be helpful in arriving at the final choice.

2. The required preparation for a career depends mostly on your career goal. Some careers, like carpentry and plumbing, are entered through apprenticeship and on-the-job training programs. Other careers like secretarial services require training in the appropriate vocational or technical school. A wide variety of careers require a two-year or four-year college degree, or in the case of professions like medicine, an advanced degree. Although college graduates continue to have the

[10]Elwood N. Chapman, *Career Search* (Chicago, IL: Science Research Associates, Inc., 1976), 119.
[11]*O.O.H.,* op. cit., 3.

highest lifetime earnings and lowest unemployment rates, they also face increasing competition for appropriate jobs.

3. The projected growth in jobs is better in some careers than others, with a bright future expected in many of the technological and service-oriented careers. Yet many other factors, like your abilities and personal drive, should be taken into consideration in evaluating your future. We also stressed the importance of changing your career goal if you're uncertain or unhappy about your career. Approximately one out of nine workers changes his or her career each year.

SELF-TEST

1. The process of choosing a compatible career involves:
   a. knowing your interests and abilities
   b. discovering the careers available to you
   c. matching yourself with a compatible career
   d. all of the above

2. Instruments such as the *Strong-Campbell Interest Inventory* help to predict _____ in a given career.
   a. how successful you'll be
   b. how likely you are to remain
   c. how happy you'll be
   d. how competent you'll be

3. Conscientious, efficient people who prefer well-ordered jobs, like clerical workers and traffic managers, score high on John Holland's _____ personality-occupational type.
   a. investigative   c. social
   b. conventional   d. artistic

4. People who want to become a carpenter or electrician usually get trained in:
   a. an apprenticeship   c. a two-year college
   b. military service   d. a technical school

5. Workers are trained in the special skills requred by a particular company like General Motors in _____ programs.
   a. university education   c. vocational school
   b. on-the-job training   d. two-year college

6. More than half of all students in their first two years of college are enrolled in:
   a. state universities   c. two-year community colleges
   b. four-year colleges   d. vocational schools

7. People interested in a nursing career could obtain the necessary education in a _____ program.
   a. two-year community college nursing
   b. hospital-affiliated nursing school
   c. four-year nursing school
   d. all of the above

8. The projected job openings are greatest in which of the following
   careers?
   a. secretaries   c. plumbers
   b. farm workers   d. unskilled laborers

9. _____ educated youth with few marketable skills will continue to have the highest unemployment rates.
   a. college   c. poorly
   b. high school   d. vocational school

10. Students may be reluctant to change their career goals out of fear that
    switching may be:
    a. disappointing to their parents
    b. seen as an admission of failure
    c. excessively expensive
    d. all of the above

EXERCISES

1. *Identifying your career interests.* Make an exhaustive list of all the activities
   you've enjoyed doing. Include school courses, projects, hobbies, sports,
   and full- or part-time jobs. Be certain to include some recent activities
   as well as those from earlier periods in your life.

   Now select a dozen or so of the most satisfying activities, and
   list them in order from the most enjoyable down. For each activity, ask
   yourself what made it so satisfying? Was it the activity itself? Was it the
   people you did it with? Or was it mostly the recognition or money
   involved? Generally, activities which are intrinsically enjoyable give the
   best indication of what you'll like to do in your career.

2. *Matching your personality with compatible careers.* Review Holland's six
   personality-occupational types or themes explained earlier in the chapter. Then select the three types that best characterize your personality-
   occupational type in order.

   Now look at the sample careers listed under each personality-
   occupational type you've selected. Also, rotate all the rankings in your
   selected types. For example, if your top three choices were RIE, then
   examine the careers for IRE, EIR, and ERI too. Check to see if your

library or counseling center has the *Occupational Finder Booklet* that accompanies Holland's Self-directed Search. If so, look up the careers associated with your most compatible occupational-personality types.

3. *Use the balance sheet to clarify your career goal.* If you're uncertain about your career goal, use the balance sheet to weigh the pros and cons of your career. Reread the explanation of the "balance sheet" technique earlier in the chapter, and follow the model given in Table 11–1. To arrive at a decision, examine the relative importance of the various points as well as comparing the number of positive and negative points respectively.

4. *Complete a career interest inventory.* Do a self-directed career inventory or one that requires professional supervision. Representative inventories are described briefly in the section of the chapter on identifying compatible careers. The most appropriate place to find these inventories is the counseling or career guidance center in your school. Perhaps an interested teacher or counselor could suggest the most appropriate one for you to take.

5. *Exploring your chosen career.* How much do you know about your chosen career? You might find it helpful to look up some basic information in a resource like the *Occupational Outlook Handbook.* Copies of this book or comparable resources can be found in your college library or counseling center.

Look up your chosen career, or one you're interested in. Then write down information on the following: (1) description of the work; (2) places of employment; (3) educational and entry requirements; and (4) employment outlook. This exercise should give you a more realistic view of your career goal and how to achieve it.

Finding
a Job

12

IDENTIFY POTENTIAL EMPLOYERS
    Creative job hunting
    Group job hunting
    Suggested resources

CONTACT POTENTIAL EMPLOYERS
    Telephone calls
    The résumé
    The letter
    The application

PREPARE FOR THE EMPLOYMENT
INTERVIEW
    Be prepared
    Questions you can expect
    Some do's and don'ts

KEEP AT IT
    Be persistent
    Make follow-ups
    Keep a positive attitude

SUMMARY

SELF-TEST

EXERCISES

Kim recently received a two-year degree in human services and now she is looking for a full-time job in her field. Meanwhile, she's working part time at the senior citizen's center where she did her internship. During a coffee break, she talks with Denise, a friend who works full time at the center.

"I'm having trouble finding a job," sighs Kim.

"It's tough these days," says Denise.

"I must have sent out fifty résumés. But I've had very little response."

"That's so discouraging."

"You can say that again."

"Have you seen anything promising on the human services bulletin board?" asks Denise.

"Not really."

"Has the college placement office been helpful?"

"They gave me several places to check out. But so far I haven't heard from them."

Then Denise asks, "Did you go to Tom Jackson's workshop on 'Guerilla Tactics in the Job Market' last spring?"

"No. I wanted to," says Kim, "but I had to work that afternoon. Did you go?"

"Yes, It was good," replies Denise.

"What did he say?" asks Kim.

"One thing that stuck with me," Denise says, "is that it's not the most qualified people who get the best jobs. It's those who are the most skilled in finding jobs."

"You mean those with the best connections," Kim says.

"I don't think that's what he meant," laughs Denise. "His main point was that more than three-quarters of the available jobs aren't listed. So people like you and me have to take the lead in finding these jobs."

"I don't understand."

"Well, as I get it," continues Denise, "it takes large companies two to six months to get a job listed. So by the time we see the job notices in the newspaper, it may have already been filled by someone inside the company. That's why Jackson says you have to take the initiative to find out about the available jobs in the early stages—ahead of the mob."

"That makes sense," muses Kim.

"Hey," says Denise. "I just remembered. We were given a several-page outline of Jackson's presentation at the door. Why don't you check to see if the counseling center has some left?"

"I sure will."

IDENTIFY POTENTIAL EMPLOYERS

Kim is looking for a job in the usual way, and with typical results. She's frustrated and discouraged. She may be tempted to take the first job offer, whether it's right for her or not. Unhappily, Kim's experience will be repeated by millions of people each year. Because there is no real system of job placement in our country, finding a job is mostly a trial-and-error affair. The job-hunting process is so dependent on luck that the average applicant secretly hopes for a miracle. If you just persevere, someone will offer you the right job. But it seldom happens this way.

The conventional approach to job hunting has been called the *numbers game*. That is, in order to get the job you want, you must have two or three job offers to choose from. In order to have several job offers, you should have at least six interviews with different employers. And in order to get six interviews— so runs the usual advice—you must send out fifty to one hundred résumés or more. But as most job hunters will attest, the typical result is a great deal of frustration and very few job offers.

Today, some experts in the field are suggesting a different approach, which has been called the *creative approach*. We'll begin by describing some of its main features. Then in the rest of the chapter we'll explain the basic strategies involved, including identifying potential employers, contacting employers, and handling the employment interview. Finally, we'll discuss some general suggestions about creative job hunting as a whole.

Creative job hunting

Well-known authorities like Richard Bolles and Tom Jackson suggest that you begin looking for a job by taking stock of yourself rather than scanning the want ads. Instead of sending out résumés in a "shotgun" fashion, you're urged to sit down and determine what you really want to do and what you have to offer. Once you've clarified your career goal, you'll have a better idea of what type of job you want and where to look for it. Much of this has already been discussed in the preceding chapter on choosing a career.

Bolles and Jackson repeatedly emphasize that the key to successful job hunting is to become an active, self-directed participant in the process. Remember that most available jobs never appear in print. Also, by the time jobs are listed in print, many of them are already filled. Accordingly, job seekers are urged to take the initiative and become resourceful in identifying potential employers, and not just to stick to the jobs in the classified ads. Once you've made a list of potential employers, you're encouraged to make personal contact with them, either by phone or in person. Résumés thus play a subordinate role in creative job hunting. You're also encouraged to prepare for the employment interview. Become knowledgeable about the company and try to discover its needs. Then show how you can help fulfil the company's needs. Finally, applicants must realize that job hunting is itself a full-time job which takes the average person about six months. Because of this it's natural to become discouraged; successful job applicants must strive to keep a positive attitude and to take the inevitable rejections in stride.[1]

When I first heard of the concept of creative job hunting, I thought it was rather demanding, if not unrealistic, for the typical job applicant. Yet after a little reflection, I realized I'd been using this approach all along. For example, when I wanted to publish my first textbook, there were no ads for prospective authors. So I began by asking myself what I had to say and what kind of book I was best qualified to write. Then I wondered where to begin. I decided to visit the publishers' exhibits at the annual convention of the American Psychological Association. I spoke with the editors who were present at the booths as well as the field reps who visit the various colleges. I asked about the types of books they were interested in and how to go about submitting a

[1]Mike Marcon and Margot Worthington, *Twelve Steps to Finding a Job Under $30,000 in Four Weeks* (Englewood Cliffs, N.J.: Prentice-Hall, Inc., 1984), 2.

manuscript. By the end of the day, I'd made a list of five publishers who were in the market for the kind of book I wanted to write. Upon my return home, I wrote three sample chapters and sent them off to the five publishers. Later, three of the publishers offered me a contract. I chose to work with Prentice-Hall in the end, and the book I wrote is still in print.

As you can see, I didn't just wait for an invitation to write a book. I didn't even accept the first publisher's offer. Instead, I took the time and effort to determine what type of book I wanted to write, which publishers were in the market for such a book, and eventually, which publisher I wanted to work with. Successful job hunting is a lot like this.

How Have You Found Jobs?

Think back to the way you've found jobs. Include past and present jobs, and part-time as well as full-time jobs.

How did you find out about the job? Where did you see it listed? Did a friend tell you about it? What role has good luck played in getting a job? Would you agree that successful job hunting demands that you take the initiative?

Keep in mind that the average worker changes jobs ten times or more in his or her lifetime. Are you willing to leave such important moves to chance? Or are you interested in developing job-finding skills you can use throughout your career?

Group job hunting

Too often, job hunting is a lonely endeavor. But now job hunters are getting together, and *group job hunting* is the result. One of the most popular group approaches is Nathan Azrin's job-finding clubs, of which there are over one hundred now established throughout the country. Azrin stresses that the group approach may provide many individuals with the specific job-seeking skills and group support they need.

In an early experimental project, 120 job hunters were recruited into the job-finding club. Most were in their mid-twenties and had an average of fourteen years of education. Individuals were matched into pairs according to the probability of their finding a job. Then one member of each pair was randomly assigned either to the job-finding club or a *no-treatment* control group. Those in the latter group were simply encouraged to find work on their own.

Members of the job-finding club pursued employment on a full-time basis. They were seen daily in small groups consisting of two to eight members. They were encouraged to contact relatives and friends about job openings. They wrote letters, made telephone calls, and attended interviews. Supervision was given on writing résumés and letters of application. Members participated in role playing to improve their skill at making telephone calls and being interviewed. They were also shown how to dress appropriately for an interview, keep records of their contacts, and make follow-up calls. Personal contact was emphasized throughout the project. Individuals were encouraged to see the employer in person whenever possible, or at least to speak with this person on the phone using the name of the referring party.

The results showed that two-thirds of the club members found jobs within one month, compared to just one-third of the control group. Members of the job-finding clubs found jobs within an average of fourteen days, versus fifty-three days for others. Furthermore, club members were more likely to find higher-level, professional jobs, with an average pay one-third higher than non–club members. Among the sixty members of the job-finding club, there were only five failures. Most of these had either attended irregularly or dropped out early.[2]

If you're interested in joining a job-finding group, you may inquire about this at your college placement office or local state employment service.

Job hunters may benefit from group guidance and support.

[2]N.H. Azrin, T. Flores, and S.J. Kaplan, "Job-finding Club: A Group-assisted Program for Obtaining Employment," *Behavior Research and Therapy* 15 (1975): 17–27.

Suggested resources

Because there is no one foolproof strategy for job hunting, it's advisable to use a variety of resources to identify potential employers. Richard Bolles readily admits that the creative job hunter uses many of the same resources as the conventional job hunter does, but with a different attitude.[3] Well aware of their limitations, the creative job hunter uses such resources as part of an overall strategy rather than relying on them alone. The major resources for identifying potential employers are incorporated in the following suggestions.

1. *Register with your college placement center.* These are increasingly common in today's tight job market. Usually you fill out an application, giving information about courses taken, grades, activities, and work experience. Letters of recommendation are often required. You may also be asked to come in for an interview to talk about your ideas for a job. Help and suggestions may be given on such matters as writing letters of application, résumés, interviewing for a job, and following up job leads. Sometimes a nominal charge may be required for reproducing and sending out placement papers.

2. *Contact your state employment office.* The United States Employment Service (USES) has a number of employment offices in every state, usually located in the major cities. Each state office provides information on labor market changes, trends, and job openings on a national basis. USES provides services for not only entry-level workers, but for the full range of job opportunities, though middle-management workers and executives tend to avoid it. After completing an extensive application, you are interviewed and classified according to your education, career preferences, and work experience. Your credentials are then matched with available job openings as these occur. Ordinarily, you're expected to contact prospective employers. No fee is charged.

3. *Check out private employment agencies.* These are springing up all over the place. Many specialize in certain types of positions, such as managerial, or certain fields, like data processing. Because these agencies vary greatly in their effectiveness, you're strongly advised to check out an agency before using it. Ask the opinions of staff members at your college placement center or friends who have been through a job search recently.

    Most commercial agencies thrive on a volume business requiring a rapid turnover of clientele, which favors the most marketable job hunters. For example, when Larry, a computer programmer, was laid

---

[3]Richard N. Bolles, *What Color Is Your Parachute?* (Berkeley, CA: Ten Speed Press, 1983), 17.

off in a cost-cutting move, he quickly found another job and his new company paid the agency's fee. Applicants in less marketable jobs would not fare so well.

4. *Contact family members and friends.* Let them know you're looking for a job. Ask them to inquire about job openings at their workplace and elsewhere. The beauty of this approach is that your family and friends already know you and believe in you. They may or may not be familiar with the type of job you want, however, so take some time to tell each of them what you're looking for. Check periodically to see if they've uncovered any leads. Also, be sure to follow up all suggested openings. Otherwise they might not be convinced that you appreciate their help. As you might expect, more jobs are found this way than any other way.

5. *Look for job openings in newspaper ads and trade journals.* Notices of job openings appear in most major newspapers as well as many community newspapers, usually in the *classified* section. Trade or professional journals are an even better source of ads, mostly because the job openings are confined to a given field of employment. Ask your college librarian to assist you in getting copies of the appropriate journals in your field. You should also be aware that most responses to classified ads, especially to newspaper ads, are quickly screened out, so that only a few are seriously considered. As a result, in answering an ad your goal should be to get invited for an interview. Accordingly, tailor your letter or résumé to fit the listed specifications as closely as possible. Avoid everything else. If the ad requests a salary requirement, either ignore it or give a salary range, adding the words *depending on the nature and scope of responsibilities.* Why give a potential employer an excuse for screening you out?

6. *Subscribe to job registers or clearing houses.* These have become increasingly popular in recent years. Most of them serve as "job exchanges" where employers and job hunters can meet. There are both federal and private job registers. Some are general. Others are more specialized, e.g., for business or data processing. Some list employer vacancies or job hunters' abbreviated résumés; others list both. Most charge a fee.

   A typical register will list many more clients than job openings at any one time. Some registers will notify employers of every eligible client; others select only the best qualified ones. Ask what the policy is when you sign up. As with the private employment agencies, you might get more for your money from the newer, rapidly expanding registers than the older ones. Since the company pays the fee in many cases, loyalty probably goes to the employer rather than to the job hunter.

   A variety of job registers are described in Richard Bolle's annual edition of *What Color is Your Parachute?*

7. *Use as many resources as you find helpful.* According to one survey, the greater the number of resources used by the job hunter, the greater

his or her success in finding a suitable job.[4] In most cases, you'll want to use a combination of the above resources. Perhaps you can think of others. You're limited only by your imagination, energy, and resourcefulness.

Kay began looking for a job during her last semester in the hospitality management program. She put in her application with the college placement center, and began looking in the classified ads in a couple of appropriate trade journals. The best job offers came through the program director and the trade journals. But most were inconveniently located. Meanwhile, she responded to an ad for a part-time job on the college placement center bulletin board, thinking it would be just for the summer. After two months on the job, Kay's employer was so pleased with her work that she was offered the job on a full-time basis. A couple of years later, she found an even better job through one of the contacts suggested by her program director at the college. Like so many people, Kay has learned that it's best to pursue as many different leads to jobs as you can; you never know which will result in the best job offer.

CONTACT POTENTIAL EMPLOYERS

Once you're ready to contact potential employers, keep in mind the following: First, try to make personal contacts with potential employers, whether on the phone or in person. A personal contact helps you to stand out from the crowd and avoid getting lost in the impersonal paperwork of the employment process. Second, whenever possible make direct contact with the person who has the power to hire you. For example, if you're looking for a sales job, contact the sales manager of the company you're interested in. In many cases, especially with entry-level jobs, you may have to go through the personnel department or its equivalent. But when in doubt, it's usually better to go too high rather than too low in the company hierarchy. The person you contact can always refer you back to the appropriate department.

Telephone calls

About three-quarters of all want ads offer a phone number for reply, making the telephone a major means of initial contacts with employers.[5] By using the phone you avoid wasting your time, gas, and tires, not to mention avoiding the aggravation of finding the person you've gone to see is busy or out. Also you can set up a week or more of appointments on your own terms.

[4]Ibid., 17.
[5]Marcon and Worthington, op. cit., 127.

Most calls will be answered by a receptionist or secretary. Some people in these positions are overprotective of their bosses, and may begin asking a lot of questions. Others, especially those in large, established companies, may simply ask, 'Who's calling?" and connect you with your party. The opening of the conversation may go something like this:

RECEPTIONIST: National Computer Company.

YOU: Good morning. May I please have the name of your sales manager?

RECEPTIONIST: That would be Mr. Hughes.

YOU: Thank you. May I speak with Mr. Hughes, please.

If you're going to have trouble reaching your party, this is the point at which you're likely to encounter resistance. The receptionist might ask, "May I tell Mr. Hughes the nature of your business?" To reply, "I'm looking for a job," is to invite certain rejection. This is understandable in a time when many employers feel overwhelmed with calls and letters from job hunters. To avoid being screened out at this stage, it's best to state your purpose in calling in a more subtle way. You might say something like, "I'd like to speak with Mr. Hughes about a matter pertaining to the marketing division of your company," and let it go at that.

When you reach the person you're calling, begin by addressing that person by his or her name. Then identify yourself, and when possible the name of the person who has referred you. According to one strategy, you shouldn't go after a job too directly at this point. Be more subtle. Ask about what sort of opportunities are opening up in the field, and whether the person foresees any such openings at his or her company. However, many people in management positions are busy and might appreciate a more direct approach. If you feel this is the case, state your credentials, the type of job you're seeking, and ask if you can come in, fill out an application, and speak further about this matter. If the answer is *yes,* your call is a success. If not, then reply you'd like to send a résumé in case something opens up in the future. If the person discourages this, you might simply write a thank-you letter and include your telephone number, your qualifications, and the type of job you're seeking. After all, neither you nor the other person can be certain if or when such a position might open up.

How many calls should you make? If you're going by the numbers' game, you can expect to get about one interview for every ten calls. But if you've done your homework and make calls more selectively, you may get more interviews with the same number of calls. Either way, it's best not to schedule more than two or three interviews in a day. Also, it's preferable to schedule your interviews on Tuesdays, Wednesdays, and Thursdays, and perhaps Friday mornings. But on Friday afternoons and on Mondays, employers, like other workers, may be mentally preparing for, or getting over, the weekend.[6]

[6]Ibid., 123.

How Am I Doing?

Have you ever wondered how you're coming across to a potential employer on the phone? Telephone calls are one of the most effective ways of contacting employers if you know how to use the phone. Yet many job hunters don't know how to talk on the phone. Worse still, they keep repeating their mistakes because no one is there to give them immediate feedback.

A helpful way to improve your telephone calls to potential employers is to use a buddy system, as required in Azrin's job-finding clubs. Ask a friend who is also looking for a job to join you. Then when you contact a prospective employer by phone, have your buddy listen in on an extension and afterwards make suggestions to improve your conversation. Later, you can listen in while your buddy makes similar phone calls, and suggest ways for improving his or her approach.

The résumé

The résumé, usually pronounced rez'-e-mā, is a summary or short account of your education and employment experience, prepared for potential employers. Applicants usually prepare their own résumé, though in today's tight job market many individuals are seeking consultation as they go about it.

A résumé may serve several functions. First of all, preparing the résumé may act as a kind of self-inventory and help you to organize the essential information. Second, a résumé may serve as a guide for the employment interview, thereby allowing you to help set the agenda for the interview. Third, résumés may serve as an extended calling card, with the primary purpose of getting you invited for an interview. Résumés are most frequently used for this purpose. Finally, a résumé may serve as a memory jogger for the employer after the interview.

In writing a résumé, you should observe several principles. First, make it brief—preferably one page. Second, make it clear and readable, not only in regard to the selection and order of the contents but their presentation on the page. Third, tell the truth about yourself, but select carefully what you say. Never say anything negative about yourself that might cause you to be screened out. Last, but not least, have your résumé professionally typed and duplicated.

There is no one résumé format which you *must* use. But there are several common types which may be used for various purposes, as described in Tom Jackson's book *The Perfect Résumé.* You should decide which type of résumé best displays what you have to offer an employer.[7]

The *chronological* résumé puts the emphasis on your work experience, with your job history spelled out from the most recent job backward. Titles and

[7]Tom Jackson, *The Perfect Résumé* (Garden City, N.Y.: Anchor/Doubleday Press, 1981), 65–68.

organizations are emphasized, with duties and accomplishments described. Advantages of this type of résumé are that it emphasizes continuity and career growth, highlights the names of employers, and is easy to follow. It's best used when you're looking for a job which is directly related to previous positions held, or when the name of your last employer is prestigious.

The *targeted* résumé is focused on a clear, specific job target. It lists only those abilities and accomplishments that relate to the job target. Even if you lack much experience in a particular field but have acquired relevant skills and

---

Sample Résumé
(Functional Form)

Marilyn Morris
892 Hemlock Avenue
San Jose, California 95132
(408) 655-9813

OLDER ADULTS

Worked with older adults in a senior citizens' center, including supervision of educational and social programs.

Served as volunteer in an outreach program maintaining daily telephone contact between single adults living in the community.

Wrote paper on "Sex Differences in Aging."

TEACHING AND COUNSELING

Served as counselor and teacher in summer camp for mentally retarded adults.

Taught in tutorial program for learning disabled adolescents.

WORK EXPERIENCE

1984–85   Human services intern in the Senior Citizens Center, Collegeville, California

AWARDS

1982   Sarah Mitchell Award for Volunteer of the Year, San Jose Optimist's Club

EDUCATION

1985   A.A.S. in Human Services, Woodstock Community College

knowledge through education, a targeted résumé may be suitable. Sometimes, a combination of chronological and targeted résumé works well if you have some related job experience and also possess skills obtained through training. Advantages of the targeted résumé include the fact that it makes a very impressive case for the job you select, and demonstrates a strong understanding and ability in the targeted area. It is best used only when you're clear about your job target.

The *functional* résumé highlights your major strengths and accomplishments but allows you to organize them in a way that best supports your work objective. Actual titles and work history are put in a subordinate position or left off entirely. Advantages of the functional résumé are that it provides considerable flexibility in your emphasis, eliminates repetition of job assignments, and deemphasizes experience. It's best used when you're seeking your first job, reentering the job market, or changing careers.

The letter

The letter has several uses in the job hunting process. First, you may choose to send a cover letter with your résumé, highlighting certain points in the résumé. A letter may also be sent instead of a résumé, especially by those with little work experience or background. Someone you've contacted by phone may ask you to put your qualifications in writing. Or you may be sent an application to complete, in which case an accompanying letter would be appropriate.

A letter says a lot about yourself, not only in what you write but how you write it. Your letter should be clear, neat, and to the point, preferably one page. It is very important to observe the rules of good grammar, especially spelling. If in doubt, have someone to check your letter before you type up the final copy.

The form of the letter depends partly on personal taste. Two of the most popular forms are the blocked letter and the indented line letter. In the

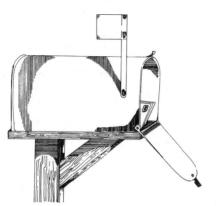

Figure 12-1

blocked letter all the lines of the body of the letter begin with the left hand margin. Only the return address, consisting of the writer's address and date, and sometimes the complimentary close, start from the right hand side of the page. In the indented line letter, the more traditional form, the opening line of each paragraph is indented, usually five spaces. It is also important to be consistent in the number of spaces indented.

The body of the letter—your message—should be brief. Ask yourself what the purpose of the letter is. Everything should be directed to this purpose. If you're responding to an ad or applying for a particular position, then state this in your opening sentence. Otherwise, use the opening sentence to attract the attention of the reader. The middle paragraph should describe your qualifications for the job. Here you might elaborate on anything in your résumé that would strengthen your chances of getting the job, including your education or work experience. The concluding paragraph should request an interview. Ordinarily, the interview is scheduled at the employer's convenience. But if you're available only at certain times because of your present employment, you should state this here.

Sample of Blocked Letter Form

1630 Maple Hill Road
Ambler, Pennsylvania
April 12, 1985

Mr. William Palmer
Personnel Director
Samson and Associates
Certified Public Accountants
2460 Chestnut Street
Landsdale, Pa. 19446

Dear Mr. Palmer:

Dr. David Lander, Chairman of the Business Department at Montgomery College, suggested that I write you about a position in your firm. I would like to apply for a position as an accounting clerk.

I've been majoring in accounting at Montgomery College and expect to receive my degree this June. I've also gained some professional experience the past two summers. I've worked for Mr. Fred Hansen, C.P.A. of Ambler, who said he would be glad to serve as a reference for me.

I would welcome an opportunity for an interview at your conveninece. I can be reached at the return address above or by telephone at 643-6417.

Yours sincerely,

Matt Benson

Matt Benson

The application

Ordinarily, you'll have to complete an employment application, which prospective employers will read before interviewing you. The initial impression you make depends partly on how well you complete the employment application. If you can obtain the application form in advance, take it home and type out the informationn. Otherwise, *print* the necessary information as neatly as possible. Also, use *black ink,* as tests have shown that black ink makes a better impression on interviewers.[8]

Although the required information varies somewhat with the employer, be prepared to provide the following items:

1. NAME. Print your full name, indicating the name you prefer to be called.
2. SOCIAL SECURITY NUMBER. Always carry this with you.
3. DRIVER'S LICENSE NUMBER.
4. PRESENT ADDRESS. House or apartment numbers are preferable to post office box numbers.
5. PERMANENT ADDRESS. Simply write *same as above* if this is the case. Otherwise, supply your home address.
6. TELEPHONE NUMBER. Always include your area code. If you don't have a phone, arrange for someone to take calls for you.
7. EDUCATION. Include the school name, curriculum, diplomas or degrees, and dates of graduation.
8. SPECIAL SKILLS.
9. PREVIOUS EMPLOYMENT. Include name of employers, job titles, and dates of employment.
10. REFERENCES. Get permission from people before using their names.
11. POSITION. If you're not certain, ask someone for the exact title of the job you're seeking.
12. SALARY. It's best to jot down a term like *negotiable* to keep this important matter open for discussion.

Employers are not supposed to ask for irrelevant personal information because of the legislation concerning equal employment opportunities. Such information includes your sex, race, religion, national origin, marital status, mental handicaps, and past arrests. Employers do have a right to know if you've attained the necessary qualifications for employment. But other personal information is not required unless it is for the purposes of national security.

[8]Marcon and Worthington, op. cit., 106.

Suppose you were fired, or quit your last job under unfavorable circumstances. Should you list the employer? Much depends of course on your particular situation. But generally, honesty is the best policy. If you omit a former employer, how are you going to explain the gap in your work history? It's best to list all past employers, and be prepared to deal with potential trouble-spots. If possible, make a personal visit to your former employer and find out where you stand with this person. If you feel the person's reference might hurt you, then be prepared to explain your views when you're interviewed. Explain your view as briefly and objectively as possible. If you realize you were in the wrong, say so, and point out the steps you've taken to correct your mistakes. The wisdom of being honest in such matters is implied in Sir Walter Scott's poetic warning, "O what a tangled web we weave, when first we practice to deceive."

PREPARE FOR THE EMPLOYMENT INTERVIEW

Interviewing is something you do throughout the job-hunting process. Even in the initial contacts with the company, you need basic interviewing skills to get what you want from the receptionists and secretaries. Once you've reached the desired person in the company, many of the early interviews are largely for the purpose of getting information. At this stage you're active in the interview, building contacts and tracking down leads. At a later stage, you're more likely to be interviewed for hire. Having narrowed down your choices, you want to demonstrate why you're the best person for the job. In a given job search, the typical job hunter will have a dozen or so interviews to get three or four job offers. So it is important to learn how to handle interviews well.

Be prepared

The single most important requirement for a successful interview is to be prepared. Familiarize yourself with the types of questions applicants are asked. Then think through your own answers to them. Learn something about the organization interviewing you. What are its strengths? What are some of its needs and problems? How can someone like you be helpful to this organization? Know what you're looking for in a job. During the interview find out what sort of future there is for you with this organization. These are some of the issues you need to think through before you go to the employment interview.

You should be aware that there are different types of interviews. Many employers prefer an informal, or "free" interview, in which the interviewer follows no organized plan and may ask whatever questions come to mind. The biggest dangers are an uneven coverage of the applicant's background and credentials, with the personal bias of the interviewer contaminating the results. Speaking of the psychological interview required of police in one department, one recruit said, "All the psychologist did was to ask questions like 'When your son disobeys, how do you discipline him?' What does this have to do with police work?" I assured him that despite the apparent irrelevance of this question, such an indirect approach may be a valuable way of finding out how a potential police recruit handles authority and aggression—an important consideration in police work.

Interviewers may follow a patterned or standardized format in which the applicant is allowed to do most of the talking, but the conversation is steered along lines pertaining to his or her background, such as education, work experience, job history, and special skills. Some critics claim the planned interview usually follows a slavish pattern without regard for the client's individuality. But in my experience interviewers inevitably adapt this format to each applicant. For example, I served on a search committee to find a new head for the nursing department in our college. Although a set format was agreed upon, the interviews varied considerably from one applicant to another. Part of the explanation is the spontaneity inherent in a group meeting. Another reason is the applicant's personality and background. I was amazed at how much each applicant influenced the course of the interview, not only by her manner of answering the questions, but by initiating questions of her own as well.

Questions you can expect

A good way of preparing yourself for the interview is to mentally rehearse your answers to some of the questions commonly asked by employers. You might even ask a friend to role-play an employer and practice your answers orally. Richard Bolles suggests that most companies, whether they beat around the bush or come right out and ask, want your answers to several basic questions.[9]

1. *Why are you here?* Employers naturally want to know why you're leaving your present job. If you're unemployed, they'll want to know why you left your last job. Most important of all, why have you chosen their company? Also, are you applying to other companies? If so, which ones?

2. *What can you do for us?* Questions like this provide you with an opportunity to demonstrate your awareness of the company's needs and problems. You should let them know what special skills you possess and how these may help the company do a better job. Also, be careful to listen to what the interviewer has to say about the company.

---

[9]Bolles, op. cit., 182.

Being well prepared will help you relax during the job interview.

3. *What kind of person are you?* This concern may be expressed in a variety of specific questions such as: What are your goals and values? What are your job-related strengths and weaknesses? How do you see yourself in this company ten years from now?

4. *How much are you going to cost us?* Sometime during the interview, the employer will probably mention the salary. If not, you should ask what the salary is, and indicate whether that amount is satisfactory for you. If the interviewer mentions a salary range, you might respond in terms of an alternative salary range. But make certain to set your minimum near the top of their salary range, adding you're more interested in the opportunities and challenges of the job than the money.

Employers may also ask you a number of other legitimate questions, depending on your background and their special needs. But they should not inquire about such personal matters as your marital status, as mentioned earlier. Your privacy is protected under equal employment legislation.

Look Your Interviewer in the Eye

Did you know that interviewers form a more favorable impression of you when you look them in the eye? Eye contact conveys interest, sincerity, and honesty. Avoidance of eye contact creates the impression, rightly or wrongly, that you're bored, insincere, or holding something back. Unfortunately, by not meeting the eye of others, shy people risk creating an unfavorable impression.

But be careful not to overdo it. In their zeal to make a positive impression, some people look at others so intently they make them feel uncomfortable.

Typically, partners in conversation adopt an alternate "look" and "look-away" pattern. It's as if constant looking would be distracting. Throughout the conversation, both the speaker's eyes and listener's eyes will meet briefly for a few seconds before looking away. The listener of the moment is more apt to initiate eye contact as if to say, "I'm listening." To create a favorable impression, all you need do is be aware of this natural pattern and look your interviewer in the eye, as long as you don't overdo it.

Some do's and don'ts

The overall impression you make depends on many other factors. An interviewer often forms an impression of you, positive or negative, in the first five minutes of the interview. Much of what you're judged on involves factors like your appearance, grooming, and nonverbal behavior. Practical wisdom on such matters can be summed up in some do's and don'ts in interviewing.

When interviewing, try to *do* the following:

1. *Dress appropriately for the job.* Ordinarily, this means wearing a good-looking suit or dress. If in doubt what to wear, notice what others working for the organization wear, and dress similarly.

2. *Observe good grooming.* This includes clean teeth, clean fingernails, and the use of deodorant. The more trimmed the hair and beard on males, the better the impression.

3. *Be attentive.* Sit up straight in your chair. Look the interviewer in the eye. Show interest in the job. Most important of all—listen. By listening closely, and by skillful questioning, you may learn a great deal about the job.

4. *Express yourself clearly.* Speak in an audible voice. Use proper grammar and complete sentences. Don't be afraid to ask questions.

5. *Think and talk about the work—not about yourself.* Concentrate on the company's needs, and how your education and skills can help them to do a better job. Be sure to let them know you can get along with others.

6. *Ask for the job.* Express an interest in the position. Don't be afraid to ask if your qualifications fit the job, or what your chances are of getting it.

Next to knowing what to do, it is important to know what not to do. Therefore, when interviewing, *don't* do the following:

1. *Don't dress casually or sloppily.* The wearing of jeans, shorts, sandals, or dispensing with bras, creates a negative impression on most employers.
2. *Don't create annoying distractions.* Among the more common ones are restlessness, fidgeting with your hands, or worse still, handling some object on the interviewer's desk, chewing gum, and (in most situations) smoking.
3. *Don't interrupt needlessly.* If you must interrupt, try to follow with a retrieval, helping the speaker reestablish his or her train of thought.
4. *Don't act in a stilted manner.* When you try too hard to make a good impression, you risk doing the opposite. Tense, strained facial expressions and self-conscious mannerisms make a worse impresion than just being your usual self.
5. *Don't talk too much about what you want.* Dwelling on matters of salary, fringe benefits, or chances for advancement gives the impression you care more about what you want to get than what you have to give.
6. *Don't prolong the interview.* Ask the secretary how long such interviews usually run, and keep this in mind. It's better to leave an employer wanting to know you better than to risk resentment by staying too long.

KEEP AT IT

Bill and Ron attended Tom Jackson's workshop, "Guerilla Tactics in the Job Market." Both were seniors in a criminal justice program and interested in finding jobs in the police. They took notes, read the literature, and were favorably impressed by what they learned at the workshop. Inspired by Jackson's enthusiasm, they began looking for jobs in earnest. About eight weeks later Bill gave up, saying that police departments were just not hiring "these days." Soon afterward he accepted a sales job with a company that made security equipment.

Ron admitted he was discouraged. He also took a lot of kidding when he accepted a part-time job as a security guard at a large department store. But he needed the money while he kept up the job search. Finally, five months later, Ron landed a job in one of the larger police departments in the area. It wasn't exactly the job he had in mind, but he felt fortunate to find a job in his field. He told his friends that to find the job you want, "You gotta keep at it."

Be persistent

The single most important ingredient of successful job hunting is persistence. Richard Bolles once examined a number of highly successful job-hunting systems, hoping to find their common characteristics. But they all seemed so different from each other. Some stressed the importance of doing your homework or researching the companies you approached. Others spent much of the time on rehearsing, videotaping, or role-playing employment interviews. Eventually, though, he discovered all these systems had something in common. They treated job hunting as a full-time endeavor. Job hunters went at it five days a week. They came in at nine in the morning and worked at it until four or five in the afternoon. Eventually, the job hunter's persistence paid off with a good job.[10]

A major reason you may not persist in looking for a job is the amount of rejection involved. Nobody likes rejection. Yet in looking for a job you must constantly call or write to potential employers, realizing full well that most of them are going to say *no*. Worse still, you may be tempted to take the rejection personally, when this is not the case. You tend to lose sight of the fact that eventually someone will say *yes*. Tom Jackson has graphically characterized the job hunt as NO NO NO NO NO NO NO NO NO NO NO NO NO NO NO NO NO NO NO NO NO NO YES. The more *NOs* you get out of the way, the closer you get to the job. That's why it pays to keep at it.[11]

Make follow-ups

Persistence in job hunting is especially valuable in making follow-up contacts. You can't call, write, or contact an employer just once and expect to be automatically remembered. You have to follow up your initial contact. Many

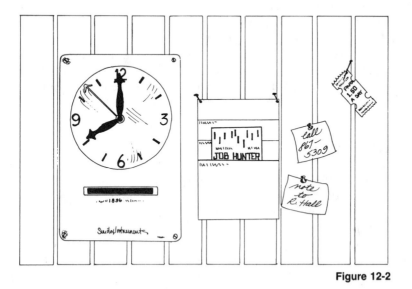

Figure 12-2

[10]Ibid., 50.
[11]Tom Jackson, *Guerrilla Tactics in the Job Market* (New York: Bantam Books, 1978), 118.

employers are so preoccupied with the day-to-day pressures of the job that a record of your call or visit, or your résumé, easily gets put aside or "forgotten." The larger the number of applicants and the bigger the organization, the more likely this is to happen. A follow-up call or letter serves to jog the employer's memory and make you "visible" again. Such contacts also let the employer know you mean business. In many cases, it's the follow-up contacts that make the difference in getting the job.

An ideal type of follow-up is the *thank-you* note. Most experts in this field suggest writing a short letter or note to this effect. Yet it's the one aspect of job hunting that is most frequently omitted. This is most unfortunate, because such notes are easy to write and evoke gratitude rather than rejection. Thank-you notes express your appreciation for the common courtesies shown during a visit. When a manager or personnel director takes time out of a busy schedule to see you, why not thank that person for doing so? Also, don't forget the help of the secretaries. When you address them by name, your note will be even more effective. Thank-you notes also afford you an opportunity to correct an impression you made, or to confirm your understanding of things. Most important of all, thank-you notes let others know you have one of the most sought after skills, namely the ability to treat another as a person. Expressing kindness and consideration has become highly valued in an age of large, impersonal organizations.

Mark got his job with a well-known real estate firm partly because of his persistence in writing thank-you notes. When an original request for an interview was refused because of the manager's busy schedule, most job hunters would have forgotten about that company. But not Mark. He wrote and thanked the manager for his letter requesting another interview at a later date. After the interview, he wrote another thank-you note expressing some of his positive impressions of the company. Eventually, Mark was hired over many other applicants, some with more impressive credentials. His employer commented, "We were favorably impressed with your motivation, and especially with your sensitivity to the people here."

Keep a positive attitude

In recent years, the government has begun furnishing statistics for a new category labeled *the discouraged worker*. When an unemployed individual has not looked for work in four or more weeks, he or she becomes a *discouraged worker*. About two-thirds of these people blame market conditions; another one-third blame race, sex, or age discrimination for their unemployment. All of them have one thing in common: They have become discouraged and depressed, and have given up hope of finding a job. Unfortunately, such a negative attitude tends to perpetuate their unemployment.[12]

[12]Marcon and Worthington, op. cit., 6.

Keeping a positive attitude is more a matter of *emphasizing* the positive, rather than denying the reality of job hunting. It has been said that in every experience there are two sets of data. One evokes hope and encouragement, inspiring us to try harder. The other arouses discouragement and hopelessness, tempting us to give up. The optimist attends more to the first set of data; the pessimist pays more attention to the second. So it is with job hunting. People with a positive attitude view the inevitable rejection in job hunting as a necessary part of the process of elimination, rather than as a personal attack. Each interview that doesn't result in a job may nevertheless produce valuable leads to a better job. Naturally, it's easy to become discouraged; but it pays to keep a positive attitude. It may even help to enlist the aid of a friend or supportive group to maintain such an attitude. As Richard Bolles says, "What you believe will happen helps to determine what does happen." If you really believe you'll eventually find a suitable job, that positive attitude in itself helps you to make it happen. But, remember, you must keep at it.[13]

SUMMARY

1. We began by emphasizing the importance of becoming an active, self-directed participant in the job hunting process. Applicants must draw on a variety of resources to identify potential employers, and not simply rely on existing job listings. Family, friends, and supportive groups may all become valuable allies throughout the job search.

2. Potential employers may be contacted in a variety of ways, including the telephone, résumé, letter, and the employment application. Although sending out résumés is a common practice, we stressed the value of making personal contact with potential employers, especially the person who has the power to hire you.

3. The key to a successful employment interview is to be prepared. You should think through your answer to such basic questions as why you are contacting the employer, what you have to offer, what kind of person you are, and how much money you expect from the job.

4. To succeed at job hunting, you must keep at it. Finding a job is itself a full-time job. Successful job hunters must be persistent in the face of rejection, make follow-up calls, write thank-you notes, and keep a positive attitude throughout.

[13]Bolles, op. cit., 204.

SELF-TEST

1. _____ job hunting involves taking the initiative in determining what you want to do, where you want to do it, and contacting the people who can hire you.
   a. computerized   c. conventional
   b. creative   d. unrealistic

2. Compared to people looking for jobs on their own, individuals in Azrin's job-finding club found:
   a. jobs quicker   c. better-paying jobs
   b. higher-level jobs   d. all of the above

3. Your local _____ provides information on labor market changes and job openings on the basis of a national network.
   a. state employment office   c. chamber of commerce
   b. college placement center   d. all of the above

4. Many employment counselors suggest you make your initial contact for a job by:
   a. letter   c. telephone
   b. personal interview   d. résumé

5. The _____ résumé highlights your major strengths and accomplishments in a way that makes it especially appropriate when seeking your first job.
   a. chronological   c. targeted
   b. functional   d. classic

6. In job hunting, a letter may be used:
   a. to accompany your résumé
   b. in place of a résumé
   c. to accompany an application
   d. all of the above

7. The most important requirement for a successful job interview is to:
   a. dress neatly   c. be prepared
   b. talk a lot   d. sit erect

8. Most employers want to know your answers to the question:
   a. why are you here?
   b. what can you do for us?
   c. how much are you going to cost us?
   d. all of the above

9. When being interviewed for a job, you should:
   a. dress casually   c. prolong the interview
   b. be attentive   d. never ask for the job

10. The most important ingredient for successful job hunting is:
    a. looking attractive   c. keeping at it
    b. using the telephone   d. sending out résumés

EXERCISES

1. *Identify some potential employers.* If you were looking for a job, which resources would you use? Which placement and employment offices are available to you? Which job registers or exchanges are you familiar with? Which individuals would you ask to help? Which trade journals would be most appropriate for you? List them by name. List as many different resources for identifying potential employers as you can.

2. *Attend a job fair.* Many colleges and communities hold job fairs that bring together college students and area employers. A job fair offers you an invaluable opportunity to distribute your résumé and talk with company representatives about the possibilities for employment. If there is no job fair or its equivalent in your area, ask your college placement office, state employment office, or local chamber of commerce about the possibility of holding one.

3. *Use the buddy system to practice telephone calls to potential employers.* If you're looking for a job, have a friend listen to your calls to potential employers on an extension and make constructive suggestions for improving them. Whenever possible, ask someone who is also looking for a job so that you can help each other.

4. *Write up a résumé of your education and experience.* First of all, decide which type of résumé is best for your background and vocational goal—chronological, targeted, or functional. Write a one-page résumé and have several of your friends give you feedback on it.

5. *Write a letter applying for a job.* Select a specific position you're interested in. Then write a brief cover letter to accompany your résumé. Have your instructor or friends read your letter and make suggestions for improving it.

6. *Prepare for an employment interview.* Select a specific position you'd like to apply for in a company. With this in mind, write out your answers to the four critical questions posed by employment interviews: (1) Why are you here? (2) What can you do for us? (3) What kind of person are you? and (4) How much are you going to cost us? If possible, ask a friend to help you role-play the employment interview.

7. *Write up your experience in finding a job.* If you've had experience getting either a full-time or part-time job, write it up. How did you find out about the job? Were friends helpful? What did you do to get it? How much luck was involved? How typical or atypical was your experience in the past compared to the search for a desirable full-time job in today's tight job market?

Getting Along on the Job

13

WORK ADJUSTMENT AND SATISFACTION
   The first job
   Job satisfaction
   The challenge of technology
   Growing in the job

WOMEN IN THE WORKPLACE
   Women at work
   Working mothers
   Reducing the earnings gap

IS THERE A FUTURE IN IT?
   Promotion
   Discrimination
   Changing jobs

SUMMARY

SELF-TEST

EXERCISES

Ron has been working as the assistant manager of a large restaurant for about six months. He likes his job, but occasionally finds it frustrating to work with Fred, his boss. Fred is a compulsive, fussy person. Ron is more casual, though conscientious in his work. He feels the difference in their personalities makes for problems at work. During the morning coffee-break, he confides in Rita, the bookkeeper, who shares many of the same complaints about Fred.

"Fred wants the banquet room set up by noon today," says Ron, as he pours a cup of coffee. "Of course, the wedding party isn't due here until 6:30 this evening."

"That's about par for the course," chuckles Rita.

"The problem is," explains Ron, "one of my best workers can't come in until later today. On top of that, one of the student workers had an exam this morning."

"Explain that to Fred, and see how far you'll get," says Rita with a laugh.

"I already know," groans Ron.

"You're not the only one who's getting the heat around here, you know," says Rita. "Monday he asked me for a printout of last month's expenses. I told him I was too busy getting out the W-2 forms to all the workers. But he said, 'Well, you can come in Saturday and do it.' I blew my stack. The nerve of that guy!"

"Well," asks Ron, "did you come in?"

"Are you kidding?" says Rita. "I stayed late a couple of afternoons and did it. But I still resent it. That work could have waited."

"I know. I'm not the only one who's frustrated around here," says Ron. Then he adds, "Say, why don't you help us set up the banquet room today."

Rita laughs as she reaches for the phone. "That'll be the day," she says.

WORK ADJUSTMENT AND SATISFACTION

Conversations like this occur in practically every workplace. Look around at any office or plant. No matter how busy the workers seem to be, they can always find a few minutes to share their gripes, their good news, or the latest gossip. Such informal talk serves as a safety valve, helping to make the daily annoyances at work more bearable.

All this is a reminder that how well you get along on the job depends on more than liking the work activity itself, important as this is. A lot depends on your working conditions and the psychological climate of the workplace. In this section, we'll look at several important aspects of work adjustment and satisfaction, including your first job, satisfaction on the job, the challenge of technology, and the importance of growing in the job.

The first job

Recent graduates tend to approach their first job with mixed feelings. They're relieved finally to have a job. They may even be enthusiastic. But most new employees are also apprehensive. They may not simply be afraid of not being able to do the work satisfactorily; they may also be fearful about meeting repeated challenges and asserting their autonomy. Also, new employees are concerned about being accepted. How well will they get along with their superiors? Will they be accepted by their colleagues? Still other fears center around whether or not they have made the right choice. The more unsure of themselves and their abilities workers are, the more they will be bothered by the demands of a new job. Those with more experience and self-esteem may make a smoother adjustment to a new situation.

The first job may also be a source of disappointment. New workers are frequently ambitious, sometimes entertaining unrealistic expectations about the job. More often than not, the realities of the situation soon dampen their ambitions. They may find the job boring and routine. They may feel they are overtrained, and that they are not being given enough responsibility. Some workers cope with their disillusionment by learning to be satisfied with a mediocre job. Others may simply change jobs. The most effective strategy is usually to wait and work for advancement. This is what Lisa did. A top student in her class in nursing school, she was disappointed her first job was on the night shift. However, she resolved to be efficient in carrying out her responsibilities, and to be caring toward the patients, and this was noticed by the night supervisor. When an appropriate position on the day shift opened up several months later, Lisa got the job.

Job satisfaction

Typically, a recent graduate's first job pays a low income and requires little responsibility. Despite this, recent graduates are likely to have high morale in the early months of their first job. Part of the reason is the thrill of having a job, the novelty of the work activity itself, and the stimulation of getting to know new people. In fact, the first year on the job is frequently called the *honeymoon year.* After the first two or three years, morale and satisfaction drop considerably. After three to five years, job satisfaction is at its lowest point. If employees remain with the same company for five years or more, however, job satisfaction increases. Apparently, seasoned workers adjust to the realities of the job, reevaluating their job aspirations in the process.[1]

Despite the daily gripes heard on the job, surveys consistently show that most workers like their jobs. Depending on the survey, from two-thirds to three-quarters of workers are either "somewhat" or "very" satisfied with their jobs. Managers, executives, and professionals are generally more satisfied with their jobs than other workers. Much of this has to do with intrinsically satisfying work, greater freedom on the job, and higher financial rewards. Semiskilled, unskilled, and clerical workers generally express lower job satisfaction, with supervisors and skilled workers falling somewhere in between. The most dissatisfied workers tend to be young (under thirty-five), black, at the lowest income levels, and overqualified for their jobs. Such workers are especially apt to cite low pay and lack of advancement as the causes of their dissatisfaction. But much of it has to do with the clash between the worker's expectations and the realities of the job. On the other hand, the older the workers and the longer they have been on the job, the more satisfied they are regardless of income. Such workers have not only made their adjustments to the job but enjoy greater job security as well.[2]

[1] J. Halloran, *Applied Human Relations,* 2nd. ed. (Englewood Cliffs, N.J.: Prentice-Hall, Inc., 1983), 132.
[2] Ibid., 133.

More established workers, those with job security, tend to be satisfied with their jobs.

What makes for job satisfaction naturally varies somewhat from one person to another. Yet certain factors like job security, opportunities for promotion, and pay turn up repeatedly in surveys on the subject. The more inadequate the pay, the more important this factor is. But once the pay is adequate, other factors pertaining to job satisfaction become important, such as how interesting and enjoyable the work activity itself is. A carpenter who genuinely likes making things with wood is more likely to be happy in his work than someone who is doing it largely for the money. Working conditions are generally an important, if not the most important, source of job satisfaction. The most frequently cited working conditions in this regard include the friendliness of co-workers, the amount of freedom there is in the job, the way one is treated by others at work, and job security.[3]

[3]P.A. Renwick, E.E. Lawler, and the *Psychology Today* staff, "What You Really Want from Your Job," *Psychology Today* (May 1978): 56.

Shift Work

Julie is a nurse who works the eleven-to-seven night shift in a local hospital. She became accustomed to these hours while in college, and now prefers them. Brad, her husband, has a daytime job in the office of a trucking firm. He's usually home by about 5:30 P.M. each day.

Julie and Brad are among the growing number of couples with at least one partner who works changing or unusual hours. In due time, individuals find their body rhythms adapt to the new hours, but adjusting their domestic and social lives usually proves more difficult. In some cases, shift work is temporary; in other cases, it's a regular arrangement. Among some workers, like police and firefighters, individuals rotate shifts, which can be even more trying for one's marriage.

Julie says she and her husband have a good marriage and have worked out a satisfactory arrangement. Brad is conscientious about getting home promptly after work, and Julie regularly sets aside part of the evening for time with Brad, and occasionally for socializing. They also have most weekends off. But what about other couples? How does shift work affect the intimacy of their relationships, especially when there are already problems in the marriage? What does shift work do to the management of household chores and the quality of child-care? Researchers are just beginning to find out.

The challenge of technology

Work conditions are rapidly changing with the use of new technologies. Machines for precision work demand new skills on the part of workers. Industrial robots are taking their place in manufacturing and assembling jobs. And computers are changing the methods of work in just about every field—from banking, printing, and weather forecasting to payroll and billing functions.

The new technologies promise greater efficiency and productivity at work. Yet they also exact a price in terms of the worker's satisfaction. Work skills are now often linked to machine operations, with the end product being dependent mostly on other machines and workers. As a result, the mechanized worker stands at a psychological distance from his or her work and is less identified with the end product than the cabinet maker or blacksmith of the past. Also, assembly-line workers may be confined to a fixed work station which they can leave only with permission. Such restrictions can't help but affect the worker's attitude toward the job.

An important factor in work satisfaction is the length of the job cycle, that is, how long it takes you to perform an operation before starting again. For an author or architect, it may take two or three years. For a skilled craftsman, it may be weeks or months. But for an assembly-line worker, it may be only minutes. One automotive worker said, "No sooner do you get through with one operation than another one is coming at you. It's demoralizing." Another factor is the variety in a job. Most people like to vary their work rhythm and routine. They may work fast for a while, then gradually slow down as the day wears on. Such a change in pace helps to reduce fatigue and boredom. Yet the set pace of a production line becomes a coercive influence on the worker.

White-collar workers such as computer programmers and laboratory technicians fare better in some respects. In the first place, their jobs demand more intellectual than physical effort. Such jobs also involve deeper concentration and a more varied work pace, both of which make the work more interesting. White-collar jobs are also less likely to be tied to strict quotas, and allow more flexible working hours. The upgrading of the job title with advancement may also enhance the worker's morale. Being called a *staff assistant* rather than *chief clerk* does something for one's self-image on the job, even though the work may be the same. Yet as higher levels of education have become available to Americans, the status of white-collar jobs has declined. Many white-collar workers feel they are in dead-end jobs. An executive secretary put it this way: "I've been told I can't get a raise because I'm at the top of the pay scale for my job. So what incentive do I have to improve?"

Growing in the job

Growth in your job depends partly on how compatible you feel with the work activity itself. If you really like what you're doing and feel it's a challenge, it is probable that you'll grow in your job. Much depends on how motivated you are, and how strong your desire for achievement is. When you're sufficiently motivated, you keep looking for opportunities to grow and accomplish things. I once knew a man who quit college and began working on an assembly line making precision instruments. Many of his college-educated friends looked down on his new job; they thought he could do better. But Fred really enjoyed making mechanical things with his hands. Later, he began developing specialized medical instruments. He became so successful that he formed his own company, and is now a millionaire several times over. He credits his success largely to doing something he liked, and which continues to be a challenge to him.

Growth in the job also depends on the psychological climate you work in and especially on the incentives offered by the company. Praise and recognition for a job well done encourages you to do your best. Common complaints among workers at all levels are that nobody appreciates what they do, and that they are "just a number." Badges, pins, medals, and plaques all provide recognition of a job well done. One company invited production teams to describe their successes to the board as a form of recognition. Promotions too are important incentives. Advancement in your field not only acknowledges publicly your accomplishments, but also increases responsibility and self-direction, all of which may further growth in the job. A pay raise is often an effective incentive. Some companies wisely review each worker's salary level every few

Figure 13-1

months as a way of providing monetary incentives. Money is a particularly powerful incentive in part because it provides a concrete form of feedback for a job well done.

Greater freedom at work also facilitates growth in the job. It provides workers with more flexibility and makes them feel more accountable for what they do. The degree of freedom on the job is also a major source of job satisfaction, as you may recall from worker surveys cited in an earlier chapter. Another important consideration is participation in decision making, especially in matters in which the worker's expertise is appropriate. Also, it is important to help workers see the end results of their job, either in terms of the quality of the final product or service, or the impact on sales and profits. This often benefits the company as well as the workers, as was the case at the General Motors plant in Tarrytown, New York. By the late seventies, 7 percent of the workers were failing to show up for work, and the number of worker grievances against management totalled two thousand a year. By increasing worker participation in company policies, management reversed declines in morale and production. Within a few months, absenteeism fell by half and the percentage of bad welds dropped from 35 to 1.5 percent.[4]

[4]"Stunning Turnaround at Tarrytown," *Time* (May 5, 1980): 87.

Getting Along with a Difficult Boss

Michael Lombardo and Morgan McCall asked seventy-three highly successful executives about their experiences with intolerable bosses. About two-thirds of the executives had encountered such bosses, mostly males. The labels of the more frequently encountered types suggest their respective characteristics: snakes-in-the-grass, Attilas (as in Hun), heel-grinders, egotists, dodgers, incompetents, detail drones, Rodneys (as in Dangerfield), slobs, and miscellaneous types.

Although there was no one best way to cope with all these different types of bosses, suggested strategies included:

1. *Learn to be patient and cope with adversity.* Difficult bosses may help us to learn how to handle disagreement and conflict without destroying the relationship. They may also remind us we work for the company rather than the boss.
2. *Look for common ground.* Don't take the easy way out, blaming everything on your boss. If you must differ on one matter, be supportive on others.
3. *Try modifying behavior.* Chances are better for modifying your behavior to fit the situation than changing your boss's behavior. Emphasize cooperative responses to your boss's positive behavior; minimize complaints.
4. *Make it a learning experience.* Many successful executives learned what *not* to do by observing their boss's bad habits.

No one should remain in an intolerable situation indefinitely, especially if your principles are being compromised or your health suffers. But it's best to treat a difficult boss more as a problem situation that may be improved, if not resolved, before taking the ultimate step of quitting your job.

M.M. Lombardo and M.W. McCall, Jr., "The Intolerable Boss," *Psychology Today,* (January, 1984): 44–48. Reprinted from *Psychology Today* Magazine Copyright © 1984 American Psychological Association.

WOMEN IN THE WORKPLACE

Around the turn of the century, fewer than one out of five women worked outside the home. Then in response to the labor demands of World War II, the proportion increased dramatically. The new breed of women workers, symbolized by "Rosie the Riveter," filled many jobs closed to women before the war. Today, nine out of ten women work outside the home at some time during their lives; one out of every two women at any given time.[5] Prior to World War II, most women workers were young and single. At present, women employed outside the home come from all age groups, and include both married and unmarried workers.

[5]U.S. Bureau of the Census, *Statistical Abstract of the United States, 1984,* 104th ed. (Washington, D.C.: U.S. Government Printing Office, 1984), 413.

Women at work

Now that it is illegal to discriminate in hiring on the basis of sex, women are breaking down job barriers in a variety of fields. Women work as carpenters, welders, and astronauts as well as doctors and lawyers. In recent years, a woman was appointed to the United States Supreme Court. Another woman was nominated for the vice-presidency on the Democratic ticket. The distribution of women varies widely from one career to another, however. More than three-quarters of the women in the workplace are crowded into just twenty of the Labor Department's 427 categories. Women are over-represented in such occupations as waitress, house servant, nurse, elementary-school teacher, and secretary. But they are under-represented in such jobs as auto mechanic, police officer, miner, and construction worker. Only a small proportion of women belong to unions and apprenticeship programs in the trades.[6]

Some claim that women are not capable of the physical exertion demanded in such jobs as mining and construction work. But the rise in labor-saving machinery, documented knowledge of sex differences, and the actual experience of women workers in these fields has made this argument less convincing. A stronger case can be made for the influence of sex-role stereotypes. Many women simply don't want to take jobs that threaten their sense of femininity. Similarly, many men are reluctant to enter fields such as nursing because they are afraid of appearing unmasculine or gay.

At least one survey has found that women work longer and harder on the job than do men. Workers who expended the greatest effort at work were unmarried women, professionals, union members, part-time workers, and those employed less than thirty hours per week. Unmarried women scored the highest on the work-effort scale and took the least amount of break time. On the other hand, craftspersons, machine operators, males, young people, and those with high monthly incomes spent the most time in either formal or informal work breaks. How does this compare with your experience? Would you agree that much depends on the person and the working conditions in a particular job?[7]

Women are generally as satisfied with their jobs as men are. At least, this is the finding in the *Psychology Today* survey on work attitudes, which admittedly included a large proportion of young, college-educated women. Curiously, job satisfaction was not affected by the boss's sex. Women with female supervisors, women with male supervisors, men with female supervisors, and men with male supervisors, all seemed equally satisfied or dissatisfied with their jobs. However, women were much less satisfied with certain aspects of their jobs. Women were more likely to complain about inadequate

---

[6]T. Lewin, "A New Push to Raise Women's Pay," *New York Times* (January 1, 1984): 15.
[7]From *ISR Newsletter,* Institute of Social Research, Ann Arbor, Michigan, Summer 1977.

opportunities to learn, insufficient freedom on the job, not "being in on things," promotions, and lower pay.[8]

Sexual Harassment on the Job

At a workshop on this subject, women were asked to share their experiences. A middle-aged woman said, "A male colleague can't keep his hands off me." A young married woman complained, "One man makes these suggestive remarks like 'You seem happy today—it was that kind of night, eh?' " A recently hired college graduate said, "My boss hinted I'd get a raise faster if I went out with him."

Sexual harassment on the job takes many forms. A familiar one is directing catcalls, whistles, and demeaning words like *baby* at women. Another is repeated, offensive flirtation. Although most sexual harassment is verbal, unwelcomed sexual advances, including physical intimidation, are not uncommon. Soliciting sexual favors for advancement on the job is often cited in lawsuits against large companies.

Although each situation is different, here are some suggested strategies for dealing with sexual harassment on the job.

1. *Make it clear when you disapprove.* Say directly but tactfully something like, "I find that remark offensive."
2. *Share the incident with other workers.* Other women may have been harassed too. Take positive steps in raising the awareness of male workers.
3. *Jot down the time, place, and manner of such incidents.* Who are the biggest offenders? Under what circumstances?
4. *If necessary, complain to your employer.* This may be done orally or in writing, depending on the situation. As a last resort, contact federal agencies, like the Equal Employment Opportunity Commission.

Working mothers

Until recently, most women followed the interrupted career pattern. That is, they worked at their chosen job for a few years. Then they married, began a family, and remained at home while the children were small. Later, when their children were well along in school, many women would resume their career. Today, however, more young women are opting for the dual-career pattern, simultaneously combining career and family responsibilities. Yet because of the traditional emphasis on the homemaker role for women, they are keenly aware of competing priorities, especially if they have small children.

Women soon discover that working outside the home doesn't spare them the usual housekeeping chores. This is especially true with divorced mothers who don't have help at home. Married women do not always fare much better. In most homes, women continue to do most of the grocery shopping, cooking, and clearing away after meals. Where there are children, women generally take care of them, or share responsibilities with their husbands. The younger the couple, the more likely it is that household chores and parenting responsibilities are shared equally.

[8]Renwick and Lawler, op. cit.: 55.

Figure 13-2

The effect that a mother's working has on her family depends on so many factors that it's hard to generalize. Most young children develop normal attachments to their mothers, even though working women have less time to attend to the physical needs of their families. Much depends on the quality of the mother's relationship with her children, how she spends her time with them, and the availability of daycare services and help at home. The same is largely true of the mother's relationship with her older children and adolescents. When there are rigid role expectations in the home, the eldest daughter often gets trapped into doing many of the mother's household tasks. The more mutual sharing of roles there is, as in many middle-class homes, the more boys and girls may share housework cooperatively and achieve greater independence in the process.

A lot also depends on the woman's attitude toward her job and her family. If she goes to work reluctantly, possibly to help with expenses, and the children resent her job, the family atmosphere suffers. However, if the woman likes her job and has a supportive husband and children, working outside the home greatly enriches the home atmosphere. The more emotionally involved a woman becomes in her job, the more the positive and negative effects on her family are accentuated. If she is deeply involved in her work, and likes it, this enhances her overall satisfaction. But if she's very involved and frustrated at work, this may spill over into the home as well. Actually, married couples report the highest level of marital happiness when *both* partners have moderate rather than high emotional involvement in their careers.[9]

Flexible Schedules

Many companies permit their workers to follow a flexible work schedule, or *flextime*. Such schedules are common among professionals, technical workers, managers, and administrators, for example. About one out of every four persons in sales works on a flexible schedule.[10]

Workers may set their own schedules as long as these meet the company's needs and are sufficient for the workers to get their assignments done. One person may work eight to four, while another works twelve to eight. Some large companies have four or even five shifts. A variation of flextime is the compressed workweek, typically the four-day workweek. In many instances, workers may choose their days off, and so enjoy a three-day weekend.

Some companies have established a "mother's shift" which allows women to adjust their work schedules to the hours their children will be in school. Flextime thereby encourages mothers to continue in the work force during their childbearing years. College students may also coordinate work hours with their class schedules, allowing them to work while going to school.

Generally, flexible schedules have resulted in less worker absenteeism, lateness, and turnover, and heightened morale and productivity.

Reducing the earnings gap

The Equal Pay Act of 1963 requires equal pay for equal work. The Civil Rights Act of 1964 prohibits discrimination in hiring, firing, or promotion on the basis of race, ethnic origin, or sex. You might think, therefore, that discrimination against women in the work force has ended, and that women now earn as much as men. This is not the case, however. Women employed outside the home full-time earn an average of only sixty cents for every dollar paid to men. Those without a college education receive even less.[11]

Why has there been so little progress in reducing the earnings gap between men and women? One reason is the lack of effective enforcement powers to back up the legislation passed. Another reason is a court system overburdened with a backlog of cases, most of which have been brought against federal and state agencies and large corporations. Still another explanation is that the majority of women continue to choose low-paying occupations like secretary and waitress. Also, women take time off to take care of their children, and

[9]A.C. Ridley, "Exploring the Impact of Work Satisfaction and Involvement on Marital Interaction When Both Partners Are Employed," *Journal of Marriage and the Family* 35, 2 (1973): 229–237.

[10]U.S. Bureau of the Census, op. cit., 438.

[11]Ibid., 469.

reenter the labor force later in life, with the result that the jobs they take have less seniority. But despite all these claims, critics of the present system say that the existing wage gap cannot be explained by anything but sex discrimination.

In recent years, many of the lawsuits aimed at reducing the earnings gap have been based on the concept of *comparable worth*. This goes beyond the idea of equal pay for equal work and demands instead equal pay for different jobs of comparable value. For example, AT&T set up *affirmative action programs* which encouraged women to go into predominantly male craft or trade jobs. Yet most telephone operators are still women and most of the higher-paying craft jobs are still held by men. In a further effort to eliminate the earnings gap, the company carried out an extensive evaluation program. Each job was evaluated in terms of 14 factors, such as the level of skills required and the mental as well as the physical fatigue involved. As a result, workers are to be paid according to the comparable worth of their jobs, rather than the subtle judgments about which skills society values most.[12]

IS THERE A FUTURE IN IT?

Is there any future in your job? The answer is vital, for when the future looks bleak, the job grows stale. Eddie felt lucky to have found a desk job in a steel fabrication plant where his father worked. But with the poor outlook for domestic steel, retrenchment had begun to haunt him. "I think it's a matter of time before I'm laid off," admitted Eddie. "I'm already looking for another job." Christine, on the other hand, felt enthusiastic about her first job, mostly because of the bright future it promised. Disappointed when she wasn't hired by one of the major airlines, she took a stewardess's job with a small, newly formed airline. Along with her co-workers, Christine agreed to do other jobs as needed as well as her stewardess duties. On occasions, she answered the phone at the reservation desk or checked tickets at the loading gate. She threw herself into her job because she felt that her share of the company's profit-sharing plan, and the expected promotions, would more than make up for her modest beginnings.

Promotion

Lack of advancement, along with low pay, continues to be a major cause of worker dissatisfaction. As one disgruntled firefighter put it, "when you keep getting passed over for people with less training and seniority, it says something about you." In this person's case, failure to win a promotion after years on the same job led to problem drinking and eventually a move to another situation.

A promotion means more than just a pay raise. A promotion is also a way that your abilities and accomplishments are recognized. It usually brings added responsibilities, which stimulates growth in your job. All of this helps

[12]Lewin, op. cit.: 15.

Figure 13-3

you to feel good about yourself and what you do. So it is not surprising to find that promotions and worker morale go hand in hand.

It is important to know how promotions are made in the organization you work for. Sometimes company policy on promotions is made clear in advance. If not, find out what the policy is. Many organizations claim their promotions are based on performance, but you may need to clarify this. For example, Marty was hired by an air conditioning manufacturer to bolster a division with sagging sales. He did so in record time—but no promotion was forthcoming. When he asked why, he was told there were too many complaints about his abrasive, high-handed style of leadership. Marty had expected to be promoted on the basis of his results, but his superiors judged him instead on the means he used to attain these results. Such misunderstanding could have been avoided had either Marty or his superiors clarified the standards by which his performance would be judged. Another matter is the difficulty in evaluating a job objectively. Many jobs simply don't lend themselves easily to such an evaluation, as we pointed out in discussing the *comparable worth* concept. On the other hand, an over-reliance on such measures as sales quotas may be counterproductive in the long run. Also, those who are not promoted may complain of favoritism. Almost half the workers in the *Psychology Today* survey felt that getting ahead in large organizations depends more on whom you know than how well you do. Since this response was given more frequently by dissatisfied workers, a certain amount of the cynicism may be "sour grapes." Nevertheless, it is an attitude often expressed in private company and, as a result, many organizations base promotions on a combination of factors like education, experience, and accomplishments, as well as seniority.[13]

[13]Renwick and Lawler, op. cit.: 56.

Workaholics

Frank moonlights at a second job in the evenings. Lisa makes out a long list of things to do each day. These lists have become so detailed she now makes them out on yellow-lined legal pads. Mark, the self-employed head of a cleaning supplies company, brags, "I love my work. Why do I need a vacation?"

All these people are *workaholics*. What sets them apart is more their attitude toward work than the hours they keep. Workaholics love to work. Their self-esteem is tied up in their work. They can't tolerate inactivity. When they finish one thing they find an excuse for beginning something else. Frequently, workaholics are driven by a fear of failure, and suffer from worry and guilt when not working.

Much of the negative image of workaholics comes from the obvious association of the term with the word *alcoholic*. Also, there are the well-publicized accounts of the workaholic's stress-related illnesses, as well as the complaints of spouses who must compensate for what workaholics don't do at home.

But do you also know what's right with workaholics? They're among the world's most productive people. Many highly successful people are confessed workaholics. Some companies would like more of these people. Furthermore, as a group, workaholics are generally happy, well-adjusted people who are satisfied with their lives.

Workaholics who suffer from ulcers or high blood pressure or unhappiness at home may benefit from modifying their work habits. Even with such changes, most workaholics will probably remain workaholics at heart.

Discrimination

Ever since the Civil Rights Act of 1964, it has been illegal to discriminate against workers, or treat them unfairly because of characteristics like age, sex, race, or ethnic background. Yet you and I know that much discrimination still exists both on the job and off. Frequently, targets of discrimination are people who make up minority populations within our society, like blacks, Hispanics, Asians, American Indians, and Eskimos. Curiously, people may also feel they are victims of "positive" discrimination, like those Asians who complain that employers see them as people who will work hard for low wages. In recent years, we have become more aware of discrimination against older people. Yet "old" is often a matter of personal opinion. Women and working-class men are commonly regarded as old when they reach sixty, while middle-class professional men are not viewed as old until they are seventy. Conversely, some employers tend to discriminate against the young. They may feel that young people are lazy, expect too much, and are preoccupied with sex and drugs. Whatever your age or sex, have you ever felt you were the victim of discrimination in the workplace? Are you aware of having discriminated against someone else at work?

An important way to reduce discrimination in the workplace is the use of more accurate job analyses by employers. For example, until the mid-1960s,

Figure 13-4

police organizations had height and weight requirements that excluded
women. Candidates had to be at least 5′6″ tall and weigh 135 pounds. With the
passage of civil rights legislation, such groups made more use of tests of
strength that were presumably fairer. In one northeastern state, for instance,
applicants for the state police were required to drag a 140 pound weight 100
yards in a certain number of seconds. Since many deer were killed by cars, this
was thought to be equivalent to dragging a dead animal off the road. Not
surprisingly, few women were able to pass the test. Yet a subsequent job analysis showed that very few police officers actually dragged dead deer off the
highway. Maintenance workers usually did it. Furthermore, the average dead
deer weighed closer to 100 pounds, and the distance was more like 10 yards.
Nor did it really matter how quickly the task was completed. The point is that
the more realistic and fairer job requirements become, the less the discrimination because of irrelevant factors.[14]

Changing jobs

Experts are now confirming what many of us have long suspected, that people are
changing jobs more frequently than in the past. The average length of time a
person keeps a job has steadily declined to about $3\frac{1}{2}$ years. The typical American
worker holds ten different jobs (or employers) in his or her lifetime, compared to
about six jobs during the 1950s. An individual usually has a number of very brief

[14]F.J. Landy, *Psychology: The Science of People* (Englewood Cliffs, N.J.: Prentice-Hall, Inc.,
1984), 645.
[15]U.S. Bureau of the Census, op. cit., 414.

Moonlighting

   After the working day is over, most people go home to relax. But some eat a hasty dinner and head for their second job. These people are *moonlighting*. As many as a third of all workers have moonlighted at one time or another. Moonlighting is done by virtually every type of worker, though it is more common among wage-earners and salaried workers and individuals who combine farming with a nonfarm job.[15] Those in higher-status jobs tend to take on some type of self-employed activity, like selling real estate or dealing in investments. In some instances, moonlighting jobs turn into full-time careers. One man who began selling calculators out of his basement eventually built his moonlighting job into a multimillion dollar business.

   People moonlight mostly for extra money. When they can hide the extra income from the tax department, moonlighting becomes even more attractive. Employers often look favorably on moonlighters because they are usually paid less and receive fewer fringe benefits than other workers.

   Moonlighting doesn't seem to affect the worker's performance of his or her full-time job. Moonlighters tend to be a special breed; they are energetic, have a stronger work ethic, and are often even more active in volunteer organizations than other workers.

jobs in the first few years after leaving school, then settles into a position that lasts several years. If someone in his or her thirties stays with the same employer for five years or more, it is probable that that person will remain in the job for a long time. As workers get older, they make fewer changes, and there are few differences in this pattern among men and women. By the age of forty, workers will make about two more job changes; at fifty, only one more. Few people change jobs in their sixties, and most of them are probably moving into second careers. Of course there are exceptions to this general pattern. A small minority of workers exhibit extremely stable job patterns throughout their careers. Others change jobs every few years until they reach retirement age.[16]

   People change jobs for many reasons. Some may feel they aren't being treated fairly in their present position. Others may feel the chances for promotion are better elsewhere. Still others simply tire of doing the same old thing and want more challenge. Then there are the people who are fired, sometimes for good reason, but often for reasons that have nothing to do with their job performance: it may simply result from their company's strategy for strengthening their competitive position, or, in some cases, survival.

   As we suggested in the previous chapter, finding a job is an indispensable lifetime skill. It has been estimated that at any given time, about one-third of all technicians and middle-managers have résumés making the rounds. It is clear that workers now expect more from their work than in the past, and are more willing to switch employers to find a satisfying job with a future.

[16]A. Crittenden, "One Life, Ten Jobs," *New York Times* (November 23, 1980),

SUMMARY

1. The recent graduate's first job is usually a mixed experience, with the initial high morale soon fading. Satisfaction at work generally increases with the worker's adjustment to the job, re-evaluation of his or her job aspirations, and greater job security. Those who continue to grow in their jobs not only enjoy the work activity itself, but benefit from favorable working conditions too.

2. About half the women in this country are employed outside the home at any given time, many of them in low-paying service jobs. More women are also combining career with family responsibilities, often with the help of supportive husbands and families. Women earn on the average only about two-thirds of what men earn in the same job, and efforts continue to reduce this earnings gap.

3. Satisfaction at work depends partly on how much future your job has. A promotion means more than a pay raise; it also conveys recognition for a job well done. Although some workers still suffer from discrimination in hiring and promotions, equal employment practices and more accurate job analyses are helping to diminish discrimination among women and minorities. Workers today change jobs more frequently than in the past, with the average worker holding ten different jobs in his or her lifetime.

SELF-TEST

1. Recent graduates tend to approach their first job with:
   - a. mixed feelings
   - b. a fear of failing
   - c. unrealistic expectations
   - d. all of the above

2. Surveys show that the most dissatisfied workers are those:
   - a. in the upper class
   - b. under thirty-five years of age
   - c. with the highest incomes
   - d. nearing retirement

3. Among the major factors determining job satisfaction are:
   - a. friendliness of co-workers
   - b. freedom on the job
   - c. job security
   - d. all of the above

4. _____ workers experience greater psychological distance from their work and identify less with the end-product of their efforts than workers in earlier eras.
   - a. carpentry
   - b. assembly-line
   - c. secretarial
   - d. medical technicians

5. Women are over-represented in such careers as:
   - a. lawyer
   - b. nurse
   - c. auto mechanic
   - d. high-school teacher

6. Today, more women are opting for:
   a. having larger families
   b. marrying earlier
   c. doing all the house chores
   d. combining marriage and career

7. The average income of women employed outside the home is _____ men's income.
   a. two-thirds that of
   b. about the same as
   c. half of
   d. slightly more than

8. A major cause of worker dissatisfaction is:
   a. working hours
   b. physical surroundings
   c. educational requirements
   d. lack of advancement

9. An important way to reduce discrimination in the workplace is the use of more:
   a. accurate job analyses
   b. social affairs
   c. management consultants
   d. employment tests

10. The typical American worker now holds about _____ different jobs in his or her lifetime.
    a. five
    b. ten
    c. fifteen
    d. twenty

EXERCISES

1. *Job satisfaction.* Write a short paragraph describing how satisfied or dissatisfied you are with your present job. If you're a full-time student, you might apply this exercise to a part-time job or your last job. What are the major sources of satisfaction or dissatisfaction at work? How satisfied are you with your present job?

2. *Freedom on the job.* In most jobs, there is considerable discretion regarding how hard you work as well as the quality of your work. Also, some employers encourage more worker input on decisions affecting their jobs than others. How much freedom do you have in your job? How does this affect your satisfaction and productiveness at work?

3. *Handling a difficult boss.* Write a brief paragraph describing your experiences working for a difficult boss. What made your boss so difficult? How did you manage to get along with this person? To what extent was this a learning experience for you?

4. *Your experience as a woman in the workplace.* Describe your experience working outside the home. Comment on some of the issues raised in this chapter, such as discrimination and fairness at work, sexual harassment on the job, salary and promotion, and job satisfaction.

5. *Are you a working mother?* If so, describe how you've managed to combine family and career responsibilities. If you're married, how suppor-

tive is your family? If you're a single parent, what special problems has this presented for you? If you're the husband, son, or daughter of a working mother, you might comment on how the woman's working outside the home has affected your family life and your attitude toward working mothers.

6. *Job changes in your life.* Reread the section on this topic and apply it to your own job history. How does the number of job changes in your career so far compare to the average worker in the same age bracket? If you've changed jobs more often than the average or less often than the average for your age bracket, explain the reasons for this.

Leisure

14

LEISURE AND NONLEISURE
  What is leisure?
  Types of leisure

WORK AND LEISURE
  Views of work and leisure
  Work and leisure patterns

USING LEISURE POSITIVELY
  Outdoor recreational activities
  Entertainment and cultural activities
  Vacations
  Leisure and personal growth

SUMMARY

SELF-TEST

EXERCISES

Tom and Kevin work at the same plant. They also play on the company softball team and occasionally go fishing together. Ordinarily, they don't see each other much during the winter months. Then one afternoon in March they meet on their way out to the parking lot.

"Hey, Tom, it won't be long before fishing weather," says Kevin.

"I can't wait," Tom says, shaking his head. "These last few days have been rough here."

"Well, in that case," says Kevin, "why don't you come bowling with us tonight?"

"I'd like to," replies Tom. "But I've got to do my income tax return this evening."

"Ugh," groans Kevin. "I get a CPA to do mine."

"I like to do my own," Tom explains, "Of course, I'll probably get so frustrated I'll end up watching TV before the evening is over."

"Oh, why don't you do your tax another evening and come bowling with us," Kevin persists.

"To tell you the truth, I'm too tired."

"That's even more reason to go bowling. It will do you good," Kevin says. "We'll go out for beer and pizza afterwards. What do you say?"

"It's tempting," says Tom. "But I'd better take a rain check. Maybe some other time."

"Okay, buddy, it's your life."

"Thanks for asking me anyway."

"Sure. If you change your mind before seven o'clock," Kevin says, "just give me a call."

"I'll keep that in mind," Tom says, as he opens his car door and slides into the driver's seat.

LEISURE AND NONLEISURE

Tom and Kevin, like most of us, are happy to be heading home after a hard day's work. Kevin is obviously planning to spend his evening in recreational activities and socializing. Yet Tom's plans for the evening remind us that not all time away from work is leisure. Much of our nonworking time is spent in *maintenance activities*. Chores like food shopping, preparing meals and cleaning up after meals fall into this category. So does preparing your income tax. But what about Tom's plan to watch TV? Isn't this leisure? It all depends. If Tom watches TV primarily for entertainment, that's leisure. But if Tom watches TV mostly because he's too tired or frustrated to do anything else, then he's using TV as *recuperation time,* which serves a maintenance function. All of this brings us to the question of what leisure is, and what purpose it serves.

What is leisure?

The concept of leisure comes from two well-known traditions developed by the ancient Greeks and Romans respectively. According to Aristotle and the Greeks, leisure has to do with the cultivation of the self and the pursuit of the higher things of life. Work is secondary. In fact, leisure was so important to the good life that the Greeks defined work as the absence of leisure. In due time, the more practical-minded Romans reversed the relation between work and leisure. For them, leisure meant the opportunity to rest from work, or free time. Much of our present-day meaning of *leisure* follows the Roman usage of the term, and usually refers to recreational and social activities.

The proper understanding of leisure includes something from both traditions. Ordinarily, leisure means something we've freely chosen to do, usually in our spare time. But leisure doesn't simply refer to recreational activities; it refers to the *way* we use our free time. In this sense, leisure has to do with the personal motivation and meaning of leisure activities, and how they affect our lives. Accordingly, leisure can be understood in terms of the following characteristics:

1. *Nonwork context.* Leisure generally occurs outside work situations. Examples are hiking, camping, and playing a musical instrument primarily for the enjoyment we get.

2. *Freely chosen.* For the most part, swimming and listening to music are leisure activities we choose to do. By contrast, maintenance activities such as buying food and cleaning up after meals are things we have to do. Such maintenance activities are excluded from leisure.

3. *Prescribed activities.* Recreational activities and vacations involve planning and, to a certain degree, prescribed activities. On the other hand, "doing nothing" is more likely to be an opportunity to recuperate from work, and may soon become boring.

4. *Intrinsic motivation.* We engage in leisure activities mostly because they are personally meaningful and enjoyable in themselves. Accordingly, leisure is somewhat individual. Playing tennis may be leisure to one person but more of a social obligation to someone else.

5. *Absence of monetary rewards.* We do things like bike riding mostly because of the enjoyment we get from it, not because of pay. Professional athletes, on the other hand, should not consider their chosen sport a leisure activity, no matter how much they claim to enjoy it, as long as they are getting paid for it.[1]

Figure 14–1. Types of Leisure. Adapted from John R. Kelly, "Work and Leisure: A Simplified Paradigm," *Journal of Leisure Research,* 4 (1972): Figure 3. Reprinted by permission of the publishers. © Copyright National Recreation and Park Association.

		CHOICE	
		Freely chosen	Determined
WORK	Nonwork Related	Unconditional leisure	Complementary leisure
	Work Related	Coordinated leisure	Nonleisure

[1]B. Kabanoff, "Work and Nonwork: A Review of Models, Methods, and Findings," *Psychological Bulletin* 88 (1980):60–77.

Types of leisure

John Kelly has suggested that leisure can be classified according to two criteria: the amount of choice the individual has, and the relation of leisure to work. Accordingly, we can distinguish four basic types of leisure, as shown in Figure 14–1.

Unconditional leisure includes activities we do primarily for enjoyment and personal fulfilment. This is leisure at its best. Examples would be attending a concert, playing a musical instrument, bowling, hiking, camping, swimming or any other activity undertaken for its own sake. *Coordinated leisure* refers to activities that we choose to do, but are essentially work related. Taking a customer to lunch or attending the office Christmas party are typical examples. *Complementary leisure,* though not work related, includes activities that are more or less expected of us. Examples would be participation in civic clubs, churches, and community organizations. *Nonleisure* includes a variety of activities that are not clearly leisure or work. Much of our nonleisure consists of maintenance activities, such as preparing a meal, working in the yard, and recuperating from work.

According to this scheme, then, the meaning an activity has for you is important; it's not simply the activity itself that makes it leisure. So attending a movie or play may be an unconditional leisure for the average person, but more of a coordinated leisure for the drama critic who must write a review of it. The woman who voluntarily helps with a church bake sale may be engaging in complementary leisure, though the clergy who drop by during the sale would probably consider it a part of their job. Those who watch a specific program on television for entertainment are probably using TV as a form of leisure; but the tired truckdriver who opens a beer, plops into a chair, and starts watching whatever happens to be on because he's too tired to do anything else, is trying to recuperate, which is a form of nonleisure.

WORK AND LEISURE

In the earlier years of our country people worked in shops and fields near their homes, making for a closer association between work and leisure than there is today. Much of this changed during the Industrial Revolution. The rise of cities and factories, and the separation of workplace and living areas, eventually led to a sharper distinction between work and leisure. In the morning, people went off to work. At the close of the day, they came home to relax and socialize, either in the privacy of their homes, in the pubs, or on the village green. Ever since, experts have been investigating the relationship between people's work and their leisure.

Figure 14-2

Views of work and leisure

Social scientists have come up with several major views regarding the relationship between work and leisure, though none clearly predominates over the others. One view holds that people engage in leisure mostly to compensate for the deprivation and frustration experienced at work. According to this view, those who are the least satisfied in their jobs use their leisure time to "let off steam." Assembly-line workers, for example, have jobs which are boring and unfulfilling, and you'll often find bars located near large industries. A significant number of plant workers will be active in recreational activities; bored to death at work, they eagerly look forward to going fishing, hunting, and camping.

A second view holds that there is a positive association between emotional involvement with work and leisure. By this view, those who are enthusiastic about their jobs are also likely to invest themselves in voluntary leisure activities. An example would be the self-employed professional who works hard in her job. She also has well-developed leisure activities, such as gourmet cooking, sailing, and civic club activities. Likewise, workers who feel little involvement in their jobs may engage in very few social and recreational activities. An example would be the unskilled laborer who does what is necessary to keep his job, but little more. His idea of leisure consists of opening a can of cold beer and sitting down in front of the television.

According to a third view, work and leisure are quite independent of one another: there is little relationship between our involvement and satisfaction at work, and our recreational activities. There is some evidence for this view too. In one study, a representative group of American workers was interviewed about their satisfaction in work and leisure, and their overall quality of life. The results showed that satisfaction both at work and in leisure activities was related to overall quality of life satisfaction, but that there was very little direct relationship between satisfaction at work and at leisure.[2]

Leisure and Compatibility

You might be interested in comparing your leisure preferences with those of your close friends or spouse. Compatibility with others is as important in leisure as it is at work.

Rank the following types of leisure activities from 1 to 16. Put a 1 next to the activity you like best, a 2 next to your second best, and so forth, until you have ranked all 16 activities. Then compare your list with that of a friend.

_____	Engaging in an active sport like tennis	_____	Taking part in community or church activities
_____	Listening to music	_____	Helping those in need
_____	Making something with my hands	_____	Doing what I please, with a minimum of planning
_____	Enjoying sexual relation-ships	_____	Working with nature, such as growing things
_____	Driving a vehicle, boating, or flying	_____	Enjoying the companionship of a close friend
_____	Watching TV or a movie	_____	Getting together socially with co-workers
_____	Engaging in family leisure, like camping	_____	Visiting, sightseeing, or traveling
_____	Watching sports, whether live or on TV	_____	Seeking intellectual stimulation

---

Work and leisure patterns

Just as people work for a variety of reasons, so they pursue leisure out of different motives. Some people engage in recreational activities mostly to expend excess energy; others, for exercise or self-expression. Also, there is a variety of possible interactions between our work and our leisure. One of the most helpful ways to classify these interactions is to rate them by involvement and satisfaction in each area. Several work and leisure patterns have already been identified in this way, along with the personal characteristics of people who exemplify each pattern.[3]

[2]M. London, R. Crandall, and G. W. Seals, "The Contribution of Job and Leisure Satisfaction to the Quality of Life," *Journal of Applied Psychology* 62 (1977): 328–34.

[3]B. Kabanoff, and G.E. O'Brien, "Work and Leisure: A Task Attributes Analysis," *Journal of Applied Psychology* 65 (1980):596–609.

1. *Passive involvement.* This pattern includes low levels of involvement and satisfaction in both work and leisure. Although this pattern may be seen among many types of people, such as those who are marginal, resigned, or alienated in society, it is especially characteristic of men with little education and low income. For example, Harold always felt somewhat left out in the large family he grew up in. He dropped out of high school, and has had difficulty holding a job. Eventually, he got a clerk's job in an auto parts store, mostly "to make a living." He remains unmarried, has few friends, and his leisure life consists mostly of frequenting bars and watching TV.

2. *Live for leisure.* This pattern describes low involvement and satisfaction in work but high levels of satisfaction in leisure. Such a pattern is characteristic of many young men and women whose attitudes and values fit the compensatory view of leisure. But it is especially prevalent among older women in dead-end menial jobs. For example, Thelma never considers leaving her low-paying secretarial job at the high school. She feels the security of the job outweighs its disadvantages. She is quite active in her church, and enjoys "having the girls over" for lunch in her off-hours. She also takes a good deal of satisfaction from working in her garden.

3. *Job-centered.* As the title implies, this is a pattern of high involvement in work, but little involvement or satisfaction in leisure. Since men are expected to be "breadwinners," it isn't surprising that the largest single group who exhibit this pattern are men. For example, Fred is well paid

Figure 14-3

for his work in pharmaceutical sales. His job involves traveling, and he feels he spends most of his week at work. Since Fred is hoping to be promoted to sales manager, he's working harder than he has to. To Fred, work isn't so satisfying in itself, but it is the means to status and to the money to give his family the goods things in life. Leisure consists mostly of taking his wife out to dinner at the country club and playing an occasional game of golf.

4. *Self-actualizing.* People who fit this pattern report high levels of involvement and satisfaction in both their work and leisure. For the most part, they are well educated, well paid, and enjoy their work. Their leisure activities serve largely to fulfil self-actualizing needs not met in their work. An example of the type is Monica, a highly successful, self-employed industrial designer. Although she enjoys her work, much of it is done at home and over the phone. She misses direct contact with people. Consequently, in her leisure time she participates in the community drama group and enjoys family outings with her husband and two children.

Naturally, not everyone fits neatly into the above patterns. But most of us come closer to one than to the others. Which pattern best reflects your involvement in work and leisure? How would you account for this?

USING LEISURE POSITIVELY

Today, the average worker spends thirty-five hours a week on the job, compared to almost forty hours a week in 1960.[4] Less time at work does not automatically result in more leisure, of course. Much of the newly available time may be taken up with maintenance activities, moonlighting at another job, or simply watching more TV. Nevertheless, people already spend as much time in some type of leisure activity as they do at work. As a matter of fact, people in the eighteen-to-twenty-five-year-old group and those over fifty spend twice as much time in leisure as they do in work.[5]

Most people enjoy their leisure. According to surveys, six out of ten people derive a great or very great satisfaction from their leisure. Another three out of ten get moderate satisfaction. Only one out of ten persons reports getting little or no pleasure from their leisure.[6]

[4]U.S. Bureau of the Census, *Statistical Abstract of the United States, 1984,* 104th ed. (Washington, D.C.: U.S. Government Printing Office, 1984), 425.

[5]U.S. Bureau of the Census, *Social Indicators* III (Washington, D.C.: U.S. Government Printing Office, 1980), 526.

[6]Ibid., 526.

Some individuals prefer more daring leisure activities like skiing.

The positive use of leisure requires a certain amount of choice and planning. Ideally, you should select an activity that is compatible with your interests and lifestyle, rather than doing whatever is convenient at the time. In many instances, you may have to acquire the necessary skills to enjoy a given recreational activity or sport. You must also budget your time and money to keep it up. People who play tennis regularly probably derive greater satisfaction from it than those who play only a few times each summer.

The great variety of available leisure activities makes it impossible to examine all of them. So we'll take a look at some of the more familiar types of leisure in several major categories, including outdoor recreational activities, entertainment and cultural activities, and vacations. Finally, we'll point out the importance of using leisure for personal growth.

Outdoor recreational activities

Among the most popular outdoor activities are visiting zoos, aquariums, and fairs, and going to amusement parks. Picnics are almost as popular, and a large number of people go on picnics regularly. These activities are popular in part because they lend themselves to family-centered outings. A family may find it convenient to combine a picnic with a visit to the zoo or amusement park. The development of large recreational facilities, including commercial, state, and national parks, especially those with overnight accommodation, has helped to maintain the popularity of such activities.[7]

Attendance at sports events has grown steadily in popularity in recent years, with paid admissions totaling several billions of dollars a year. Two of the most popular spectator sports are baseball and football, as indicated in Table 14–1.

Baseball tends to be most popular among middle-aged spectators; football more so among young adults. One reason may be the relatively fast-paced action in football. The popularity of these sports also reflects the well-developed leagues of college and professional teams, as well as increased television coverage. Other sports, such as boxing, tennis, golf, bowling, gymnastics, and auto racing, tend to be viewed more selectively.

As for active participation in sports, individual preferences differ widely. A few people have a very active lifestyle and engage in a wide variety of sports. Many more people play sports on an occasional basis. Tennis and golf remain popular, though racquetball has increased in popularity in recent years. There is also a relatively large proportion of people who prefer to engage in leisure activities that will simply keep them in shape. Some walk or jog; others prefer to do exercises. The increased concern for physical fitness in recent years has led to the popularity of aerobic (a-er-ó bik) exercises, which stimulate

Table 14–1. Attendance at Selected Spectator Sports: 1970, 1982.

SPORT[1]	1970	1982
Baseball, major leagues	29,191	45,415
Basketball		
college teams	NA	31,106
professional teams	7,113	10,732
Football		
college teams	29,466	36,539
professional teams	10,071	8,504
National Hockey League	5,992	10,710
North Amer. Soccer League	NA	3,229
Horseracing	69,704	76,858
Greyhound racing	12,660	21,375

[1]Attendance in millions
U.S. Bureau of the Census, *Statistical Abstract of the United States, 1984,* 104th ed. (Washington, D.C.: U.S. Government Printing Office, 1984), 241.

[7]Ibid., 542.

heart and lung activities sufficiently to produce beneficial changes in the body. Jogging, running, swimming, and cycling are typical aerobic exercises.

Entertainment and cultural activities

When asked to identify their favorite way to spend an evening, the majority of people cite watching television. The United States now has more TV sets than bathtubs, automobiles, or telephones. These sets are on an average of six hours a day per household. However, the various individuals in each household only watch television about four hours a day on the average. Men and women of fifty-five years and older watch television the most. Evening is the prime time for watching television, with more individuals watching TV on Sunday evening than at any other time. Most people watch television primarily for entertainment.[8]

But people also watch television for the news. Two-thirds of the population list television as their principal source of news on current events, with newspapers ranking second. There has been a slight decrease in television-viewing time during the past several years, probably reflecting a growing disenchantment with television programming. We'd like to think people are watching televison programs more selectively. But most people watch television

Figure 14-4

[8]*The World Almanac and Book of Facts 1984* (New York: Newspaper Enterprise Association, Inc., 1983), 428.

Table 14–2. Household Participation in Leisure Activities.

TYPE OF ACTIVITY	Number (mil.)	Percent[1]	TYPE OF ACTIVITY	Number (mil.)	Percent[1]	TYPE OF ACTIVITY	Number (mil.)	Percent[1]
Watching television	68	81	Camping	17	20	Golf	10	12
Listening to music	54	64	Vacation trips in U.S.	29	34	Swimming in own pool	7	8
Sewing/needlepoint	27	32	Bicycling	19	22	Horseback riding	8	9
Going to the movies	36	42	Tennis	10	12	Racquetball	6	7
Vegetable gardening	35	42	Workshop/home repair	25	29	Skiing (downhill)	5	6
Pleasure trips in cars	37	44	Jogging	16	19	Boating (power)	8	10
General exercise/ Physical fitness	26	31	Bowling	17	20	Vacation trips outside U.S.	5	6
Watching professional sports (TV)	33	39	Hunting	14	16	Snowmobiling	3	4
Fishing	26	31	Photography	17	20	Cross-country skiing	3	4
			Hiking	12	14	Archery	3	4

[1]Percent of all households.

Based on a national sample survey of 1,500 households as of mid-July 1983 conducted by the Gallup Organization. U.S. Bureau of the Census, *Statistical Abstract of the United States, 1984,* 104th ed. (Washington, D.C.: U.S. Government Printing Office, 1984), 238.

more according to time slots than the programs. Bill's television-viewing habits are typical. By the time he's driven home after a hard day's work, eaten dinner, and checked the kids's homework, he's too tired to do much else. Usually, he watches television in the family room. Sometimes his wife will join him for the late movie. Despite being kidded about sitting in front of the "boob tube," Bill realizes his television time is as much an opportunity to relax and unwind as it is leisure.

Movies have declined in popularity since the advent of television. Weekly attendance has sunk from the 100 million mark set in the 1920s and 1950s to about one-third of that number in the 1980s. Now that people are watching more films on television, including cable TV and video cassettes, they go out to the movies much less frequently. Although people of all ages occasionally take in a commercial movie, the typical moviegoer is under thirty years of age. The youthful makeup of movie audiences is reflected in the overwhelming popularity of science fantasy films like *Star Wars* and its sequels. How often do you attend the movies?

Music continues to be a favorite form of leisure, both as entertainment or "pop" culture, and as "high" culture. Radio, once threatened with extinction by television, has found new life in catering to the musical tastes of diverse groups, especially from adolescence on. Radio music is usually programmed for particular audiences, and most stations specialize in one type, with a rock station rarely playing classical music and vice versa. The continued development of new technology in music, as in the improved quality of blank tapes and the appearance of video discs, may well change the way individuals listen to music, but not its popularity.

Among the other cultural leisure activities are visiting museums and art galleries and attending performances. Included here are symphony concerts, live performances at theaters, ballet, dance, and the opera. Audiences at such cultural events tend to be college educated. Apparently individuals become more familiar with the performing arts as they pass through higher levels of education. Anyone can learn to appreciate good music, art, and drama, however.

Vacations

A *Psychology Today* survey on how Americans view vacations is most informative. Although respondents of all ages and educational levels were included, the sample was somewhat younger and better educated than the population at large. Half of the respondents took a one- or two-week vacation in the year of the survey, with almost the same number taking an even longer vacation. Yet among the general population, only about forty percent of the people took a vacation the same year, with another one-third of them taking no vacation at all.[9]

[9]C. Rubenstein, "Survey Report: How Americans View Vacations," *Psychology Today* (May 1980), 62–76.

Most respondents felt little or no guilt at taking time off for a vacation. About half of them felt they deserved even more vacation time. Judging from the survey, most people feel a need to escape the everyday routine and relax. Favorite ways to spend a vacation include visiting a park or national forest as well as traveling. Relatively few people are content to stay home and putter around the house. However, workaholics are apt to resent vacations, and often take work with them.

Respondents were asked to indicate five main reasons for taking a vacation, and were given twenty-two different choices. An analysis of their answers showed six basic patterns, reflecting different motives for taking vacations. (1) The most common motive for taking a vacation is to relax, with about one-third of the respondents saying they needed time off to recharge their batteries. Many of these were professionals with advanced degrees. (2) Another motive for taking a vacation is to get intellectual stimulation. Most people who fall into this pattern are active in civic and social organizations and enjoy seeing places they've never been to. (3) Family togetherness is a third motive for vacations. Those who exhibit this pattern tend to have young children and use vacations to be with their children or visit friends and relatives. (4) Another group of people are mostly interested in finding excitement and exotic adventure in their vacation. These are the most adventurous and least cautious vacationers, and not surprisingly, they enjoy their vacations the most. (5) Self-discovery is another motive for taking a vacation. People who are so inclined usually want time to mull over some personal problem or simply to be alone. (6) Still others, mostly women, use a vacation to escape routine life and get a tan. These people are more apt to travel to the Caribbean, to Hawaii, or to a local beach. But as a group, they enjoy their vacations the least. As you read over these various motives for vacations, which comes closest to your preference?

Most people are glad to come home from a vacation, and are eager to return to work. Only a few feel depressed at the prospect of getting back to the everyday routine. A majority of people continue to feel that their work is more important than leisure. What they seek is not so much a leisure-filled life as a

Figure 14-5

better balance between work and leisure. In fact, as family life changes, work and leisure patterns are changing too. Now that more women are working outside the home, leisure becomes more essential. Also, a shorter working week along with flexible schedules will enable people to take more long weekends, which promises to make vacations a regularly recurring experience rather than a once-a-year affair.

Leisure and personal growth

Our leisure should serve a more positive aim than simply restoring us for work, important as this is. Leisure should also foster personal growth. Because of the difficulty of finding work in a tight job market, and the abundance of routine jobs, two trends which promise to continue, it seems likely that many people will derive little satisfaction from their jobs. Even those fortunate enough to have satisfying careers rarely employ all their abilities in their work. Leisure may help people to utilize more of their potential and to express themselves more fully.

Table 14–3. What Is Your Dream Vacation?

	All Respondents	Under 30	Over 30	Men	Women
Spending a year living in a foreign country	31%	28%	33%	30%	32%
Taking an ocean voyage on a luxury liner around the world	29%	29%	28%	24%	32%
Being marooned on a tropical island with several members of the opposite sex	8%	11%	6%	14%	5%
Doing something creative (composing a symphony, writing a book, painting or drawing)	7%	6%	8%	8%	6%
Spending time, anywhere, with my spouse and kids	6%	4%	9%	8%	6%
Going on a charter tour of Western Europe	5%	6%	4%	3%	6%
Climbing Mt. Everest	4%	5%	3%	6%	3%
Going on a spending spree in the best shops in Paris	3%	5%	2%	1%	5%
Taking a slow barge down the Nile	2%	2%	3%	2%	2%
Taking a gourmet trip through the South of France	2%	2%	3%	2%	3%
Taking a religious pilgrimage	1%	1%	1%	1%	1%

When individuals in the *Psychology Today* survey were asked, "If money and time were no object at all, which one of the following vacations would come closest to being your ideal fantasy trip?" they responded in the manner shown above. Which of these preferences comes closest to your vacation fantasy?

Source: Carin Rubenstein, "Survey Report on How Americans View Vacations," *Psychology Today,* (May 1980): 72. Reprinted from *Psychology Today Magazine.* Copyright © 1980 American Psychological Association.

I'm constantly amazed how much more interesting people are, even so-called ordinary people, once I get to know them through their leisure pursuits rather than just through their jobs. Michael, a school counselor, is well thought of by his students, which is an accomplishment in itself. Yet those who know Michael well realize he is an even more interesting and well-rounded person than his students suspect. He's an avid photographer who has exhibited at state and national shows. He also plays a good game of tennis, which he feels affords him an outlet for his physical energies and competitiveness. In addition, he and his wife operate a nonprofit summer camp for retarded children. All of these activities help Michael to actualize himself as a person in a way that would not be possible in his career alone.

Much the same can be said for Lauren. Although she enjoys her work as a dental hygienist in a small private clinic, she sometimes feels a bit stale on the job. She has taken up painting, and enjoys doing portraits. She also likes playing golf with her husband, socializing with other couples, and going camping with her husband and their two children. When friends ask how she can bear looking into people's mouths all day long, Lauren replies, "Most of the time, I find it interesting. But I've got to admit, sometimes I can hardly wait to go home and get back to my painting."

The link between leisure and personal growth is also evident in the *Psychology Today* survey cited earlier. When asked which of a number of goals they wished they had more time for, about half the respondents indicated that personal growth was more important than work. A full 27 percent of them wanted more time for "developing special skills"; another 20 percent wanted more time for developing "intellectual abilities." Fewer than one out of ten wanted more time for advancing their careers. Furthermore, over one-quarter of the respondents said they would take from one to six months off without pay, if they had the option.[10] Apparently, many people have a need to actualize themselves outside their career and family responsibilities.

SUMMARY

1. Leisure has been defined as "free time" from work, and much of it is spent in recreational and social activities. We classified leisure along two dimensions: the amount of free choice involved, and its relation to work. Unconditional leisure, such as playing a musical instrument primarily for pleasure, is leisure at its best. At the other extreme are nonleisure activities, such as food shopping and cleaning up after a meal. These are things which we must do to maintain life apart from work.

2. We described four general patterns in which people's involvement and satisfaction in work and leisure are related. Some people are

[10]Ibid., 64.

only passively involved in their work or leisure. Others endure their work, living mostly for leisure activities. Then there are those whose lives are job-centered. And finally, there are the self-actualizers who exhibit high involvement and fulfilment in both their careers and leisure.

3. Most people spend as much time in leisure as they do at work, and derive great satisfaction from it. We discussed selected activities in several categories of leisure, including outdoor recreational activities, entertainment and cultural activities, and vacations. It was also pointed out that leisure does more than simply restore us for work; leisure also helps us to actualize ourselves more fully.

SELF-TEST

1. Leisure refers to activities we do:
   a. in our free time   c. because we want to
   b. without pay   d. all of the above

2. A typical example of unconditional leisure is:
   a. mowing the grass   c. playing golf with a
   b. attending a concert   customer
                                d. attending church

3. Watching television while recuperating from work is a _____ activity.
   a. leisure   c. maintenance
   b. work   d. coordinated leisure

4. People who are the least satisfied in their jobs tend to use leisure to:
   a. blow off steam   c. actualize their potential
   b. earn extra money   d. attend evening school

5. _____ are especially apt to exhibit low levels of satisfaction in both work and leisure.
   a. older women   c. managers and executives
   b. men with little   d. young adults
      education

6. _____ are the most likely to be heavily involved in their work, with little time for leisure.
   a. women   c. men
   b. teenagers   d. low-income females

7. People in the eighteen-to-twenty-five-year-old age group spend twice as much time in _____ activities as in work.
   a. leisure   c. sports
   b. school   d. sexual

8. _____ is one of the most popular outdoor recreational
   activities of all.
   a. cross-country skiing   c. visiting zoos and parks
   b. archery   d. scuba diving

9. For most people, a favorite way to spend an evening is:
   a. listening to music   c. engaging in a hobby
   b. watching television   d. socializing with friends

10. The most popular reason given for taking a vacation is:
    a. relaxing   c. intellectual stimulation
    b. family togetherness   d. adventure and excitement

EXERCISES

1. *Classify your leisure time.* Review the types of leisure in Figure 14–1.
   Then keep notes on your various leisure activities during one week,
   and classify them into the respective types. Which type of leisure do
   you engage in the most? Do you find that much of what you regarded
   as leisure really amounts to maintenance activity?

2. *Your work and leisure pattern.* Look over the four general patterns relating work and leisure, described in the second section of the chapter.
   Which most resembles your own pattern of work and leisure? How do
   you account for this? In what ways would you like to change your
   involvement in work or leisure?

3. *Your television viewing habits.* How do your television-viewing habits compare to those described in the chapter? How many hours of television
   do you watch each day? Every week? Do you watch television mostly by
   the program, or more according to the time slots? What would you
   most like to change about your television-viewing habits?

4. *What's your favorite outdoor recreational activity?* List some of your favorite
   outdoor recreational activities. How do these compare to the list of
   activities described in the text? Are you more interested in watching
   sports or engaging in active recreational activities?

5. *What is your dream vacation?* Look over the options given in Table 14–3,
   then list five of your favorites from 1 (most favorite) to 5 (least valued
   of the favorites). Which vacation fantasy most appeals to you? Why?

6. *In what sense do you consider leisure an opportunity to "recreate" yourself?* Do
   you think leisure is mostly an opportunity to get restored for resuming
   career and family responsibilities? Or would you agree that leisure is
   also a time for actualizing yourself more fully?

Coping with Loss

15

SEPARATION AND LOSS
>Types of loss
>The experience of loss

DEATH AND DYING
>Awareness of death
>The experience of dying
>Dying the way you live

BEREAVEMENT
>The grief process
>Unresolved grief
>Good grief

SUMMARY

SELF-TEST

EXERCISES

Stan and Bernice are having difficulty getting over the death, several months earlier, of their oldest son Alex. He was killed in a single-car accident having apparently fallen asleep at the wheel while driving home from college. His parents were especially saddened to learn that the alcohol content in Alex's body had been near the level of legal intoxication.

Friends commented that Stan had held up like a rock during the funeral, never shedding a single tear. But Bernice had taken an extended leave of absence from her job because of unpredictable crying spells. After dinner one evening, the topic of Alex's death comes up again.

"I thought of Alex again today," says Bernice. "I saw a car like his in front of me at a stoplight. I just can't get him out of my mind."

"It takes time."

"I don't know. I feel as badly about his death now as I did last April."

"Part of the reason," Stan says impatiently, "is that you dwell on your feelings too much. I thought going back to work would help with that."

"I just can't turn off my feelings the way you do," replies Bernice.

"I have feelings too," Stan say emphatically. "I feel just as badly as you do about Alex's death. But I don't feel it helps to moan and groan about it all the time. It's not going to bring him back."

"Well, I still feel you should have warned him about driving home so late at night, especially after drinking."

"I can't anticipate *everything* the kid is going to do," Stan says angrily. "He was old enough to know better. Besides, I *did* warn him about driving after drinking. You know that."

"I still feel we let him down."

"That's water over the dam now."

"I can't help feeling bad about the way he died," says Bernice. "I feel like it wouldn't have happened if we had been in better communication with him."

"It's natural to feel like that occasionally," Stan says. "But I refuse to wallow in guilt, much less talk about it all the time. Now, can we talk about something else for a change?"

Looking away from the table with a vacant stare, and heaving a subdued sigh, Bernice says, "I suppose so."

"Good," Stan says as he picks up his empty coffee cup and heads for the kitchen.

SEPARATION AND LOSS

Stan feels like crying at times. Yet he holds his tears in check because he knows that "grown men" don't cry. Although Bernice is more in touch with her feelings, she tends to flounder in guilt and self-pity. Perhaps each can help the other in a time of grief. By urging Stan to express his feelings of sadness more openly, Bernice may help him to grieve in a healthier way. Similarly, by insisting that Bernice resume her work activities, Stan may help his wife come to grips with their son's death more realistically.

Life is a series of separations and losses, with death being the most devastating loss of all. Coming to terms with death, either our own or that of a loved one, often depends on how well we have learned to handle our lesser losses. This is why we begin the chapter with a look at separation and loss in everyday life before turning to the discussion of death and bereavement.

Types of loss

A favorite pet dies. You lose your house keys. A close friend moves away. Your car is damaged in an accident. The promotion you expected at work is denied. Your parents get divorced. Your grandmother dies suddenly. These are but a

Figure 15-1

few examples of loss—the state of being deprived of an object or a relationship you once had.

Many types of loss are incurred in the course of everyday life. One is the loss of friends because of a move from one place to another. It is estimated that one out of every five families moves each year. The most common reason is a change of employment, often because of promotion. No matter how voluntary the move, it's a stressful experience. Everyone in the family is uprooted, and must begin working with new people in new settings. It's not surprising that each member of the family tends to experience more minor illnesses than usual for up to a year after such a move.

Losing your job is almost always a serious loss. It's bad enough to be fired or to quit a job because of basic differences with your boss. But during the economic recession of recent years, many people have lost their jobs through no fault of their own. In either case, people who are unemployed experience multiple losses. Not only are they faced with the loss of security and income, but they often lose such things as health benefits and retirement pensions as well. They also feel a loss of esteem and morale. The disappointment and rejection suffered daily in the search for a new job only aggravate the problem. Middle-aged and older workers are likely to become demoralized with the loss of their jobs.

Divorce is an especially difficult loss because of the intense emotions involved. Even when a husband and wife are unhappy in their relationship, they have usually grown accustomed to married life and become emotionally dependent on each other. In some cases, the marriage may have become so turbulent that divorce comes as a welcome relief. But in most instances, the severance of close attachments is very painful. Children and adolescents are especially vulnerable to the loss of emotional security afforded by their parents' marriage. Divorce also has wide-reaching effects because of the variety of changes involved. Included are a change in residence, loss of neighborhood friends, change in community status, an altered lifestyle because of a more modest budget, the children's separation from one of their parents, and, at least for one parent, separation from one's children.

Bill's experience is typical. He has recently moved into his own apartment. He is hurt because some of their friends have sided with his wife. Also, visits to his kids are restricted to Saturdays and special holidays. Even then, his older son hardly speaks to him during these weekly visits. Bill readily admits, "Life is kind of mixed up right now."

Certain types of loss are inherent in the process of growing older. Adolescents may regret the loss of their childhood, as seen in the girl who keeps her teddy bears and dolls lined up on her dresser as a reminder of that happy, secure period of her life. Her middle-aged parents might well understand. They too are keenly aware of getting older. As one middle-aged man put it, "I just don't have the energy I once had anymore." The loss of vigor and health that accompanies aging also entails giving up things. An older woman bemoaned having to cut back on her social life because of the difficulty of getting around with a cane. An older man finally gave up gardening because he wasn't up to it anymore. Retirement usually means not only giving up one's career involvement but also the way of life associated with it. Finally, as you reach old age, you gradually lose more and more of your friends through death.

Learning How To Say Goodbye

In several ways, the two women were similar. Both had grown children and were in their late fifties. Also, both had recently lost their husbands through death. Yet in one important way they were quite different. One woman envisioned a new chapter in her life, filling her days with friends and activities. The other woman felt devastated, and wallowed in self-pity. The difference lay in the fact that the first woman had learned how to say goodbye, while the other woman had not.

Although death is the most significant goodbye of all, life is a series of separations. People who can comfortably say goodbye when a child goes off to school or college or gets married, are better prepared to survive the death of a loved one. People who handle separation best are those who have a strong self-identity, and other interests, and don't think of themselves solely in terms of their role as a parent or spouse. By the time their children reach their twenties, a healthy parent may say, "It's time to be on your own. I want some time for myself." Similarly, a healthy spouse is able to say, "If I have to, I can make it on my own."

Think of how you handle separations, such as leaving home, changing jobs, or breaking up with a friend or spouse. Have you learned how to say goodbye?

The experience of loss

The way we cope with loss varies considerably from one person to another. Healthy-minded people tend to take disappointments and losses in stride. On the other hand, pessimistic people with fragile egos may find the experience of loss quite frustrating, if not overwhelming. Most of us probably fall somewhere in between. Furthermore, our reaction to loss fluctuates from time to time. During happy times, we may take serious setbacks like the loss of a job in stride. Yet in our low moments, we may have difficulty even coping with minor losses such as receiving a disappointing grade on a test.

Our experience of loss also varies with the type of loss and the circumstances surrounding it. Losing our wallet or having a long-awaited date cancelled may be frustrating. But it won't be as upsetting as having to face serious surgery or the death of a close friend. Sudden losses like damage to your car from an accident or an unexpected death are usually more traumatic than predictable losses. The jolt to our daily routine catches us by surprise. We usually make a better adjustment to gradual, predictable losses like the breakup of a close relationship that has been in trouble for some time, or the death of an ailing grandparent. Similarly, most of us take the changes due to aging in stride because they occur so gradually we have plenty of time to become accustomed to them.

How people perceive and react to loss greatly affects their overall experience of loss. For example, faced with the involuntary loss of their jobs because of company cutbacks, two men reacted quite differently. Soon after Howard was told, he spent much of his time in bars complaining about the raw deal he was getting. He even considered suing the company. Joe reacted differently. At first, he was deeply disappointed. Then he started a business out of his garage. For Joe, the loss of a job became an opportunity to do something he had always dreamed of. Something similar occurs with couples getting divorced. Some partners are consumed with anger and self-pity and contest the legal divorce. Others feel they're getting a new lease on life.

In the course of a bereavement, each individual's reaction to loss usually changes. In the early stages of grief, it's typical to be preoccupied with frustration, bewilderment, and anger. But in the latter stages, it's not only normal but healthy to view loss as an opportunity for change and growth. After all, a certain degree of loss is inherent in the course of living. Even though many losses are not under our control, we can control our understanding of and reaction to them.

When you see someone suffering from a terminal illness, you may wonder how you would deal with it. Probably the best indication can be found in how you cope with everyday losses. Each day we face unforeseen changes in our schedules, unexpected problems, disappointments at the hands of others, and unfulfilled expectations. How do you cope with these frustrations? Do you curse and pout? Or do you try your best to take them in stride? Whatever your response, the way you handle these little losses will go a long way in shaping your responses to the major losses.

DEATH AND DYING

The ultimate experience of loss is death. The prospect of our own death or that of a loved one is so frightening we tend to deny it. This denial of death assumes many forms. We avoid talking about death unless we have to. If you doubt this, the next time you're at a party or social gathering ask a friend, "Have you made a will?" or, "Do you have plans for your burial?", and notice the response. Another way to deny death is by avoiding old people. It's as if old people remind us that death is coming faster than we think. Also, much of the frantic search for pleasure is motivated in part by an unconscious anxiety over death. The difficulty of dealing with death can also be seen in the words we use to describe it. We speak of people being "terminally ill" instead of dying. Or we speak of someone who has "passed away" or "departed" rather than saying, "He's dead."

Awareness of death

Despite such denials, almost every one has some awareness of death. When a cross section of the population was asked, "How often do you think about your own death?", over half of them said, "Occasionally." Fewer than one-quarter said, "Frequently" or, "Very frequently." Another one-quarter claimed they rarely thought about their own death. For the most part, people admitted that thoughts of death made them feel glad to be alive and caused them to resolve to live more fully. Only about one-third of them said thoughts of their own death made them feel depressed. What about you? Do you occasionally think about the prospect of your own death? How does this affect you?[1]

As people get older, they think of death more often. Older people have already lived a reasonably long life and may have less to look forward to. Also, aging, the increase in chronic illnesses, and the death of close friends are all reminders of death as the natural end of life. Yet as a group, older people are not as plagued by the fear of death as young people imagine. Those with a deep religious faith, especially with a belief in some kind of afterlife, tend to have even less fear of death. When I asked an eighty-two-year-old man how he felt about death, he put it this way: "I've already lived more than that 'three-score and ten years' the Bible speaks of. So I'm ready to go." "Don't you have any fear of death?" I asked. "Well, mostly I worry about dying a drawn out painful death, or being a burden to my children," he said. "Otherwise, I've made my peace with death."

[1]E.S. Shneidman, "You and Death," *Psychology Today* (June 1971): 77.

The prospect of our own death is so terrifying we often lack a realistic awareness of it. In one survey, students were given actuarial tables on life expectancies and asked to estimate how long they expected to live. Most of them estimated they would live 10 to 20 years longer than their projected ages. When asked to explain why they would live so long, typical remarks were, "It won't happen to me," "I'm not like other people," "I'm unique."[2] Do you often feel this way? Actually, there's a great deal of misunderstanding about the risk of death from various causes. Because of mass media coverage, people greatly over-estimate the danger of death from sensational causes like accidents and homicides. But they under-estimate the danger of death from nonspectacular causes that claim one victim at a time, like diabetes, heart attacks, and strokes. They also under-estimate the risk of death from familiar hazards such as driving a car, smoking, and X rays. And yet these are the very things each of us can control to increase our chances of living.[3]

Do You Ever Dream You're Dying?

When asked this question, even older adults reply, "Not very often." Yet an analysis of their dreams tells another story. Their dreams usually reveal the emotional themes and symbols of death.

One sixty-year-old woman reports, "I am trying to find my way home. But all sorts of roads crisscross in front of me. I'm confused." A seventy-eight-year-old man says, "I'm delivering a package to my daughter's home and am attacked by a pack of dogs. I yell for help, but nobody hears me." An eighty-two-year-old woman says, "While we are out for a sail, the rudder falls off the boat and we can't get back to shore."

In all of these dreams, the dreamer is represented as weakened, helpless, lost, or going away on a long trip—all symbols of death. In many instances, such dreams indicate the dreamer is making his or her peace with death. Do you ever have such dreams?

The experience of dying

Not too long ago, people died at home, often with little more than the aid of home remedies and the support of their families. Today people are more apt to die in a hospital, surrounded by sophisticated equipment and health workers. Such changes are bound to affect people's experience of dying. In an effort to investigate this, psychiatrist Elisabeth Kübler-Ross and her colleagues interviewed more than four hundred terminally ill paitients. Such individuals were asked what it was like to be sick, how it felt, and what changes they experienced. One of the first things she discovered was that most patients

---

[2]C.R. Snyder, "The Uniqueness Mystique," *Psychology Today*, (March 1980), 76–80.
[3]P. Slovic, B. Fischhoff, and S. Lichtenstein, "Risky Assumptions," *Psychology Today* (June 1980), 44–48.

realize they are seriously ill whether so informed or not. They could even predict the approximate day of their death with surprising accuracy. Dr. Kübler-Ross also observed that patients tend to go through several stages in the process of dying, with considerable overlap between the stages.[4]

1. *Denial.* Initially patients respond to the news of their serious illness with shock and denial. This may last from a few seconds to several months. Such denial gives them time to come to terms with the disturbing reality of their impending death. But as family and friends come in with red faces and awkward smiles, or talk excessively about trivial things, patients are quickly forced to face the truth.

2. *Anger.* As the individual's denial weakens, negative emotions surface. The mere sight of others enjoying the glow of health evokes envy, jealousy, and resentment. Unfortunately, individuals tend to displace their negative feelings onto those closest to them, mostly because of what they represent—life and health. They may complain about the way the nurses give the medications, or criticize family members for seemingly trivial matters. It's important for hospital personnel and loved ones alike not to take these negative remarks personally. Such outbursts should be viewed as part of the person's attempts to answer a deeper question—"Why me?" In some instances, people may conclude their illness is God's way of punishing them for some wrongdoing.

3. *Bargaining.* At this point people can admit, "I know I'm dying, *but* . . ." Then they proceed to indulge in a bit of magic. They may promise God or the doctor something in exchange for an extension of life. They may promise to donate their kidneys or eyes, or if they're able to they may attend church every Sunday. They may ask God to let them live another six months until their son or daughter graduates from college or gets married.

4. *Depression.* When individuals can drop the *but* and admit, "Yes, I'm dying," they tend to become depressed. At this stage, they should be encouraged to share their feelings of sadness. Too often, doctors, nurses, and loved ones attempt to cheer up the patient, mostly because of an inability to accept their own feelings of sadness. Yet it would be more helpful for dying people to express their grief more openly. After all, such "preparatory grief" is normal at the prospect of having to separate oneself from life and friends and loved ones.

5. *Acceptance.* Some people simply become resigned to their fate. Others reach a more positive acceptance of their impending death. Either way, dying people ask for fewer visitors, and eventually just one, usually the husband or wife, or in the case of children, their parents. Few people want to die alone, which is why most would prefer to die at home, even

---

[4]Elisabeth Kübler-Ross, *On Death and Dying* (New York: Macmillan, 1969), 39–137.

though they are more apt to die in a hospital. Toward the end, people who are dying may not feel like talking. They simply want the companionship of someone they feel comfortable with, who will just sit and hold their hand.

Elisabeth Kübler-Ross would be the first to point out that the above sequence is not a fixed, inevitable process. Each individual experiences dying differently. One person remains resentful throughout the entire process; another may express little or no resentment. Robert Kastenbaum, who also has considerable experience with dying people, denies that there are any stages of dying. Instead, he claims, each person dies in his or her own way, and the experience is affected mostly by factors such as personality, age, and sex, and by the characteristics of the particular disease.[5]

Dying the way you live

Your own lifestyle also furnishes important clues about the way you may die. The most obvious example is of people who hasten their own death through self-destructive habits. One survey of doctors showed that almost half of their patients under fifty who died in hospitals had contributed to their own deaths in some way. Many of those who died from heart attacks were grossly overweight or smoked. Practically all those who died of cancer of the throat or lungs were addicted to cigarette smoking. Many diabetics failed to follow the prescribed treatment. In other cases, aggressive or foolhardy people increased their chances of dying in an accident, especially after combining drinking and driving. Also, those who are low in self-esteem, overly self-critical, and impulsive, are more apt to end their lives through suicide.[6]

Figure 15-2

[5]R.J. Kastenbaum, *Death, Society, and Human Experience,* 2nd ed. (St. Louis: C. V. Mosby Company, 1981).
[6]*The Philadelphia Inquirer* (October 24, 1978).

Fortunately, people may also prolong their lives by altering their life-styles. A man named Bernie once told me that most of the men on his father's side of the family died of heart attacks before they reached their fifties. As a result, he had pursued an "eat, drink, and be merry" philosophy of life. Finally, at the urging of his wife, Bernie agreed to have corrective by-pass surgery on his heart. He also agreed to modify his lifestyle, consume less high-cholesterol food and exercise more. Now in his late fifties, Bernie has a healthier lifestyle and a more positive outlook on life.

At the other extreme are those people with a strong will to live. Even if they are afflicted with a life-threatening illness, they will do everything possible to conquer it. Such people often defy medical opinion and live longer than would be expected without the use of life-saving machines. Yet, when convinced that their time has come, these people may face death with equal determination. One man who despite his good health felt that he would soon die, consulted his lawyer, sold his house, and was dead of natural causes within a month.

People who have taken pride in controlling their lives also like to have some control over the manner of their death. Psychiatrist Edwin Shneidman tells of elderly people suffering from terminal illnesses who ended their lives in the same manner as they had lived. Many of these patients took out the needles and tubes from their arms, climbed over the bed rails, opened heavy windows, and threw themselves to the ground below. When their records were examined, they had one thing in common—they had never been fired from a job; they had always quit first.[7]

How about your own lifestyle? Do you take care of yourself? Or do you have some "bad" habits like overeating, smoking, or excessive drinking? If you're over forty, do you have a medical checkup every year or so? Do members of your family live a shorter or longer than average life? What do you think you'll eventually die of?

BEREAVEMENT

Many of our friends and loved ones will die during our lifetime. The process of coming to terms with such loss is called *bereavement* ("to be deprived of"). Generally, the experience of bereavement includes *grief,* the intense emotional suffering that accompanies loss, as well as *mourning,* the outward expression of bereavement.

Since death is one of the universal rites of passage, most societies have mourning customs to facilitate the expression of grief. Formerly, widows dressed in black and widowers wore black armbands. Such dress excused any oddities of behavior on the part of the bereaved and afforded them an

---

[7]E.S. Shneidman, *Deaths of Man* (New York: Quadrangle Books, 1973), 83.

opportunity to talk about their loss and to receive the needed sympathy. In recent years, many of these customs have been abbreviated or given up. Wakes and visitations have been replaced by brief funerals and memorial services. And the bereaved are expected to resume their usual dress and activities as soon as possible.

Sometimes, our modern customs get in the way of "grief work"—the healthy process through which we come to terms with the emotions associated with loss. Grief work consists of freeing ourselves emotionally from the deceased, readjusting to life without them, resuming ordinary activities, and forming new relationships. This takes time, so that ordinarily we work out our grief through progressive phases of the grief process.

The grief process

The grief process parallels the experience of dying, with many of the same emotions involved. Initially, we react to someone's death with shock and disbelief, especially when death comes unexpectedly. When we've been anticipating someone's death, such as in the case of a person suffering from a terminal illness, our initial response may be more emotionally subdued and accompanied by a sense of relief. In such instances, we've already begun experiencing

Figure 15-3

what is called *anticipatory grief*. Sometimes anticipatory grief works all too well. When prisoners-of-war who have been given up for dead return unexpectedly, their wives may have difficulty accepting them, having already accepted the possibility of their death.

After the initial shock wears off, we're apt to be bothered by painful memories and visual images of the deceased. We may withdraw somewhat from our usual routine, especially if we're preoccupied with taking care of the deceased person's estate or affairs. Negative emotions such as anger and guilt are likely to surface at this stage. We may blame God, fate, or those who've attempted to care for the deceased. Also, it's not uncommon to blame the deceased person for having abandoned us, especially if the person committed suicide. We may also feel guilt. Sometimes we feel guilty because of something we should have said or done while the deceased was still alive. But part of our guilt is "survivor's guilt," the feeling of guilt simply because we're still alive and the other is not.

The emotional intensity of grief often assumes the disguise of physical symptoms. During the first several months or so, bereaved people may feel depressed, cry, and have difficulties concentrating on things at work and at home. They have trouble sleeping, and may resort to sleeping pills and tranquilizers. Lack of appetite and weight loss are also common. Understanding doctors will realize that nothing organic is wrong with the bereaved, and that such symptoms are a normal part of the grief process.

The final stage of grief is marked by acceptance of our loss and the resumption of ordinary activities. This may occur from a few months to a year or more after the loss, depending on the person and the circumstances surrounding the death. At this stage, we're more likely to recall the deceased person with pleasant memories. In some ways, we never fully get over the death of a loved one, especially a parent, child, or spouse. But the more fully we work out our grief, the more likely we will be to get on with our lives. Those who are unable to do so, however, become the victims of delayed or unresolved grief.

Unresolved grief

I sometimes ask students: "Which of the following people would have the most trouble getting over the death of their spouse—the widow who sobs constantly

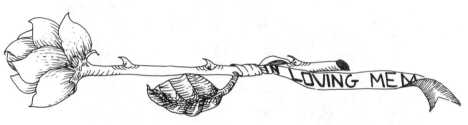

Figure 15-4

throughout her husband's funeral, or the widower who never sheds a tear during his wife's burial service?" Most students pick the latter, and rightly so. People who suppress the emotions associated with grief simply delay the resolution of grief. And the longer their grief remains unresolved, the more severe their symptoms become.

Unresolved grief may assume a variety of forms. In some instances, people can't bring themselves to return to the same hospital, home, or room associated with the deceased. A woman quit attending the church where her husband's funeral had been held. She said, "Every time I go there, I still see Peter's coffin in front of the altar." A man who had lost his older son in the second world war spent the rest of his life in bed with an assortment of unexplained physical and emotional ailments.

In some cases, unresolved grief may assume a more baffling disguise. One young man who sought therapy because of his lack of sexual desire discovered that much of his problem came from unresolved grief. In recounting his earlier life, he complained that when his father had died, his mother had

Grief often assumes the disguise of physical symptoms, especially among the elderly.

excluded him from the bereavement process. He had not been allowed to attend the funeral or talk about his father's death afterwards because of her belief that he was too young to understand. With the therapist's help, this man discovered that his unresolved grief, especially his anger toward women, had become displaced onto his wife. As he expressed sorrow and anger over his father's death, he gradually experienced the return of sexual desire and love for his wife.

Unresolved grief may also lead to premature death. A study of people who had lost their spouses found that older men are especially likely to die within a few years of the death of their spouse, but that women's mortality rates are not so strongly affected. Men between the ages of fifty-five and sixty-five who had lost a spouse died at a rate 60 percent higher than married men the same age. One explanation is that the quality of life changes more dramatically for men than for women, possibly because of their greater reliance on wives for their daily needs and emotional support. Also, the stereotype of the strong, silent male encourages men to hold their emotions in check. Women are able to express their emotions more freely and have a better support system of friends. Curiously, though, when widowers remarry they have an even lower mortality rate than their married counterparts.[8]

Out of Grief, a Reason for Living

Two days before Christmas, Frank Baldwin, a forty-five-year-old father of four, discovers he has mesothelioma, a fatal form of cancer. The disease is traced to his job in an asbestos pipe company. Ten months later he's dead.

Melissa, the seven-year-old daughter of Bill and Jean Grossman, is abducted from a school bus stop. Two weeks later, her lifeless body is found in a swamp outside town.

Tom, the nineteen-year-old son of Everett and Marianne Johnson, is killed by a drunk driver in an automobile accident.

The Baldwins, the Grossmans, and the Johnsons were all devastated by their losses. But they did not wallow in their grief. Instead, they were motivated to transform their anger and grief into action, thus rekindling their reason for living—a process called *sublimation.*

Frank Baldwin's wife launched a campaign on behalf of asbestos victims, holding a major manufacturer of asbestos accountable for the disease and death of her husband. The Grossmans helped pass federal legislation aimed at finding missing children. And Mrs. Johnson became active in MADD, Mothers Against Drunk Driving.

Faced with similar losses, most people would simply give a donation to research on the subject. A significant minority would become seriously depressed. Only a few would work for social change. These are the rare ones. How many such people do you know?

---

[8]K.J. Helsing, M. Szklo, and G.W. Comstock, "Factors Associated with Mortality After Widowhood," *American Journal of Public Health* 71 (August 1981), 802–809.

Good grief

Those who are fortunate enough to work out their grief may eventually find it becomes a positive, growth experience—sometimes called *good grief*. It seems we don't fully appreciate people until they are gone. While they are with us, we have mixed feelings toward them. Sometimes we love them; at other times we don't. Looking back, however, we can appreciate their lives more fully despite their shortcomings. We realize how much they meant to us, and we wish we had been more loving towards them. In the process, we come to value even more those friends and loved ones who are still living. In short, grief helps us to deepen our affection for those around us.

Grief also helps us to put our own lives into perspective. Far from being a morbid subject, death is an integral part of life and gives meaning to human existence. It sets a limit on life, reminding us to spend our days on the things that matter most. Perhaps one reason people are attracted to the idea of life after death is that it's hard to believe something so precious as life has an end. Yet seeing death as an inevitable companion of life may help us to live our lives more fully. Not that you should rush out and do all those things you fantasize about. Instead, realizing you only have so much time to live may help you make the most of life, including the disappointments and sorrows as well as the joys. Whatever things make your life meaningful, plan to do them before it's too late. As Elisabeth Kübler-Ross reminds us, the greatest lesson we may learn from the dying is: "LIVE, so you do not have to look back and say, 'God, how I wasted my life.' "[9]

SUMMARY

1. Throughout life we must cope with loss—the state of being deprived of an object or a relationship we once had. Whether it's the loss of a job, a friend, or a spouse, much of the experience of loss depends on how we perceive and react to it. How we deal with the "little losses" in everyday life largely determines how we'll face the major losses such as the death of loved ones.

2. The ultimate loss is death. The prospect of our own death is so terrifying that we characteristically deny it. Even those who are terminally ill usually pass through the stages of denial, anger, bargaining, and depression before accepting their imminent death. Yet each of us tends to face death in our own way, depending largely on our personality and lifestyle.

3. Bereavement, or coping with the death of loved ones and friends, includes expressing our feelings of sadness, emotionally freeing

[9]Elisabeth Kübler-Ross, *Death* (Englewood Cliffs, N.J.: Prentice-Hall, 1975), xix.

ourselves from the deceased, and forming new relationships. People who unduly suppress their painful emotions may experience delayed or unresolved grief. But those who persevere through the full cycle of grief work eventually may find grief to be a positive experience, bringing them a deeper appreciation of life and closer ties with others.

SELF-TEST

1. _____ is generally defined as the state of being deprived of something or a relationship with someone you once had.
   - a. death
   - b. loss
   - c. delayed grief
   - d. denial

2. Your experience of loss is greatly affected by your:
   - a. education
   - b. physical health
   - c. reaction to loss
   - d. social class

3. the most common attitude toward death in our society is:
   - a. acceptance
   - b. denial
   - c. fear
   - d. indifference

4. After getting over the shock of discovering they are terminally ill, patients tend to enter the stage of dying characterized by:
   - a. depression
   - b. acceptance
   - c. anger
   - d. bargaining

5. People tend to die:
   - a. shortly before their birthday
   - b. according to their own lifestyle
   - c. at an older age than they expected
   - d. all of the above

6. As many as half the patients under fifty who die in hospitals hasten their deaths through self-destructive habits like:
   - a. remaining overweight
   - b. cigarette addiction
   - c. not complying with the prescribed treatment
   - d. all of the above

7. The process of emotionally freeing ourselves from the deceased and readjusting to life without that person is known as:
   - a. the near-death experience
   - b. grief work
   - c. denial of death
   - d. unresolved grief

8. The emotional intensity of grief is often expressed in physical symptoms like:
   - a. lack of appetite
   - b. sleeping difficulties
   - c. depressed feelings
   - d. all of the above

9. Which of the following people are most likely to die within a few years after the death of their spouse?
   a. widows
   b. young adults
   c. widowers
   d. people who don't attend church

10. The process of transforming one's anger and grief into positive social action following the loss of a loved one in an accident is called:
    a. sublimation
    b. denial
    c. repression
    d. delayed grief

EXERCISES

1. *Coping with everyday loss.* Jot down some of the "little losses" you've experienced in the past few weeks, like lost keys or a broken appointment. How did you react? Did you become so frustrated and angry your entire day was ruined? Or did you take things in stride? What does your reaction to such losses suggest about the way you'll handle the major losses like the death of a parent or spouse?

2. *How long do you expect to live?* The average life expectancy for men is now seventy years, with women living about six years longer. Do the members of your family tend to live shorter or longer lives than average? How many years do you expect to live? What changes in your lifestyle might extend your life?

3. *Your personal awareness of death.* How many times today have you thought about the possibility of your own death? If such a thought hasn't crossed your mind, you probably have a low awareness of death. If you've thought about your death two or three times, you have a moderate awareness of death. If you've thought about your death four or more times, you may be preoccupied with the idea, and have a high awareness of death. Write a paragraph or so describing your personal awareness of death.

4. *Your attitude toward death.* In order to assess your attitude toward death, jot down brief answers to the following questions:

   Does hearing about a friend's death depress you?

   Have you made a will?

   Have you considered donating your body parts through a living will?

   Do you dread visiting someone who is dying?

   Are you afraid of dying?

   All things considered, do you tend to be overly fearful of death? Or do you have a fairly realistic attitude toward death?

5. *Reflections on your experience of bereavement.* Think back to some experiences of personal loss, like a divorce or the death of a loved one. Then describe your experience of bereavement in a page or so. Keep in mind the following questions: To what extent did you experience the appropriate grief work? Did you initially react with shock? Were you able to express your feelings of sorrow, anger, and guilt? How long did it take before you eventually resumed your ordinary activities? Finally, how have you been affected by your grief? Has it made you bitter? Or has it made you more appreciative of life and other people?

6. *Write your own obituary.* Major newspapers keep a file of obituaries about celebrities while they are still alive, updating these accounts at the time of death.

   Write your own obituary in several brief paragraphs. Be sure to supply the basic information—your name, age, and family survivors. What else would you include? What are some of your major accomplishments? Which community activities would you mention? What do you most want to be remembered for?

   What are your burial plans? Would you prefer that people send flowers or make contributions to your favorite charity? Where do you want to be buried?

Answers to Self-Tests

Chapter 1:   1(b),   2(a),   3(c),   4(d),   5(b),   6(d),   7(a),   8(b),   9(c),   10(d).

Chapter 2:   1(c),   2(b),   3(d),   4(a),   5(c),   6(b),   7(c),   8(c),   9(a),   10(b).

Chapter 3:   1(b),   2(d),   3(b),   4(d),   5(d),   6(d),   7(c),   8(b),   9(c),   10(a).

Chapter 4:   1(b),   2(c),   3(b),   4(d),   5(a),   6(b),   7(a),   8(d),   9(c),   10(b).

Chapter 5:   1(d),   2(a),   3(b),   4(d),   5(c),   6(b),   7(c),   8(b),   9(d),   10(a).

Chapter 6:   1(a),   2(b),   3(c),   4(d),   5(b),   6(c),   7(b),   8(a),   9(d),   10(a).

Chapter 7:   1(a),   2(c),   3(b),   4(c),   5(d),   6(c),   7(b),   8(c),   9(a),   10(d).

Chapter 8:   1(b),   2(d),   3(d),   4(b),   5(c),   6(a),   7(d),   8(c),   9(b),   10(d).

Chapter 9:   1(b),   2(a),   3(b),   4(d),   5(c),   6(a),   7(b),   8(c),   9(c),   10(d).

Chapter 10: 1(d),   2(b),   3(d),   4(b),   5(a),   6(c),   7(c),   8(a),   9(c),   10(d).

Chapter 11: 1(d),   2(b),   3(b),   4(a),   5(b),   6(c),   7(d),   8(a),   9(c),   10(d).

Chapter 12: 1(b),   2(d),   3(a),   4(c),   5(b),   6(d),   7(c),   8(d),   9(b),   10(c).

Chapter 13: 1(d),   2(b),   3(d),   4(b),   5(b),   6(d),   7(a),   8(d),   9(a),   10(b).

Chapter 14: 1(d),   2(b),   3(c),   4(a),   5(b),   6(c),   7(a),   8(c),   9(b),   10(a).

Chapter 15: 1(b),   2(c),   3(b),   4(c),   5(b),   6(d),   7(b),   8(d),   9(c),   10(a).

Glossary

addictive relationships: Love relationships that are characterized by excessive dependency and the need for approval.

altruistic egoism: The balance between the pursuit of self-interest and altruistic impulses to help others.

androgyny, psychological: The ability of an individual to combine the desirable traits of both sex roles.

anticipatory grief: The process of coming to terms with the death of someone who is dying or lost and presumed dead.

apprenticeship program: A training program that prepares individuals for the skilled trades like carpentry.

approach-approach conflict: A conflict between two desirable alternatives.

approach-avoidance conflict: A conflict between a desirable and an undesirable alternative.

approach-avoidance conflict, double: A conflict between two alternatives, each of which presents desirable and undesirable consequences.

assertive approach to stress: A problem-solving approach to stress which involves saying or doing things that will directly modify stressful influences in your surroundings.

assertiveness: The act of expressing your own thoughts, feelings or rights, but in a way that respects those of others.

avoidance-avoidance conflict: A conflict between two undesirable alternatives.

balance sheet: A helpful strategy of weighing one's potential gains and losses in making an important decision.

barriers to communication: Anything which gets in the way of effective communication, such as anxiety or passing judgment on others.

bereavement: The experience of coping with loss, especially the death of a loved one.

capitulation: Giving in to others in the face of a conflict.

career: One's occupation or life work, as seen in the sequence of jobs held throughout one's life.

commitment: The pledge or promise to make something work, as in committing ourselves to a relationship with someone.

communication: The exchange of information, signals, or messages between two or more people.

comparable worth: The view that people should receive the same pay for different jobs of comparable value.

compatibility: A state of harmony between two or more people.

compatible career: A career that is especially appropriate for a given person's interests, abilities, and experiences.

complementary leisure: Non–work-related activities that are more or less expected of someone in a given job.

complementary needs, theory of: The view that when people act out their own needs in a way that simultaneously complements the needs of others, these people are especially attracted to each other.

compromise: A realistic way of handling conflict or stress through each person making certain concessions.

conflict: The experience of antagonistic or incompatible forces.

conflict-habituated marriage: A stable marriage relationship involving frequent quarreling between the spouses.

conformity: The willingness to change our behavior because of real or imagined pressure from others.

contraceptives: Chemical or mechanical techniques designed to prevent fertilization of the female's egg during sexual intercourse.

cooperation: Working together for a common purpose.

cooperative problem solving: A cooperative approach to resolving conflicts in which the emphasis is on what both parties gain rather than what they give up.

coordinated leisure: The leisure activities we choose that are also related to our work.

creative job hunting: The concept of taking stock of yourself and your career goals before looking for a job, in contrast to the conventional practice of starting with the want ads.

death: The biological cessation of life, usually determined in terms of brain death as well as heart and respiratory failure.

defensive coping: The reliance on automatic, unconscious reactions to stress to protect our self-esteem; sometimes called defense mechanism.

denial: The unconscious refusal to see or hear unpleasant or threatening things.

devitalized marriage: An "empty" marriage relationship in which the partners often remain together for the sake of their children or community standing.

discrimination: The unfair treatment of workers because of their age, sex, race, religion, or ethnic background.

displacement: The unconscious mechanism by which we redirect threatening impulses onto less dangerous objects.

distress: Stress that has a harmful effect.

divorce: The legal termination of marriage, usually accompanied by psychological, social, and financial adjustments.

earnings gap: The difference in pay between women and men doing the same work, with women receiving less.

employment application: The official application form employers require of prospective workers.

employment interview: The face-to-face interview between an employer and prospective worker that is usually required before someone is hired.

erogenous zones: Any part of the body that causes sexual arousal when stroked.

eustress: Stress that has a beneficial effect.

false cues: Various signals and indirect suggestions which unconsciously trigger off certain associations in our minds.

first impressions: The initial image and feelings you get of someone on the basis of such characteristics as the person's physical appearance, speech and behavior.

flextime: The policy which permits individual workers to follow a flexible work schedule.

friendship: The affectionate attachment between friends of either sex.

gain-loss theory of attraction: The view that the more someone increases his or her liking for me, the more I'm attracted to that person.

general adaptation syndrome: The complex chain of bodily and mental reactions in response to stress.

genital herpes: A venereal disease transmitted through sexual activity, which in addition to the discomfort of the symptoms may lead to serious medical complications.

getting/giving contract: The unwritten rules that govern what we give in relation to what we expect in return in our work, marriage, and relationships.

gonorrhea: A venereal disease characterized by inflammation of the mucous membrane of the genitourinary tract.

good grief: The positive personal growth that comes with the eventual acceptance of an experience of loss.

grief: The intense emotional suffering that accompanies an experience of loss.

grief work: The process of freeing ourselves emotionally from the deceased, and readjusting to life without that person.

group job hunting: The practice of providing individuals who are job hunting with specific job-seeking skills and group support.

halo effect: The notion that someone I like can do no wrong, as if that person wears a halo over his or her head.

homosexual: Any adult who seeks out and prefers members of the same sex for sexual contact.

hyperstress: Excessive stress.

hypostress: A state in which too little stress leaves us bored and unchallenged.

"I" message: The expression of your feelings about another person's behavior in a nonjudgmental way.

inhibited sexual desire: The lack of sexual desire or a low level of such desire.

intimacy: The warmth and closeness

between people in which they share their innermost thoughts and feelings.

job: A position of employment; the set of work activities and responsibilities associated with a given position.

job satisfaction: How well you like a given job, depending on such factors as the people you work with as well as your pay.

leisure: Time free from work that may be spent in recreational and social activities.

listening: The perception of meaningful sound, usually through paying attention to what someone is saying.

loneliness: Feelings of emptiness and isolation resulting from the absence of satisfying relationships.

loss: The state of being deprived of an object or a relationship.

love: A complex emotional state characterized by deep feelings of affection and attachment to another person.

lovestyles: Characteristic individual differences in experiencing and expressing romantic love.

maintenance activities: A variety of activities that are not clearly leisure or work but are necessary for maintaining everyday life. *See* nonleisure.

marital conflict: Disagreements between spouses over such things as breakdown in communication and sexual compatibility.

marital infidelity: Sexual unfaithfulness through a husband or wife engaging in extramarital sex.

marriage roles: Widely held social expectations regarding the appropriate behavior for husbands and wives in marriage, which continue to change with time.

masturbation: Self-manipulation of the sex organs to produce pleasure.

mate selection: The characteristic process by which individuals choose their romantic partners, especially in marriage.

memorandum of agreement: A written letter or memo reminding both parties of their commitments in regard to a specific matter of agreement.

mistaken impressions: The inaccurate perceptions we have of other people, usually because of insufficient information.

moonlighting: The practice of holding an extra job, in addition to your regular one.

mourning: The outward expression of bereavement, such as the wearing of black.

mutuality: The state in which two or more people have the same relationship toward each other.

negotiation: A cooperative approach to bargaining, synonymous with cooperative problem solving.

nonleisure: A variety of activities that are not clearly related to leisure or work, such as preparing a meal. *See* maintenance activities.

nonreflective listening: The simplest form of listening, which includes the use of attentive silence and minimal responses like "mm-hmm."

nonverbal behavior: All those expressions of behavior that do not rely on words or symbols; sometimes known as *body language*.

nonverbal messages: Communication through nonverbal means, such as one's facial expressions or hand gestures.

organizational climate: Working conditions that affect our productivity and satisfaction on the job.

passive-congenial marriage: A stable marriage relationship characterized by low emotional involvement between the partners.

projection: The unconscious mechanism whereby we attribute our unacceptable desires or impulses to others.

rationalization: The unconscious mechanism by which we attempt to justify our unacceptable behavior through "good" reasons.

reaction-formation: The unconscious attempt to control unacceptable desires be adopting the opposite feelings and behaviors in our conscious mind.

reflective listening: The process of giving the speaker nonjudgmental feedback as a way of checking on the accuracy of what has been heard.

regression. The unconscious falling back, in the face of stress, to patterns of behavior that were more appropriate to an earlier stage of development.

remarriage: The act of marriage in which one or both partners has been divorced.

repression: The unconscious blocking of a threatening impulse or idea from consciousness.

reputation: How a person is commonly regarded or viewed by others.

résumé: A short summary of your education and employment experience prepared for potential employers.

romantic love: The strong emotional attachment to someone of the opposite sex.

search for community: The tendency for people to reach out for closer, more satisfying relationships to compensate for the impersonal individualistic aspects of society.

self-assessment in career choice: Taking stock of one's interest, abilities, and personal traits as a means of choosing a compatible career.

self-disclosure: The deliberate sharing with others of information and feelings about yourself.

self-fulfilment: The fulfilment of one's own potential as in self-actualization or personal growth.

self-fulfilment contradiction: The psychological and social limitations within the process of self-fulfilment itself.

service-producing industries: Industries that provide a service, like a secretarial service, rather than a product.

sex-role stereotypes: Widely held but exaggerated generalizations about the characteristics of males and females.

sex roles: The social expectations regarding appropriate behavior for males and females.

sexual compatibility: The state in which partners mutually enjoy the sexual aspects of their relationship, especially sexual intercourse.

sexual dysfunctions: Problems in sexual functioning, such as premature ejaculation and difficulties achieving an erection among males, and slowness of arousal or difficulties having an orgasm among females.

sexual harassment: The mistreatment of women workers because of factors relating to their sex, like unwelcome sexual advances.

sexual intercourse: The penetration of the female vagina by the male penis, characteristically accompanied by pelvic thrusting and orgasm for one or both partners.

sexually transmitted disease: an infection transmitted primarily by sexual intercourse.

shift work: Work that is done by a group of workers in a given time slot in relay with other groups.

single-parent families: Families headed

by only one parent, more often a woman.

stages of career choice: The view that career choice is a developmental process which occurs in three successive stages: *fantasy, tentative,* and *realistic.*

stereotypes: Widespread generalizations about people that have little, if any, basis in fact.

stress: Any adjustive demand that requires a response from us in order to satisfy our needs.

sublimation: The unconscious tendency to redirect unacceptable impulses toward more socially valued activities.

suppression: The conscious, deliberate control of an unpleasant thought or impulse.

syphilis: An infectious venereal disease transmitted by sexual intercourse, which if left untreated may lead to the degeneration of bones, heart, and nerve tissue.

terminal illness: The final stages of a fatal disease.

total marriage: A marriage relationship characterized by total togetherness or sharing.

unconditional leisure: Activities which we do primarily for enjoyment and personal fulfilment.

unresolved grief: The delay in the grief process which results from the excessive suppression or repression of the emotions associated with grief.

vital marriage: A marriage relationship characterized by high emotional involvement and satisfaction on the part of both partners.

vocational schools: Institutions that provide post–high-school training for careers that do not require a college degree.

withdrawal: A potentially constructive approach to stress, especially when used as a temporary strategy in the face of an overwhelming situation.

work: Physical or mental activity that produces something useful, usually as a means of earning one's living.

work adjustment: The varied adjustments to one's job necessitated by the working conditions on the job as well as the work activity itself.

workaholics: People who are so absorbed in their jobs they're unable to enjoy anything else.

Index

Addictive relationships, 63
Alone, wish to be, 14
Altruistic egoism, 27
Androgyny, 71–72
Anger, management of, 162
Apprenticeship programs, 215–16
Assertiveness, 135–36
Attitudes:
  changing attitudes toward work, 194–95
  toward job, 266
  in job hunting, 252–53
  toward work, 194–97
Attitudes, sexual, 80–83
  caution in, 81–82
  freedom in, 80
  and fulfilment, 80–81
  about homosexuality, 82
  and love, 82–83
Attraction, interpersonal, 49–54
  complementary needs, 51–52
  liking, 53–54
  nearness, 50
  physical attractiveness, 52–53
  sex differences, 52–53
  and sexual revolution, 80, 82
  and similarity, 50–52
Attractiveness, physical, 33–34, 52–53

Bargaining, mutual gains:
  (see Problem-solving, cooperative)
Bereavement, 303–8
  good grief, 308
  grief process, 304–5
  grief work, 304
  mourning customs, 303–4
  unresolved grief, 305–7
Birth control
  (see Contraceptive methods)
Brainstorming
  (see Problem-solving, cooperative)

Career choice:
  and abilities, 209
  balance sheet, 213–14
  changing careers, 227–28
  compatible career, 208–14
  and decision making, 199, 213–14
  exploring careers, 210
  female-dominated careers, 202
  influences on, 200–202
  and interests, 208–9
  male-dominated careers, 202
  mentor's influence on, 201
  Occupational Outlook Handbook, 210
  personality, 209
  personality-occupational types, 212–13
  self-assessment, 208–10
  and sex role, 202
  stages of, 198–99
  and values, 210
  work experience, 202–4

Career choice, stages of:
  fantasy stage, 198
  realistic stage, 199
  tentative stage, 199
Career choice inventories, 210–13
  Harrington-O'Shea Career Decision-Making System, 211
  Holland's Self-directed Search, 211
  Strong-Campbell Interest Inventory, 211
  System of Interactive Guidance and Information, 211
Career outlook, 221–28
  and personal assessment, 226–27
  projected employment change, 224–26
  service industries, 222–23
  trends, 222–23
Career preparation, 215–21
  apprenticeship programs, 215–16
  college education, 217–18
  government programs, 220–21
  military service, 220–21
  on-the-job training programs, 216–17
  vocational and technical schools, 218–19
Changing jobs, 272
Children in marriage, 117–18
Civil Rights Act, 267, 270
Cohabiting couples, 26, 98
  in college, 98
  and marital happiness, 98
  and marriage, 98
College education, 217–18
  college educated workers, 219, 223
  college graduates, 217–18
  community colleges, 217
  and employment, 217–18, 223
  and lifetime earnings, 217–18
Commitment:
  defined, 26
  and major life decisions, 26
  in marriage, 26–27, 123
  and personal freedom, 26
  and personal fulfilment, 27
  sexual, 81–82
Communication, barriers:
  anxiety, 132
  hidden agendas, 132
  interrupting, 132
  judging, 131
  over-reacting, 132
  stereotypes, 131
Communication, improving:
  accepting attitude, 133
  attentiveness, 133
  expressing yourself, 134–38
  listening, 133
  observing nonverbal behavior, 134
  shared responsibility, 134

Communication, nonverbal, 128, 129–31
  body movement, 130–31
  facial expressions, 129–30
  looking, 130
  one-way vs. two-way communication, 132
  and personal space, 131
Communication, process of, 127–34
  and assertiveness, 135–36
  barriers to, 131–33
  "I" messages, 136–38
  improvement of communication, 132–34
  listening, 138–44
  types of communication, 127–28
Communication, types of, 127–28
  cognitive, 128
  expressive, 128
  nonverbal, 128
  persuasive, 128
  social, 128
Community, search for, 22–24
  search for community index, 22
Companionship, preference for, 14
Comparable worth, concept of, 268, 269
Comparing opinions, 15
Compatibility, 60–61, 93–95, 113–14
  and commitment, 95
  and complementary traits, 94–95
  and emotional involvement, 95
  sexual compatibility, 113–14
Complementary needs, 51–52, 93
Conflict, 149–52
  defined, 149
  types of, 151–52
  as unavoidable, 149–50
Conflict, marital, 109–10
  among happily married couples, 110
  hidden conflict, 109–10
Conflict, types of, 151–52
  approach-approach, 151
  approach-avoidance, 151
  approach-avoidance, double, 151–52
  avoidance-avoidance, 151
Conflict management, 153–57
  cooperative styles, 155–56
  defensive styles, 153–55
  your personal style, 156–57
Conflict management, cooperative, 155–56
  compromise, 155–56
  problem-solving, 156
Conflict management, defensive, 153–55
  avoidance of conflict, 153–54
  capitulation, 155
  denial of conflict, 153–54
  domination, 154

Conformity, 15–16, 181
Contraceptive methods, 77–78
  failure to use, 78
  types of, 78
  use of, 77–78
Cooperation, 11–13, 157–60
  cooperative problem-solving,
    157–60
Cultural activities, 288
  college-educated audiences,
    288
  museums and art galleries, 288
  music, 288

Death:
  awareness of death, 299–300
  denial of death, 300
  dreams of death, 300
  experience of dying, 300–302
  as inevitable companion of life,
    308
  premature death and unre-
    solved grief, 307
  risk of death, 300
Decision making, balance sheet
  in, 214
Defense mechanisms, 175–77
  defined, 175
  types, 176–177
Defense mechanisms, types of,
  176–77
  denial, 176
  displacement, 177
  projection, 177
  rationalization, 177
  reaction-formation, 177
  regression, 177
  repression, 176
  sublimation, 177
Discouraged worker, 252
Discrimination in the workplace,
  270–71
  and job analyses, 270–71
Divorce, 118–21
  causes of, 118–19
  experience of, 119–21
  and remarriage, 122–23
  stages of, 120
Dying, experience of, 300–302
  and individual lifestyles, 302–3
  stages of dying, 300–301

Employer contact:
  application, 245–46
  employment interview, 246–50
  letters for, 243–44
  resumes for, 234, 241–43
  telephone calls for, 239–41
Employment interview, 246–50
  informal interview, 246–47
  patterned interview, 247
  practical suggestions for, 249–
    50
  preparation for, 246–47
  questions to expect, 247–48
Employment projections, 224–26
  administrative careers, 224
  clerical careers, 225
  construction workers, 225–26
  engineers, 224
  health practitioners, 224
  marketing and sales, 225
  mechanics, 225

natural scientists, 224
production workers, 226
service careers, 225
social scientists, 224
technicians, 225
transportation workers, 226
writers, artists, and entertainers, 225
Entertainment:
  movies, 288
  music, 288
  television, 286–88
Equal Pay Act, 267
Erogenous zones, 74
Eye contact, 249

Families, single-parent, 121–22
  female headed, 121
  male headed, 122
Family, starting a, 117–18
Friendship, 54–64
  activities, 55–56
  and compatibility, 60–61
  and conflict, 62
  defined, 54
  and dependency, 62–63
  intimate friendships, 58–64
  lasting friendships, 57–58
  need for, 56
  opposite sex friendships, 57
  and personal growth, 62–64
  qualities of, 55, 57
  rules of, 56–57
  and secrets, 60
  and self-disclosure, 58–60
  types of, 54–55

General Adaptation Syndrome,
  173–75
  (see also Stress, General Adap-
    tation Syndrome)
Government service, 220–21
Grief:
  defined, 303
  good grief, 308
  grief process, 304–5
  grief work, 304
  and physical symptoms, 305
  and sex differences, 307
  and sublimation, 307
  unresolved grief, 305–7

Homosexuality, 82

"I" messages, 136–38
  components of, 137–38
  examples of, 138
Impressions:
  first impressions, 32–37
  mistaken impressions, 37–41
  (see also Person perception)
Interpersonal attraction,
  (see Attraction, interpersonal)
Intimacy:
  and commitment, 26–27
  and compatibility, 60–61
  and friendship, 58–64
  and growth, 62–64
  healthy and unhealthy inti-
    macy, 61–63
  and mutuality, 24–26
  search for intimacy, 22–24
  and secrets, 60

and self-disclosure, 58–60
styles of intimacy, 62

Job:
  job analysis, 270–71
  loss of job, 296
Job hunting:
  contacting potential employers,
    239–46
  creative job hunting, 234–35
  discouraged worker, 252
  employment interview, 246–50
  follow-up contacts, 251–52
  group job hunting, 235–36
  identifying potential em-
    ployers, 233–39
  and persistence, 250–51
  and positive attitude, 252–53
  resources for, 237–39
Job hunting resources, 237–39
  classified ads, 238
  college placement centers, 237
  employment agencies, 237–38
  family and friends, 238
  job registers, 238
  multiple resources, 238–39
  state employment offices, 237
Job satisfaction, 258–59, 261–62,
  268–69
  and promotion, 268–69, 272
  among women workers, 264–
    65
  and working conditions, 259,
    262
Jobs, stressful, 174

Leisure:
  characteristics of, 278
  compatible leisure patterns,
    281
  defined, 277–78
  entertainment and cultural ac-
    tivities, 286–88
  household participation in lei-
    sure, 287
  outdoor recreational activities,
    284
  and personal growth, 290–91
  positive use of leisure, 283–91
  satisfaction in, 283
  sports, 285–86
  television viewing habits, 286–
    88
  types of leisure, 278–79
  vacations, 288–90
  and work, 279–83
  work and leisure patterns,
    281–83
Leisure, types of, 278–79
  complementary leisure, 278–
    79
  coordinate leisure, 278–79
  nonleisure, 278–79
  unconditional leisure, 278–79
Letters, 243–44
  blocked letter form, 243–44
  indented line letter, 243–44
  sample letter, 244
Liking, 50, 53–54
  and interpersonal attraction,
    53–54
  and nearness, 50
  and similarity, 50–52

Listening, 138–44
  failure to listen, 139–40
  nonreflective, 140–41
  reflective, 141–44
  self-test of, 139
Loneliness, 20–21
  among college students, 20–21
  coping with loneliness, 21
  as a state of mind, 20
  types of loneliness, 20
Loss:
  and aging, 297
  coping with loss, 297
  defined, 296
  experience of loss, 298–99
  and divorce, 296–97
  loss of friends, 296
  types of loss, 295–97
Love, 87–91
  descriptions of, 91
  folklore of, 88
  and infatuation, 90
  love ethic, 80
  mature love, 90–91
  psychological explanation of, 88
  and reasons people marry, 96–97
  romantic love, 87–88
  and sex, 82–83
  styles of, 88–90
Love, mature, 90–91
  characteristics, of 90–91
  love list, 91
Lovestyles, 88–90
  agape, 90
  eros, 89
  ludus, 89
  mania, 89
  pragma, 89–90
  storge, 89

Marital adjustment:
  changes in marriage over time, 111–12
  and children, 117–18
  and conflict, 109–10
  devitalized marriage, 111
  happily married couples, 110
  and infidelity, 116
  marital roles, 105–8
  and money management, 111
  power balance in, 108–9
  and remarriage, 122–23
  and sex, 112–16
Marital happiness, 100–101, 111
  and satisfying relationships, 100–101
Marriage:
  changes in marriage over time, 111–12
  and children, 117–18
  and cohabiting couples, 98
  and commitment, 123
  and companionship, 97
  conflict, 109–10
  devitalized marriage, 111
  and divorce, 118–21
  and engagement, 105
  and family, 97
  happiness, 100–101
  and infidelity, 116
  and mate selection, 92–96

  and premarital pregnancy, 98
  reasons people marry, 96–98
  and sex, 112–16
  and working mothers, 265, 266–67
Marriage as intimate relationship, 22–23
Marriage commitment, 27
Marriage relationship, 96–101
  and companionship, 97
  and family, 97
  and marital happiness, 100–101
  reasons people marry, 96–98
  and sex, 97
  sex differences in, 101
  types of marriage relationships, 98–100
Marriage relationships, types of, 98–100
  conflict-habituated marriage, 99
  devitalized marriage, 99
  intrinsic marriage, 99–100
  passive-congenial marriage, 99
  total marriage, 100
  utilitarian marriage, 99
  vital marriage, 99–100
Mate selection, 92–96
  and compatibility, 93–95
  and complementary needs, 93
  and computerized service for, 95–96
  explanation of, 92–93
  and nearness, 93
  and personal traits, 93
  as rational or emotional choice, 95–96
  and social characteristics, 93
Mediation,
  (see Problem-solving, cooperative)
Military service, 220–21
Moonlighting, 272
Mutuality, 24–26
  development of, 25
  and enduring relationships, 24
  and sexual satisfaction, 24
  and the "we" identity, 26

Negotiation, 181–82
  (see also Problem-solving, cooperative)

On-the-job training programs, 216–17

Personality-occupational types, 212–13
Person perception:
  basic principles of, 32
  and compliments, 44–45
  false cues in, 38–39
  and first impressions, 32
  and the halo effect, 40–41
  making a good impression, 41–45
  mistaken impressions, 37–41
  and nonverbal behavior, 36–37
  person or situation in, 38
  and physical appearance, 33–34
  and physical attractiveness, 33–34

  and reputation, 34–35
  and smiling, 37
  and speech, 35
  and stereotypes, 39–40
Problem solving, cooperative, 157–60
  helpful hints, 160–63
  steps of problem solving, 158–60
Problem solving, hints for, 160–63
  communicating clearly, 161
  and cooperative climate, 160
  managing feelings, 161
  and new information, 162
  and positive power, 162–63
  setting a deadline, 163
Problem solving, steps of, 158–60
  acknowledging the conflict, 158
  agreeing on procedure, 158
  defining the conflict, 158
  evaluating the solution, 160
  exploring solutions, 159
  implementing the plan, 160
  and memorandum of agreement, 159–60
  reaching agreement, 159

Questions in the employment interview, 247–48

Remarriage, 122–23
  and divorce, 122
Resumes, 234, 241–43
  chronological resume, 241–42
  functional resume, 242–43
  purpose of resume, 241
  sample resume, 242
  targeted resume, 242
Roles, marital, 105–8
  conventional roles, 107
  democratic decision making, 106
  expanded, 106–7
  and power, 108–9

Self, search for, 16–21
Self-actualization:
  and leisure, 283, 290–91
  (see also Self-fulfilment)
Self-disclosure, 58–60
  and secrets, 60
  topics, 59–60
Self-fulfilment, 17–18, 19–20
  contradiction, 19–20
  as a lifestyle, 18
  strong-form of self-fulfilment, 17–18
  weak-form of self-fulfilment, 17–18
Sex:
  and children, 117–18
  and compatibility, 113–14
  and expressiveness, 115
  the initiative in sex, 115
  in marriage, 112–16
  problems, 114, 116
  quality of sex life, 114
Sex roles, 68–73
  and androgyny, 71–72
  changing sex roles, 71–72, 73

Sex roles (*cont.*)
   defined, 68
   identity, 70
   and sexuality, 72–73
   stereotyped sex roles, 69–70
Sexual attitudes,
   (*see* Attitudes, sexual)
Sexual behavior, 73–80
   contraceptive methods, 77–78
   and erogenous zones, 74
   and masturbation, 74–75
   sexual intercourse, 75–77
   sexual problems, 77–80
   and sexually transmitted dis-
      eases, 79–80
Sexual harassment, 265
Sexual intercourse, 75–77
   changing habits, 75–76
   and love, 76–77
Sexually transmitted diseases,
      79–80
   genital herpes, 79–80
   gonorrhea, 79
   syphilis, 79
Sexual problems, 77–80
   and contraceptive use, 77–78
   erectile dysfunction, 77, 114
   and frequency of intercourse,
      114
   and infidelity, 116
   and inhibited sexual desire,
      116
   orgasmic dysfunction, 77
   premature ejaculation, 77, 114,
      116
Shyness, 23
   in different situations, 23
   around other people, 23
Sports, 285–86
   active participation in, 285–86
   aerobic exercises, 285–86
   attendance at sports events, 285
Stereotypes, 39–40
   changing stereotypes, 40
   and sex roles, 69–70
Stress:
   alleviation of, 13–15
   carriers, 178
   College Life-Stress Scale, 170–
      71
   control of, 172, 174
   coping devices for, 178–80
   and death, 170, 172, 175
   and defense mechanisms, 175–
      77
   defined, 168–69
   and hassles, 171
   and illness, 169–71
   individual factors in, 172–73
   management of, 180–85
   measurement of, 169–71
   personal factors in, 172
   and personality, 172–73
   stressful events, 169–71
   stress reactions, 173–78
   stress tolerance, 173, 182–84
   types of, 169
Stress, coping devices for, 178–
      80
   cognitive control, 179

and exercise, 180
and oral pleasures, 178
and physical contact, 178
and verbal expression, 179
Stress, General Adaptation Syn-
      drome, 173–75
   alarm reaction, 174
   exhaustion stage, 175
   resistance stage, 175
Stress, types of, 169
   distress, 169
   eustress, 169
   hyperstress, 169
   hypostress, 169
Stressful jobs, 174
Stress management, 180–85
   environmental modifications,
      180–82
   lifestyle changes, 182–85
Stress management, environmen-
      tal, 180–82
   and assertiveness, 180–81
   and compromise, 181–82
   and withdrawal, 181
Stress management, in lifestyle,
      182–85
   pace of life, 184–85
   relaxation exercises, 183
   thought control, 183–84
Stress reactions, 173–78
   defense mechanisms, 176–
      77
   General Adaptation Syndrome,
      173–75
Suicide, 302

Technology in the workplace,
      260–61
Television viewing habits, 286–
      88
   hours watched per day, 286
   household participation, 287
   as main source of news, 286
   by time slots, 286–88

Vacation patterns, 289
   and adventure, 289
   and escape, 289
   and family togetherness, 289
   and intellectual stimulation,
      289
   and relaxation, 289
   and self-discovery, 289
Vacations, 288–90
   dream vacations, 290
   among general population, 288
   reasons for taking a vacation,
      289
   survey of vacation preferences,
      288–89
   and work, 289–90
Venereal disease,
   (*see* Sexually transmitted dis-
      eases)
Vocational and technical schools,
      218–19

Women in the workplace, 263–
      68
   changes over time, 263

and concept of comparable
      worth, 268–69
distribution of women workers,
      202, 264–65
and job satisfaction, 264–65
and sexual harassment, 265
and work effort, 264
working mothers, 265–67
Work:
   attitudes toward, 194–97
   experience in, 202–4
   importance, of, 197–98
   and job stress, 192–93
   and leisure, 279–83
   motivation in, 195–96
   reasons for working, 190–91
   and self-actualization, 197
   and stress-related illnesses, 193
   work activity, 192
   work and leisure patterns,
      281–83
   work ethic, 195
   worker burnout, 192
   working conditions, 192–93
   work satisfaction, 197–98
Work adjustment, 257–63
   changing jobs, 272
   and difficult bosses, 263
   and dissatisfied workers, 258
   the first job, 257–58
   and growth in the job, 261–63
   and job satisfaction, 258–59
   shift work, 260
   and technological changes,
      260–61
Workaholics, 270
Work and leisure patterns, 281–
      83
   defined, 281
   job-centered pattern, 282–83
   live for leisure pattern, 282
   passive involvement pattern,
      282
   self-actualizing pattern, 283
Worker recognition, 261–62
Worker satisfaction, 258–59,
      261–62, 268–69, 270
Working mothers, 265–67
   attitude toward job, 266
   and career pattern, 265
   and earnings gap, 267–68
   and family relationships, 266–
      67
   flexible schedules, 267
   and housekeeping chores, 265
   and marriage relationship,
      266–67
Work motivation, 190–91
   extrinsic satisfaction, 195
   and identity, 191
   intrinsic satisfaction, 195
   and involvement in the com-
      pany, 196
   mixed motives, 192
   and money, 190
   and personal fulfilment, 190
   security, 191
   serving others, 191
   and status, 191
Work-study programs, 203